THE INDIAN ARMY

Frontispiece: Kundah Singh (inside turret) and Risalder Dalipsingh, crew members of a Sherman tank of the Scinde Horse, part of the Indian 31st Armoured Division in Iraq, March 1944. Photo courtesy of the Imperial War Museum, London [IWM: K 6697].

The Indian Army, 1939–47

Experience and Development

Edited by

ALAN JEFFREYS
The Imperial War Museum, UK

and

PATRICK ROSE
Defence Science and Technology Laboratory, UK

Routledge
Taylor & Francis Group
LONDON AND NEW YORK

First published 2012 by Ashgate Publishing

Published 2016 by Routledge
2 Park Square, Milton Park, Abingdon, Oxon OX14 4RN
711 Third Avenue, New York, NY 10017, USA

First issued in paperback 2017

Routledge is an imprint of the Taylor & Francis Group, an informa business

British Library Cataloguing in Publication Data
The Indian Army, 1939–47 : experience and development.
1. India. Army–History–20th century. 2. World War, 1939–1945–Participation, East Indian. 3. India–Foreign relations–1919–1947. 4. India–Foreign relations–Great Britain. 5. Great Britain–Foreign relations–India. 6. India–History–Partition, 1947. 7. India–History, Military–20th century.
I. Jeffreys, Alan. II. Rose, Patrick.
355'.00954'09044-dc23

Library of Congress Cataloging-in-Publication Data
The Indian Army, 1939–47 : experience and development / edited by Alan Jeffreys and Patrick Rose.
p. cm.
Includes index.
ISBN 978-1-4094-3553-2 (hardcover : alk. paper) 1. In-dia.
Army–History–20th century. 2. Great Britain. Army. British Indian Army–History–20th century. 3. India–History, Military–20th century. 4. World War, 1939-1945–Participation, East Indian. 5. World War, 1939-1945–India. I. Jeffreys, Alan. II. Rose, Patrick.
UA842.I529 2012
940.54'1254–dc23

2011053308

ISBN 13: 978-1-138-11006-9 (pbk)
ISBN 13: 978-1-4094-3553-2 (hbk)

Contents

List of Contributors

Raymond Callahan is Professor Emeritus of British history at the University of Delaware and a Fellow of the Royal Historical Society. He has written several books on the British war effort 1939–45, the most recent being *Churchill and His Generals* (Lawrence, KS, 2007). He is currently working on a study of the 1944 Imphal campaign.

Field Marshal Sir John Chapple is President of the Friends of the Imperial War Museum, the Friends of the National Army Museum, President of the Military Historical Society, the Indian Military Historical Society and the Society for Army Historical Research. He is the Honorary Vice-Patron of the National Army Museum, Vice President of the Army Museums Ogilby Trust, the Gurkha Museum, the 2nd Gurkha Rifles Regimental Association, the Army Benevelent Fund, the Royal Hospital Chelsea, the Gurkha Welfare Trust and a number of other associations.

Graham Dunlop was a Royal Marines officer for 32 years. He served in Northern Ireland, the Mediterranean, the United States, Hong Kong, Iraq and Bosnia/Herzegovina. He commanded the Special Boat Service and 40 Commando Royal Marines. After leaving the Service in 1997, he worked as a training consultant in the nuclear industry whilst undertaking academic studies, culminating in a PhD from the University of Edinburgh for his thesis on British/Indian logistics of the Burma Campaign, which was published as *Military Economics, Culture and Logistics in the Burma Campaign 1942–1945*. He has contributed to a number of other books as well as the *Oxford Dictionary of National Biography*. He continues to write, lecture and guide battlefield tours.

Ashley Jackson is Professor of Imperial and Military History at King's College London. His research concentrates on aspects of British imperial and military history. He is the author of numerous articles on aspects of British imperial history, and the following books: *Botswana 1939–45: An African Country at War* (OUP, 1999), *War and Empire in Mauritius and the Indian Ocean* (Macmillan, 2001), *The British Empire and the Second World War* (Continuum, 2006), *Mad Dogs and Englishmen: A Grand Tour of the British Empire at its Height* (Quercus, 2009), *Distant Drums: The Role of Colonies in British Imperial*

Warfare (Sussex Academic Press, 2010), *Illustrating Empire: A Visual History of British Imperialism* (with David Tomkins) (Bodleian Library, 2011), and *Churchill* (Quercus, 2011).

Alan Jeffreys is Senior Curator, Social History at the Imperial War Museum. He is the author of *The British Army in the Far East, 1941–45* (2005) and *Training the Indian Army, 1939–45* (Ashgate, forthcoming).

Robert Johnson is the Deputy Director of the Oxford Changing Character of War Programme, and Lecturer in the History of War at the University of Oxford. His primary research interests are conflicts of the Middle East, Afghanistan, Pakistan and India, but he also works on a range of themes including strategy, conventional operations, insurgency and counter-insurgency, and intelligence. He teaches more broadly on the History of War and Military History in the Nineteenth and Twentieth Century. He has published a number of books and articles, and is the author of *The Afghan Way of War* (Hurst-OUP, 2011), *The Iran-Iraq War* (Palgrave, 2010) and *Spying for Empire* (2006). He is currently working on Indian Army operations in Persia and China in the mid-nineteenth century.

Chris Mann is a Senior Lecturer in the Department of War Studies at the Royal Military Academy Sandhurst. He is an Honorary Research Fellow in the Department of Scandinavian Studies, University College London. His research interests lay in Scandinavia in the Second World War and more recently in the Eighth Army in North Africa and Italy.

Daniel Marston is the Ike Skelton Distinguished Chair in the Art of War at the US Army Command & General Staff College, Ft Leavenworth, a Visiting Research Fellow at the Strategic and Defence Studies Centre at the Australian National University, a Visiting Fellow at the Changing Character of War Program at the University of Oxford and a Fellow of the Royal Historical Society. His first book, Phoenix from the Ashes, an in-depth examination of how the British/Indian Army turned defeat into victory in the Burma campaign of the Second World War, won the Templer Medal Book Prize in 2003. He is in the process of completing a monograph for Cambridge University Press, dealing with the final years of the British Indian Army, 1945–47.

Tim Moreman is a freelance writer and academic. For several years he lectured in the Department of War Studies at King's College London, from where he obtained his PhD. He also held a six-month appointment as Resident Historian at the Army Staff College at Camberley. His primary interests include the British Indian Army during the nineteenth and twentieth centuries, counter-insurgency, and the British and Commonwealth armies in the Far East during World War II. In addition to a number of chapters, articles and papers, Tim has written two major books: a study of the Indian Army on the North-West Frontier 1849–1947, and a book on the war in Burma and Malaya 1941–45. In recent years he has also worked for the new Dictionary of National Biography, as well as acting as a historical adviser for the BBC and Carlton Television. He is based in Somerset, UK and is currently working on a book on the First Arakan campaign.

Ashok Nath is the author of *Izzat-Historical Records and Iconography of Indian Cavalry Regiments, 1750–2007* (2009) the definitive work on the subject. He served as an officer in the Indian Army, ran a full time specialist mountain travel exploration company in Sweden and taught and researched at Södertörns and Stockholm University. He is a former senior research fellow with the United Service Institution of India and currently on a sabbatical in Dhaka, Bangladesh engaged in counter terrorism and radicalisation issues and writing a history of the South Asian armies.

David Omissi is Senior Lecturer in History at the University of Hull. He gained his doctorate in the Department of War Studies at King's College, London, before becoming a Prize Research Fellow at Nuffield College, Oxford. His publications include '"A Most Arduous but a Most Noble Duty": Gladstone and the British Raj in India, 1868–98' in M.E. Daly and K.T. Hoppen (eds), *Gladstone: Ireland and Beyond* (Dublin, 2011) and 'Europe Through Indian Eyes: Indian Soldiers Encounter England and France, 1914–1918', *English Historical Review*, 122/496 (2007).

Patrick Rose received a PhD in War Studies from King's College London for a thesis examining command culture in the British and Indian Armies between 1919 and 1945. He is a West Point Fellow in military history, and co-editor and contributing author of the forthcoming book *Allied Fighting Effectiveness in North Africa and Italy, 1942–1945.* He is currently a senior analyst in the Defence Science and Technology Laboratory of the UK Ministry of Defence, and has twice deployed to support NATO campaign planning in Afghanistan.

Foreword

Field Marshal Sir John Chapple

The conference held on 9 May 2009 at the Imperial War Museum covered many aspects of the Indian Army in the run-up to the Second World War; through that war; and then in the hectic period up to Independence and Partition. It is a period not all that well understood and about which much historical research continues and continues to be needed. The dramatic events of war, the speed of events up to 1947 and the large number of changes of those in official appointments during this period, will all have affected the ability to record decisions and events in the same thorough and detailed manner which was normal in more peaceful times in India. Thus there is much still to be uncovered and assessed.

The Indian Army expanded to become the largest volunteer army in the world during the first half of the war. It was not particularly well prepared or equipped for this conflict. Then at the end of hostilities, having risen to the challenges, it faced a massive draw down in numbers; whilst at the same time facing the run-up towards Independence and the possibility of Partition. There are many aspects of this period which have not yet been subjected to historical analysis and assessment.

The seminar brought together many who have thrown light on this particularly interesting and important period of the history of the Indian Army. I thank them all for their contributions and also thank the Imperial War Museum and King's College London for organising this valuable event.

Introduction

This volume is the result of an international conference held at the Imperial War Museum, London, in May 2009. It was jointly organised by the Museum and King's College London, a collaboration that attracted a wide range of participants considering various aspects of a subject that fascinates the serious academic and general military history reader alike. Comprising a collection of new perspectives on the experience and development of the Indian Army in the era of the Second World War, it is hoped this volume will encourage further research into the subject as well as prove an enjoyable and informative read to those interested in the conduct of the Second World War and subsequent Partition of India.

A number of academic studies have added to the growing literature on the Indian Army published in recent years, including Kaushik Roy's *The Oxford Companion to Modern Warfare in India* and *A Military History of India and South Asia* edited by Daniel Marston and Chandar Sundaram.[1] Despite this, the history and experience of the Indian Army during the Second World War and the years immediately after, leading to and encompassing the Partition of India, remains a vast area of study that has received comparatively little scholarly attention relative to its scope and importance. One earlier volume, *The British Raj and its Indian Armed Forces 1857–1939*, edited by the Indian scholars Partha Sarathi Gupta and Anirudh Deshpande, only takes its discussion as far as 1939; its companion, originally intended to cover the subsequent period until 1947, *War and Society in Colonial India*, edited by Kaushik Roy, in fact re-covers much of the same period with a focus from 1807 until 1945.[2] Many of the chapters had already appeared elsewhere and only three dealt explicitly with the Second World War.[3] A further edited work, *The Indian Army in both World Wars*, published by

[1] See Kaushik Roy, *The Oxford Companion to Modern Warfare in India* (New Delhi: Oxford University Press, 2009). See also Daniel Marston and Chandar Sundaram (eds), *A Military History of India and South Asia* (Westport, Connecticut: Praeger, 2007).

[2] See Partha Sarathi Gupta and Anirudh Deshpande (eds), *The British Raj and its Indian Armed Forces 1857–1939* (New Delhi: Oxford University Press, 2002) and Kaushik Roy (ed.), *War and Society in Colonial India* (New Delhi: Oxford University Press, 2006).

[3] See Chandar Sundaram, 'Seditious Letters and Steel Helmets: Disaffection among Indian Troops in Singapore and Hong Kong, 1940–1, and the formation of the Indian National Army'; Raymond Callahan, 'Were the 'Sepoy Generals' Any Good? A Reappraisal

Brill in 2011 and also edited by Kashik Roy, had five of its 12 chapters dedicated to the Second World War, the authors of which also contribute to this volume on different subjects.[4] Roy himself has authored three recent articles covering the expansion, deployment, morale and loyalty of the Indian Army during the war.[5] Alongside Tarak Barkawi's article examining culture and combat in the Fourteenth Army, and the works of Raymond Callahan, Graham Dunlop, Daniel Marston and Tim Moreman (all of whom contribute to this volume), this comprises the recent historiography of the Indian Army in that conflict.[6]

The Indian Army's experience in the era of the Second World War thus remains a fertile ground for historical inquiry, and even less attention has been placed on the ensuing period of Partition.[7] Outside the studies outlined above, the Indian Army during this period has remained largely untouched since the

---

of the British-Indian Army's High Command in the Second World War' and Indivar Kamtekar, 'The Shiver of 1942' (originally published in *Studies in History*, Vol. 18, No. 1, 2002) all in Roy, *War and Society*, pp. 126–60, 305–57.

4 See Raymond Callahan, 'The Prime Minister and the Indian Army's Last War'; Alan Jeffreys, 'The Officer Corps and the Training of the Indian Army with Special Reference to Lieutenant-General Sir Francis Tuker'; Rob Johnson, 'The Indian Army and Internal Security 1919–1946', Daniel Marston, 'The War in Burma: The 7/10th Baluch Experience' and Tim Moreman, 'From the Desert Sands to the Burmese Jungle: The Indian Army and the Lessons of North Africa, September 1939–November 1942' in Kaushik Roy, *Indian Army in both World Wars* (Leiden: Brill, 2011), pp. 223–331, 359–90.

5 See Kaushik Roy, 'Expansion and Deployment of the Indian Army during World War II: 1939–45', *Journal of the Society for Army Historical Research*, Vol. 88, No. 355 (Autumn 2010), pp. 248–68; 'Discipline and Morale of the African, British and Indian Army units in Burma and India during World War II: July 1943 to August 1945', *Modern Asian Studies*, Vol. 44, No. 6 (April 2010), pp. 1255–82 and 'Military Loyalty in the Colonial Context: A Case Study of the Indian Army during World War II', *Journal of Military History*, Vol. 73, No. 2 (April, 2009), pp. 497–529.

6 See Tarak Barkawi, 'Culture and Combat in the Colonies: The Indian Army in the Second World War', *Journal of Contemporary History*, Vol. 41, No. 2 (April 2006), pp. 325–55; T.R. Moreman, *The Army in India and the Development of Frontier Warfare, 1849–1947* (Frank Cass, 1998); D.P. Marston, *Phoenix From the Ashes: The Indian Army in the Burma Campaign* (Westport, Praeger, 2003); R. Callahan, *Churchill and His Generals* (Kansas University Press, 2007) and Graham Dunlop, *Military Economics, Culture and Logistics in the Burma Campaign, 1941–1945* (London: Pickering & Chatto, 2009). In addition, although not an academic publication, Chris Kempton, *Loyalty & Honour: The Indian Army: September 1939–August 1947* Parts I–III (Milton Keynes: The Military Press, 2003) is an extremely useful reference work for the period that warrants mention.

7 See Daniel Marston, 'The Indian Army, Partition and the Punjab Boundary Force', *War in History*, Vol. 16 (2009), pp. 469–505 and his tentatively titled *Rock in an Angry Sea: The Indian Army and the End of the Raj* (Cambridge: Cambridge University Press, forthcoming).

first volume of Compton Mackenzie's unfinished history of the Indian Army, *Eastern Epic*, Major General Elliott's *A Roll of Honour*, and the volumes of the Indian Armed Forces official history published in the 1950s and 1960s.[8] A modern, inclusive historical interpretation of the Indian Army in the period 1939–47 is thus long overdue. This volume goes some way towards this goal and highlights the new research being undertaken in this field.

Ashley Jackson's opening essay is a useful introductory chapter placing the Indian Army in the global context of British colonial and Commonwealth forces ranging from early imperial military units to those still in existence in Africa, India and other former parts of the empire.[9] He looks at fighting units, volunteers, labour corps and noncombatants and examines the recruitment, expansion, organisation, development and martial races theory that underpinned these formations. For example, the Iraq Levies and the Calcutta Light Horse are examined showing the vast resources of the Army in India both before and during the Second World War, along with wider coverage of the regular forces of the Indian Army, the Auxiliary Force, India (the equivalent of the British Territorial Army), the Indian Army Reserve and the Indian State Forces. Their contribution to the maintenance of the empire during the Second World War is highlighted, with a primary focus on the Indian Army from 1939 to 1942. The rapid expansion of the Indian Army and its concomitant lack of training in this period is described, as is its responsibility in the early defeats in the Far East: the Fall of Singapore on 15 February 1942 marking the beginning of the end of the Empire in South East Asia.[10] It is well to note at this juncture that this volume is almost wholly concerned with the regular Indian Army, in which during wartime there were generally three brigades per division, typically with one British Army battalion in each brigade, alongside British field regiments from the Royal Artillery and other ancillary units.

Patrick Rose next examines the distinct Indian Army command culture of the period preceding the war. This was reflective of, and consistently maintained

---

[8] See Compton Mackenzie, *Eastern Epic* (London: Chatto & Windus, 1951), Major General J.G. Elliott, *A Roll of Honour: The Story of the Indian Army, 1939–1945* (London: Cassell, 1965) and Bisheshwar Prasad, *Official History of the Indian Armed Forces in the Second World War 1939–1945* (India and Pakistan: Combined Inter-Services Historical Section, 1954–64).

[9] See Ashley Jackson, *The British Empire and the Second World War* (London: Continuum, 2006). See also Ashley Jackson, *Distant Drums: The Role of Colonies in British Imperial Warfare* (Brighton: Sussex Academic Press, 2010).

[10] See Alan Warren, 'The Indian Army and the Fall of Singapore' in Brian Farrell and Sandy Hunter (eds), *Sixty Years On: The Fall of Singapore Revisited* (Singapore: Eastern Universities Press, 2003), pp. 270–89. See also Brian P. Farrell, *The Defence and Fall of Singapore 1940–1942* (Stroud, Gloucestershire: Tempus, 2005).

in, the North West Frontier campaigns and routine policing operations of the 1920s and 1930s. From the basis of a shared doctrine with the British Army of the same period, he demonstrates how the unique organisational and operational characteristics of the Indian Army's inter-war experience developed a manifestly different approach to command. Founded in the principles of what would now be termed mission command, this approach had its roots in the pragmatism and flexibility ingrained in the conduct of British imperial campaigns, but only became effectively institutionalised within the Indian Army because of its constant exposure to operations on the North West Frontier during this time. This persistent and routine experience formed a coherent command culture in the Indian Army officer corps quite unlike its British counterpart by the eve of the Second World War. Early fighting against the Japanese in Malaya and Burma during 1942–43 exposed some of the weaknesses of this approach and challenges inherent in effecting its use in large scale warfighting operations, but this culture of command formed a solid foundation to enable the successes the Indian Army achieved from the winter of 1943 until its final battlefield victory in August 1945.

Raymond Callahan's chapter charts Churchill's ambivalent attitude towards the Indian Army, and India itself, initially formed whilst serving with the 4th Hussars in the country during the nineteenth century. This low opinion was reinforced by the disastrous wartime defeats the Indian Army suffered in Malaya and Burma during 1941 and 1942. By the latter stages of the Second World War, Churchill was both un-interested in the feats of the Indian Army as well as its reconquest of Burma. Callahan also makes the important point that in addition to the severe challenges of expansion facing the wartime Indian Army, it was extremely short of equipment during the early stages of the war.

The doctrine and training of armies has only fairly recently become the subject of serious studies of the British and Indian Armies during the Second World War.[11] Alan Jeffreys demonstrates that the Indian Army proved particularly good at learning from experience across all operational theatres, transmitting battlefield lessons into training instructions and publications much more successfully than its British Army counterpart. The Indian Army of 1939 was a well trained, professional, Imperial policing force, but was not capable of fighting a modern army. Jeffreys shows how the Army adapted the existing training organisation to develop a comprehensive training structure and doctrine to fight effectively in the Far East and Europe during the Second

[11] See David French, *Raising Churchill's Army* (Oxford: Oxford University Press, 2000) and Timothy Harrison Place, *Military Training in the British Army, 1940–1944* (London: Frank Cass, 2000). See also Marston, *Phoenix from the Ashes* and Moreman, *The Jungle, the Japanese and the Commonwealth Armies at War*.

World War. He examines and contextualises the important role played by a small number of pre-war Indian Army officers who took training very seriously before 1939, such as Major General Francis Tuker and Major General Thomas Corbett, who inculcated a similar ethos in the next generation of senior Indian Army officers during the war.

Three Indian Army Divisions fought in the North African campaign but 4th Indian Division was the only formation to fight throughout the campaign from the Western Desert Force to its role as a founding element of the British Eighth Army in September 1941. Chris Mann's contribution considers the relationship of 4th Indian Division with its parent formation, British Eighth Army, during the fighting of 1943. It notes the self acknowledged (and encouraged) view held by those of 4th Indian Division, and its commander, Major General Francis Tuker, that the formation was 'a division outside'; a tactical innovator much at odds with the rigid, upward-looking culture the author identifies within Eighth Army at this time. This chapter examines the effect of this uneasy position upon the role of 4th Indian Division in the Battle of Wadi Akarit, and how it influenced the relationship of its charismatic commander with his peers and superiors.

The Burma campaign was primarily fought by the Indian Army. Graham Dunlop and Tim Moreman both look at aspects of this campaign in the next chapters of the volume. Tim Moreman traces how the military effectiveness of the Indian Army in South East Asia was so dramatically transformed, with particular attention to the problem of Japanese defensive bunkers first encountered in the First Arakan campaign of 1942–43. Moreman's chapter examines a fascinating case study of wartime learning, and demonstrates how this problem was studied in India to develop the successful bunker-busting tactics used in the Second Arakan campaign of 1944. Graham Dunlop charts the Burma campaign from the key battles of Mandalay and Meiktila until the re-capture of Rangoon in 1945. His analysis then examines the claim as to whether this achievement was the last and greatest victory of the Indian Army.

The Indian Army controversially acted as a post-war occupation force in both French Indo-China and the Dutch East Indies at the end of the Second World War. Although much has been published about this period very little has concentrated on the Indian Army's role in post-war South East Asia. Daniel Marston re-evaluates the military effectiveness of the 20th Indian Division, under the command of General Douglas Gracey, in Saigon in 1945–46 and the ensuing political problems of their deployment.

Addressing the neglected subject of the Indian Army's experience during the period of Partition, the innovative studies of Ashok Nath and David Omissi look at the impact of this major event on the Indian Armoured Corps and the Gurkha regiments respectively. Ashok Nath examines the difficult task of dividing the Indian Armed Forces in 1947, unprecedented in military history. The need to split units along ethnic and religious lines whilst keeping regimental identity intact presented tremendous difficulties. As Nath observes, that it was accomplished at all is a testament to the efforts of senior British and Indian Army officers. They were aided in their achievement by the existing class structure of units and sub-units within the combatant arms, combined with the mutual respect and goodwill prevalent amongst the diverse men of the Indian Army rank and file that was maintained even as their country was torn in two. The Gurkha Regiments occupied a unique place within the British Indian Army, and their peculiar status resulted in some of them becoming part of the British Army upon partition of the Indian Armed forces in 1947; the only element of the old Indian Army to do so. Omissi traces the roots of this decision back into the inter-war period, when Gurkha Regiments formed a distinct part of the Indian Army and were specifically excluded from the process of Indianisation. It concludes with an examination of the post Second World War debates about the separation of Gurkha units between Britain, India and Nepal, and how this was ultimately decided according to where the regiments were based and where in Nepal they were recruited, rather than considerations of seniority and royal patronage.

Robert Johnson's concluding chapter examines the Indian Army's role in providing 'aid to the civil power' on the North West Frontier from the 1930's to the end of imperial rule. The inter-war period was one of profound change, where rules of engagement were altered and civil primacy asserted more firmly despite the fact that frontier Pashtuns were better armed and there was greater civil unrest growing within India. The outbreak of the Second World War accelerated these changes and added further pressure on the Indian Army, which adapted quickly to manage a range of violent internal threats not only before the war, but during a period of mass unrest that had the potential to unhinge the entire defence of India in wartime.[12]

The editors would collectively like to thank all the historians, including Jahan Mahmood, who presented their research at the conference and have contributed to this volume. We acknowledge the support for the conference by John Delaney, Acting Head of the Department of Exhibits and Firearms, Imperial War Museum and Dr Helen McCartney, Senior Lecturer, Department of Defence Studies, King's College London. We would also like to thank Dr Bryn Hammond, co-convenor of the IWM History Group, and afford our sincere

[12] An earlier version of this chapter by Johnson has appeared as 'The Army in India and Responses to Low-Intensity Conflict, 1936–1946', *Journal of Army Historical Research*, Vol. 89, No. 358, Summer 2011, pp. 159–81.

appreciation to Field Marshal Sir John Chapple who opened the conference and generously contributed the foreword.

Chapter 1
The Evolution and Use of British Imperial Military Formations

Ashley Jackson

> Then the marching began, the solemn convolutions of armed men, a khaki-coloured ballet of stiff arms and stiff legs. It was a scene beloved of the British, stamped out over half the world for two centuries and more. Men and arms, moving to orders, under a blue foreign sky.
>
> – Square-bashing in Hong Kong, from Leslie Thomas, *Onward Virgin Soldiers* (1971).

This chapter considers Britain's use of indigenous armed forces during the days of empire. The Empire expanded and was defended by non-European soldiers and non-combatant military labourers. Mohawks during the Seven Years War, Africans during the Boer War, and Chinese and Egyptian labour corps during the First World War – non-European labour, forced and voluntary, was a leitmotif of imperial defence. So, too, was the ability through transport, communication, administrative, and personnel networks to recruit, move, utilise, and demobilise this enormous resource. Chinese gangers in Shanghai or tea planters in Assam were integral to the recruitment and mobilisation of labourers, as was the availability of the means by which to move them, to France, Java, Mesopotamia, or the Western Desert.

Thus the chapter reviews the role of imperial military formations and the British Empire's notable capacity to mobilise military and semi-military labour across national and colonial boundaries. It does this by considering a number of related themes: the role of imperial military formations, such as the Indian Army's activities on India's military peripheries; the expansion of the Indian Army and colonial formations during the Second World War; India's role in exporting models of military thinking and organisation throughout the Empire; and the post-imperial continuation of Britain's employment of overseas military formations and colonial infrastructure.

The Indian Army was by far the largest of a diverse range of imperial military formations that helped the British Army, the Royal Navy and the Royal Air Force, as well as colonial police forces, to protect the Empire from external and internal threats. This task was always beyond the power of the British armed forces alone. What is more, the Indian Army and the other permanent military establishments maintained in the colonies and the 'white' Dominions were aided by a host of voluntary and *ad hoc* formations, particularly during times of general war. The Indian Army was a core element of the complex, but interlinking, structures maintained to provide for the Empire's local, regional, and international security through the use of indigenous military formations. But there were many other military units drawn from the scores of territories that made up the British Empire. As James Lunt reminds us:

> From Wei-hai-Wei in North China to Port of Spain in Trinidad, and from Nova Scotia to Hobart in Tasmania there were soldiers organized, equipped, and drilled in accordance with the manuals issued by the War Office in London. Some were called Scouts, others were named Levies, or Rifle Corps, or Guides, or Rangers, or Camel Corps, or Militias, or Military Police, or Defence or Frontier Forces.[1]

Britain's utilisation of colonial and semi-colonial military resources, including physical infrastructure, is usually an overlooked or taken-for-granted aspect in studies of British military affairs. But Britain's military history is inseparably linked to the service of non-British and non-European military formations, some recruited on a permanent basis, others in an *ad hoc* manner, and the labour of hundreds of thousands of indigenous men and women. These included 30,000 people employed in Malta's dockyards, scores of thousands of Indians required to build military infrastructure in order to meet the challenge of Japan, and over 100,000 Chinese labourers employed on the Western Front.

Institutions of the British state and private institutions benefiting from state backing, such as the chartered companies and their paramilitary forces, proved highly successful, over the course of three centuries, in recruiting and utilising indigenous military formations.[2] Notwithstanding mutinies – some famous,

[1] James Lunt, *Imperial Sunset: Frontier Soldiering in the Twentieth Century* (London: Macdonald, 1981), p. xiii. Lunt was dissuaded from applying to the Indian Army because of his father's belief, in 1936, that India would be independent within a decade (his father was on the staff of the Military Academy at Dehra Dun). Lunt spent a third of his 35-year military career with the Burma Rifles, the Arab Legion, and the Aden Protectorate Levies.

[2] For a compendious bibliographical study of these formations see Roger Perkins, *Regiments: Regiments and Corps of the British Empire and British Commonwealth, 1758–1993* (Newton Abbot: The Author, 1994).

most forgotten – this is a resounding fact.[3] What is more, the longevity of the British Empire, and the projection of power from its regional power centres around the world, would have been impossible without this skill. There were never enough settlers to man the barricades and dispossess the natives, never enough redcoats to defeat internal resistance and rebellions and win later-day counterinsurgency campaigns, even had it been politic to use them. Indigenous allies, formal and informal, were always crucial. Whilst the British were naturally keen (often after a spot of violent 'pacification') to cultivate the image of harmonious civil rule, colonial control was ultimately based upon the threat of violence. Civil administration based on political alliance with indigenous leaders was real enough, and very much a feature of the edifice of imperial governance and authority; but so too was the presence and effectiveness of military power. Britain's ultimate ability to enforce its suzerainty at the point of a bayonet or through the demonstration effect of a cruiser's main armament was crucial to the functioning of a global empire.

There was always effective Military Aid to the Civil Authority available within the British imperial structure, and even in the worst case scenario, as demonstrated by the Indian Mutiny-Rebellion, though the mills of British retribution might grind slow, they ground exceeding small. Unlike pre-modern empires, the British Empire could exact its power even in the remotest corners of the earth, because of the strategic lift of its marine and the technological and organisational sophistication of its forces – metropolitan and indigenous – on land. From the early twentieth century, its capacity to police the Empire was augmented by the dawn of air power. So, although what has been referred to as the Empire's steel frame – the men of the imperial civil services – were vital, so too was the cold steel frame of the Indian Army and the gallimaufry of smaller colonial organisations, from the Trucial Oman Scouts and the Fiji Defence Force to the Sarawak Rangers and the Hadhrami Bedouin Legion.

The role of colonies in defending Britain and the Empire was better acknowledged at the time than it has been in subsequent historical memory. At Queen Victoria's Diamond Jubilee in 1897, for example, colonial military formations featured prominently in the procession through London that accompanied the Queen's carriage. There were, of course, plenty of representatives from the Dominions and India. From the subcontinent came a deputation of officers from the Imperial Service Troops, a force of 20,000 men raised by India's princes to commemorate the 1887 jubilee. There were cavalry contingents from Canada and Natal, and mounted infantry units from Cape

3 See Lawrence James, *Mutiny in the British and Commonwealth Forces, 1797–1956* (London: Buchan and Enright, 1987).

Town, New South Wales, Queensland, South Australia, and Victoria. The procession included representatives of the 48th Canadian Highlanders and the Royal Canadian Mounted Police, as well as the Perth (West Australia) Artillery Volunteers. But interspersed among these Dominions and Indian units, in all their elaborate regimental splendour, were the men of the colonial empire. Colonial units involved in the procession at the heart of this imperial jamboree were the Trinidad Mounted Rifles and the Cypriot Zaptiehs, a military police unit of 670 men. The 1,100-strong Malta Militia was represented as was the Royal Malta Artillery, a 460-strong regular corps of the British Army recruited in Malta. There was also the Trinidad Field Artillery, the West African Infantry, the Trinidad Infantry, Dyak Police of the British North Borneo Company, the Jamaica Artillery, the Sierra Leone Artillery, the Sierra Leone Force, Hausa soldiers, the British Guiana Police, the Ceylon Light Infantry, the Ceylon Artillery Volunteers, and soldiers from Hong Kong and the Straits Settlement.[4]

Indigenous military formations recruited, trained, and led by British officers and NCOs were essential in creating the colonial state throughout the world and then protecting it, gathering to the British a monopoly of lethal force by emasculating indigenous polities. This monopoly was the bedrock of the subsequent *civilianisation* of British rule. In protecting the colonial state thus founded, the British Empire never lost its dependence upon indigenous allies, in the form of military and paramilitary soldiers, political and economic allies, clerks, interpreters, and labourers. Even during the initial phase of conflict that often occurred when a new tract of foreign territory was absorbed into the Empire, the British frequently relied on local people to overcome their adversaries. In Asia, decisive forward moves such as the Battle of Plassey and the conquest of the kingdom of Kandy were achieved not just by the use of European and indigenous military formations, but by the employment of cunning and subterfuge involving British and indigenous spies and go-betweens, pretenders to thrones, and bribery. The British employed any technique that could be used to undermine, overcome, conquer, and absorb powerful kingdoms.

In its world wars and its local wars Britain required professional military structures, such as the Indian Army and the King's African Rifles, which could be expanded exponentially. These permanent formations were at the heart of the Empire's impressive force generation capability. In 1914 the strength of the Indian Army stood at 155,423, a figure that had risen to 573,484 by the time of the Armistice, 'including large armies serving in Palestine, Egypt, Iraq,

---

[4] John Johnson Collection of Printed Ephemera, Bodleian Library, Oxford. *Illustrated Programme of the Royal Jubilee Procession* (London: Prince of Wales Hospital Fund for London, 1897).

Salonika, and elsewhere'.[5] Other military formations followed suit. The King's African Rifles began the First World War with 2,300 officers and men in three battalions, and ended it with 33,300 men in 22 battalions (the same occurred again in the Second World War, the force rising from a peacetime strength of six battalions to 43 battalions by 1945). These were the major fighting forces of the Empire, permanently maintained forces readily expanded during times of war.

Alongside them, however, there were a range of other military formations, often part-time volunteer units or units created specifically for the demands of a certain war, and often designated *local*, as opposed to imperial, troops, denoting their role in home defence as opposed to overseas operations. Such units included the 2,000-strong Mauritius Defence Force – a home guard formation that like its British counterpart attracted some derision, but their members would have died as well any other men if the Japanese had invaded – and the 250,000-strong Kikuyu Home Guard formed to help the British during the Mau Mau emergency in Kenya. Another distinct category of indigenous military strength was *ad hoc* units set up specifically to answer particular wartime needs. Thus in 1941, facing a manpower crisis in the Middle East following the loss of large numbers of Pioneer soldiers in Crete and Greece, the Commander-in-Chief Middle East asked the Southern African High Commission Territories to supply soldiers. From scratch, beginning with chiefly recruitment meetings and the arrival of British base depot teams, a force of over 36,000 men was soon recruited, trained, delivered, and in service across North Africa and Southern Europe. There were then a whole range of specialist units dependent upon colonial labour: South African mineworkers served in engineer units that blasted a railway through rock to link Beirut and Haifa; Basotho muleteers were employed in the Italian mountains; Iban Dyak trackers from Borneo served with SOE during the war and with infantry regiments such as the Green Howards during the Malayan Emergency; the Royal Garrison Artillery was manned by men from Ceylon, Hong Kong and Singapore.[6] Finally, in addition to all of these permanent fighting units and hostilities-only fighting and 'rear echelon' units, there were then a host of indigenous people recruited as general workers supporting British military bases and infrastructure, such as the 'hangar boys' recruited to support the work of the Empire Air Training Scheme in Southern Rhodesia, Asian

5 *The Army in India and its Evolution, Including an Account of the Establishment of the Royal Air Force in India* (Calcutta: Superintendent, Government Printing India, 1924), p. 31.

6 For the development of British special forces and the Empire, see Ashley Jackson, 'The Imperial Antecedents of British Special Forces', *RUSI Journal*, 154, 3 (2009) and Andrew Hargreaves, 'The Advent, Evolution, and Value of British Specialist Formations in the Desert War, 1940–43', *Global War Studies*, 7, 2 (2010).

and Chinese men signed on by the Royal Navy as seagoing crew, and Sinhalese women employed to provision RAF flying-boats.

The British Empire, therefore, was buttressed by a vast military structure, and the lancers, infantrymen, and artillerymen were supported by a phalanx of miners, sappers, signallers, carriers, pioneers, and mess servants. These men and women provided the essential support to the imperial fighting arms overseas, from serving gimlets in the mess to laying down smokescreens, salvaging crashed aircraft, digging graves, performing static guard duties, growing crops for army horses, evacuating casualties, performing clerical tasks, stoking the boilers, doing the laundry, and erecting telegraph poles. This amounted to a massive outsourcing of defence tasks. Colonial manpower provided the boots on the ground and the support services without which the fighting arms could not have deployed, performing many of the *non-fighting* military tasks essential to manning an empire and to the deployment of front line combat forces. Indigenously recruited units, primarily drawn from India and Africa, also provided key elements of British combat power and supplemented the British Army in wars and counterinsurgency campaigns all over the world.

Martial Races the World Over

The evolution of India's military structure influenced British military practice in parts of the world colonised later, particularly Africa. Here, racial gradations and the identification of martial races followed very familiar lines, and the migration of British attitudes and prejudices continued its journey from medieval roots.[7] Around the world British-created military formations had profound significance in shaping colonial and post-colonial society. Military formations drawn from favoured recruiting regions and ethnicities projected into the independence years military structures that were often unrepresentative of the people of new nation-states as a whole. Having said that, in many post-colonial states the military was often the only stable institution. In Nigeria, for example, the army saw its job as to defend and protect the new nation-state, and if this meant intervening in politics, then this was considered acceptable as well as necessary.

Martial race ideas, of course, came from the belief in British superiority and the need to classify the 'others' they encountered, in a manner helpful for their own acquisition of knowledge and power, and to give them greater ability to order and conceptualise alien societies, their systems of social and political

[7] See for example Timothy Parsons, '"Kamba Warriors are Soldiers of the Queen": The Evolution of the Kamba as a Martial Race, 1890–1970', *Ethnohistory*, 46, 4 (1999).

organisation, and their differing physical and mental strengths and weaknesses as human beings.[8] It was part of the codification of knowledge of foreigners, a process that silted up the fluidity of identity and being, and it began long before the British encounter with India or Africa, practised first on the tribes of Ireland, Scotland, and Wales. As an aside to the acquisition of colonial knowledge and the role played in it by scholars, it is interesting to note the recent controversy over the use of 'embedded' anthropologists working for the Department of Defense in Iraq in an attempt to deliver better cultural understanding of the alien societies among which American forces operate. History continues to be loosely dragooned into the service of current military operations, a sometimes wrong-headed 'lessons learned' mentality surviving undiminished in modern Western militaries, and culture has come to be viewed, for the moment at least, as a sharp sword capable of loosening the Gordian knot at the heart of counterinsurgency-style warfare.[9]

Martial race theory, however, had to be hastily rethought, even abandoned, during times of general war and the chronic manpower shortages that trailed in its wake. Classic martial race categories – obedience, effeminacy, loyalty, warlike, intelligent, independent, stupid – and classic colonial aversion to towns and cities in favour of rural (and usually poor) areas, passed into abeyance as men were taken from wherever they could be found, and as the Empire's need for non-fighting or rear echelon soldiers escalated. During the Revolutionary and Napoleonic Wars, the British recruited anything that moved as its appetite for military manpower grew as new theatres of operations opened up all over the world and new territories, from Mauritius to Madeira, Kephalonia to Manila were occupied or attacked. Likewise during the Second World War, defeats to Germany and Japan meant that societies that had never been considered in a military context, or, indeed, had previously been considered completely unsuitable for martial tasks, were suddenly called upon to furnish thousands of soldiers. World war meant that martial race categorisation was quietly relegated as a recruitment factor as the Indian Army expanded to number around two and a half million men, and that people such as the Batswana of Southern Africa were turned to for soldiers.

---

[8] 'The Origins of Martial Race Theory', in David Omissi, *The Sepoy and the Raj: The Indian Army, 1860–1940* (London: Macmillan in association with King's College London, 1994), pp. 23–5.

[9] For a ground-breaking approach to the subject of Western attitudes towards 'Eastern' war and the importance of culture, encompassing a broad sweep of history right up to the present day, see Patrick Porter, *Military Orientalism: Eastern War through Western Eyes* (London: Hurst, 2009).

The love of categorization, of course, remained; in the African Pioneer Corps, the Basotho were known for belligerence, the Bechuana for docility, the Swazi for rank stupidity and a propensity to become depraved if women and drink were involved, whilst Sinhalese and Mauritian servicemen were marked for their supposedly superior intelligence and a degree of effeminacy and physical frailness. Within the trans-continental military exchange that was the British Empire during times of global conflict, there was plenty of scope for the reinforcement of a range of venerable racial stereotypes held among non-Europeans, too. These were manifest most notably in a widespread aversion towards Africans. In Mauritius people were afraid of King's African Rifles 'Zulus' and much resented their presence when they were brought in to beef up the island's defences in case of a Japanese raid.[10] Similarly in Ceylon, villagers watched African soldiers bathing in the hope of glimpsing their tails, and people actually fled areas near to African camps for fear that they would eat their children, convinced as many were that they had been brought in to eat the Japanese should they land. This wasn't confined to the ignorant; in the Ceylon State Council, racist views about Africans were expounded, and in Mauritius, well-educated troops resented being given African ration scales and being 'treated as Africans'.[11]

Martial theory was not confined to the land. As Daniel Spence's research shows, in the Caribbean martial race theory was alive and well. In searching for volunteers for the Trinidad Royal Naval Volunteer Reserve, for example Cayman Islanders were considered to be 'natural seafarers':

> The average Caymanian is probably of better physique, is healthier, and has a better intelligence than the average American or the inhabitants of any other island in the West Indies and the countries bordering the Caribbean. This is attributable primarily to his energetic life. Other factors are his higher moral standards and the absence on the island of the usual tropical diseases.[12]

---

10 Ashley Jackson, *War and Empire in Mauritius and the Indian Ocean* (Basingstoke: Macmillan, 2001).

11 Ashley Jackson, '"Defend Lanka Your Home": War on the Home Front in Ceylon, 1939–1945', *War in History*, 16, 2 (April 2009). See also Katrin Bromber, 'Heshima: British Wartime Propaganda to East African Troops in Ceylon (1943–45)' in Ashwini Tambe and Harald Fischer-Tiné (eds), *The Limits of British Control in South Asia: Spaces of Disorder in the Indian Ocean Region* (London: Routledge, 2008).

12 Daniel Spence, 'Racial Identity in the Trinidad Royal Naval Volunteer Reserve', in Ashley Jackson (ed.), 'New Research on the British Empire and the Second World War', *Global War Studies*, 10, 1 (2010).

Recruiting and Using Colonial Troops

During times of global war, in the aftermath of the violent imposition of colonial rule, or in the face of colonial mutinies and rebellions, the British often required soldiers and required them fast. As British rule was manufactured, often through the use of force or with the evident threat of force, military affairs were a lot less formalised than they later were to become or than they were later portrayed in the historical record. In the initial phases of British expansion into a colonial region, then during the decades or centuries of Britain's established presence there, and then again during the years or decades leading up to independence, the British often had cause to rely on indigenous manpower to resource various types of internal colonial warfare. These ranged from border skirmishes and 'punitive raids' to localised campaigns and the suppression of rebellions. There were many marriages of convenience as the British, often few in number and in a situation where their authority was far from being beyond contest, sought impromptu help. In making British rule a reality in colonial territories, and then in providing for their security, indigenous manpower was essential. Thus British rule was gradually extended in what became the colony of Kenya by a series of actions in which British forces acted alongside Maasai warriors in subjugating other ethnic groups, as for a decade the interests of the two parties aligned before the 1904 Maasai moves which saw them ejected from their lands for the purposes of white settlement.[13] During the period of 'established' British rule in Kenya, indigenous forces were utilised for internal security purposes as well as for the prosecution of Britain's wars against Germans and Italians between 1914–18 and 1939–45, and then again were called in to play during the war of decolonisation generally known as the Mau Mau Emergency.

The British repeatedly demonstrated agility and improvisation in ministering to the military needs of a global empire in times of war. On the news of the French conquest of the Netherlands in 1795, the East Indies Squadron and troops of the East India Company were able to seize Trincomalee and Malacca in August of that year, followed by Colombo and most of the Spice Islands in

---

[13] See Richard Waller, 'The Maasai and the British, 1895–1905: The Origins of an Alliance', *Journal of African History*, 17, 4 (1976). Colonial campaigns, usually requiring the investment of considerable military resources, were legion. Beyond those periodically reviewed in books along the lines of 'Queen Victoria's little wars – see Byron Farwell, *Queen Victoria's Little Wars* (London: Allen Lane, 1973), for example and Saul David, *Victoria's Wars: The Rise of Empire* (London: Viking, 2006) for a more recent version, there were countless others. Some of these are covered in Ian Hernon, *Britain's Forgotten Wars: Colonial Campaigns of the Nineteenth Century* (Stroud, Gloucestershire: Sutton, 2003). See also Philip Haythornthwaite, *The Colonial Wars Source Book* (London: Caxton Editions, 2000).

early 1796. In all these cases it was the strategic value of the ports as naval bases which was uppermost in ministers' minds. Soldiers of the British Army and the East India Company, commanded by Colonel James Stuart of the 72nd Foot, arrived off Trincomalee on 1 August 1795. A thousand British infantrymen were joined by four battalions of Indian troops and directed against Trincomalee. The fortress was besieged, and surrendered on 26 August. The forts at Batticaloa and Jaffna also capitulated. British forces spread across the island encountering only limited Dutch resistance and on 15 February 1796 Colombo was taken. The Swiss mercenary regiment of Count Charles-Daniel De Meuron, upon whom the Dutch had depended, was persuaded to transfer its allegiance to the British Crown after being released from its oath in October, its 1,000-plus men thereafter serving with distinction alongside British troops. British operations in Ceylon demonstrated the telling benefits of seapower and the penalties to be paid by those who could not wield it; for just as the Dutch were unable to reinforce, they were unable to prevent the British from doing so at will.[14]

Thereafter, British rule clamped itself upon Ceylon, though it took half a century before a vice-like grip was established. To bolster Britain's position the 19th Regiment of Foot (later to become the Green Howards) was dispatched to Ceylon in 1796. The Regiment was to remain in Ceylon for the next 24 years. The 19th Foot lost 10 per cent of its strength each year through disease, accidents, and battle. The regiment left behind the graves of 50 officers and 1,500 other ranks. But what the Lord taketh with one hand He giveth with the other, and when the regiment departed in 1820 a great crowd of Sinhalese women saw them off, some of them with three or four children by soldiers of the regiment. Whilst in Ceylon the regiment's task was to secure the British position from internal and external threats, and to take part in imperial campaigns in the region. Thus it took part in fighting in India (for example against Tippoo Sahib in 1799), and in the Kandyan wars that were soon to come. Ceylon thus became a garrison colony, and during the nineteenth century at least 20 British line regiments spent time on the island. Supporting them, and demonstrating the common imperial practice of blending British military resources with those recruited from amongst non-European populations, were locally-recruited units, such as the Malay Regiment of Foot inherited from the Dutch, the 7th Native Infantry from India and four battalions of the Ceylon Regiment. The Ceylon example illustrates the huge importance of indigenous military forces in gaining the Empire and subsequently providing for imperial defence.

---

[14] See Ashley Jackson, 'Ceylon: The Evolution of a Martial Colony, 1760–1960', in Jackson, *Distant Drums: The Role of Colonies in British Imperial Warfare* (Brighton: Sussex Academic Press, 2010).

In 1797 there was a revolt in the provinces around Colombo. In 1800 Governor Frederick North, son of the Prime Minister, sent Major-General Hay Macdowall to Kandy to impress upon the King the power of Britain and to show the benefits of being under British protection, Macdowall taking with him five companies of Madras foot, Malay infantry, and Bengal artillery. The mission achieved little, and Governor North wearied of endless negotiations and moved towards a military solution. Kandy was mobilising for war at the same time. In 1803 the first Kandyan war broke out, and General Macdowall was ordered back to Kandy with an invasion force comprising 1,900 British troops of the 51st and 19th regiments, two companies of Bengal artillery, a company of Malays, and 1,000 men of the newly-formed Ceylon Native Infantry, plus many thousands of camp followers. Reinforcements arrived from India, including African slave soldiers, who terrified the Sinhalese. The 'British' forces maintained on Ceylon, from the time of its conquest until the final lowering of the Union Flag over a century and a half later, were thoroughly multiethnic in their composition. Malays, originally part of the Dutch garrison, were transferred to the East India Company for service in Ceylon. In 1801 they were transferred to the King's service as the Malay Regiment. In 1802 a Sinhalese battalion was formed. In 1802–1803 more Malays were used to form the 3rd Battalion of this new heterogeneous Ceylon Regiment, recruited from among ex-Dutch Malay soldiers imprisoned on St Helena, part of the massive displacement of humanity that followed in the wake of world wars. The demands of local security, given the proximity of the warlike kingdom of Kandy and the ongoing struggle with Napoleonic France, was so great that Governor North was given permission to purchase slaves for military purposes, and in 1814 the 4th Battalion The Ceylon Regiment was formed, consisting entirely of African slaves.

At times like these, military power had to be generated quickly. Elsewhere in the Indian Ocean region during the Napoleonic Wars General Sir John Abercromby was appointed Commander-in-Chief Bombay and ordered to rid the ocean of the French menace in conjunction with the ships of the Royal Navy and the Bombay marine. In moving against Mauritius, on 12 October 1810 he wrote to Robert Dundas, President of Board of Control for the affairs of India, that 'the Force to be employed on the attack is to be drawn from Bengal, Madras, Bombay, Bourbon [Réunion] and the Cape, and when united at Rodriguez, will, I hope, not be less than 7,000 European and 3,000 Native Infantry'.[15] As soon as his forces had conquered the major French Mascerene islands, his thoughts

---

15 See Raymond D'Unienville (ed.), *Letters of Sir John Abercromby, September 1810–April 1811*, Société de l'histoire d'île Maurice (Quatre Bornes, Mauritius: Michel Robert, 1969).

immediately turned to raising troops from among their native populations, so as to release his British and Indian troops for fighting elsewhere.

There are, of course, very many other examples of the rapid generation of military force in the face of unexpected events or shifting strategic fortunes. The Indian Mutiny was a completely unexpected event and, with time needed for reinforcements from Britain, the Cape, Mauritius, Persia and elsewhere to arrive in theatre (even once they had arrived in India, it took a long time for them to get to the affected areas), forces needed to be generated on the spot. Hodson's Horse was such a unit, raised in 1857 from among the Khalsa by Lieutenant William Hodson of the 1st Bengal European Fusiliers, killed at Lucknow the following year at the age of 37. He had initially been ordered to raise a force of 100 horse and 50 foot for intelligence work and personal escorts. The lack of cavalry in the aftermath of the Mutiny meant they were soon pressed in to service to make up the deficiency. Hodson was appointed to command a 'corps of Irregular Horse, which he is directed to raise at Kurnaul', up to 2,000 strong if possible.[16] Following its extensive service in the suppression of the Mutiny, the regiment remained in existence, known from 1859 as the 9th and 10th Bengal Lancers, the 10th known as the 10th Duke of Cambridge's Own from 1878, the two regiments then amalgamated as the 10th Duke of Cambridge's Own Lancers (Hodson's Horse). The 9th served in the Suakin expedition and in France, Palestine, and Syria during the First World War. The 10th served in the Afghan War of 1878–80, in Mesopotamia during the First World War, and the suppression of the Arab rebellion in 1920.

The need for indigenous military formations could be quite specific in origin. The Ceylon Engineers was raised in the early nineteenth century and in 1821 Governor Sir Edward Barnes formed the Ceylon Pioneer Corps. This unit consisted of ten companies of 200 men each, used for the construction of military roads throughout the island. It played an important role in opening up the central highlands and the territory of the old kingdom of Kandy, ensuring the growth of local and export trade and bringing accessibility for troops should internal rebellion reoccur. Ceylon's impressive non-European military establishment was employed beyond the island itself; in 1847, for example, six of the regiment's 22 companies formed part of the Hong Kong garrison. In 1848 it took part in suppressing the Kandy rebellion, caused by land dispossession under British rule.

Ceylon also played a military role in the Boer War, and in the First World War. In October 1914 Major J. Hall Brown led 236 men of the Ceylon Planters

---

[16] Major F.G. Cardew, *Hodson's Horse, 1857–1922* (London: The Naval and Military Press, 2006), p. 4.

Rifle Corps to Egypt, where they helped guard the Suez Canal before being attached to the Australia and New Zealand Army Corps at Anzac Cove. In 1918 the Ceylon Sanitary Section in Mesopotamia was attached to the Baqubah Refugee Camp commanded by Brigadier H.H. Austin. This temporary city of 3,000 tents, 33 miles north-east of Baghdad, was home to 50,000 Assyrian and Armenian Christians who had fled oppression from Muslims in Turkey and Persia.[17]

During the First World War, hundreds of thousands of such men from the colonial world or its peripheries were sucked in to support Britain's vast military machine.[18] Thousands of non-Europeans were recruited into units such as the Cape Coloured Labour Battalion, the South African Native Labour Contingent, the Canadian Infantry Labour battalions, the Egyptian Labour Corps, the Chinese Labour Corps, the Indian Labour Corps, the Zion Mule Corps, the Jewish Labour Corps, the Maltese Labour Corps, the Seychelles Labour Battalion, the Mauritius Labour Contingent, the Fiji Labour Corps, and the East African Carrier Corps. The British also drew in the labour of non-colonial or semi-colonial regions and territories in the Middle East and Europe, from places such as Mesopotamia, Portugal, and Salonika and including units such as the 60,000 plus men of the Arab Labour Corps and Persian Labour Corps.

The Iraq Levies and Indian Forces Beyond the Indian Army

The Iraq Levies provide an excellent example of an imperial military formation and an instance of the more unusual activities of the Indian Army.[19] The Levies were very much a creation of the Indian Army and testament to the fact that the Army, and the Indian Political Service, were the dominant force in the Persian Gulf region, for long part of what Robert Blyth memorably termed 'the empire of the Raj' (which also included Aden, Zanzibar, and the Swahili coast).[20] The Levies

17 See H.H. Austin, *The Baqubah Refugee Camp: An Account of Work on Behalf of the Persecuted Assyrian Christians* (Manchester: The Faith Press, 1920). Also recently republished by First Gorgias Press, Piscataway, NJ, in 2006.

18 See John Starling and Ivor Lee, *No Labour No Battle: The Labour Corps in the First World War* (Stroud, Gloucestershire: The History Press, 2009). See also Sir Charles Lucas (author of the multi-volume official history of the Empire and the First World War), *The War and the Empire: Some Facts and Deductions* (London: Oxford University Press, 1919).

19 See J. Gilbert Brown, *The Iraq Levies, 1915–1932* (London: Royal United Services Institution, 1932).

20 Robert Blyth, *The Empire of the Raj: India, Eastern Africa, and the Middle East, 1858–1947* (Basingstoke: Palgrave Macmillan, 2003).

came into existence in 1915, becoming the Air Defence Force in 1932. Major Eadie of the Indian Army, a Special Service Officer of the Muntafiq Division in Mesopotamia, began by recruiting 40 Mounted Arabs around Nasiriyah for the Intelligence Department. They were initially known as the Muntafiq Horse, then the Arab Scouts, and were used for reconnaissance for British columns fighting the Turks. On the fall of Kut a corps of guards was formed to work on the rivers and telegraph lines. They were variously used to discipline local communities, burning villages and destroying forts and towers, and the collection of tax, as an imperial no-man's-land was gradually subjected to British rule and the realities of a new colonial state made manifest. In February 1919 the 5th Euphrates Levy operated against Sheikh Badr in cooperation with aircraft and gunboats. In September 1919 the Levies fended off a Kurdish attack on the Baqubah Refugee Camp. In forming such military units the role of political officers is noteworthy, as they became part of the paramilitary foundations of the colonial state and developed the capacity for it to police its borders, suppress internal resistance, and take part in general warfighting when called upon.

The Iraq Levies were the gendarmes of a new political regime, central to the foundation of the British colonial state in Iraq. By 1922, the Levies had grown to become an all-arms force of 6,199 men, testament to the use of indigenous manpower in making good British colonial rule and the role of the military in the foundation of the colonial (and later the nation) state. The Iraq Levies recruited from among the Arab, Kurd, Assyrian, Turkoman and Yezidi communities. When the new Iraq National Army was established and as it began to grow, the size of the Iraq Levies reduced. The Iraq National Army recruited Arabs, and the Levies came to rely more heavily on the Assyrians. At the 1921 Cairo conference, where Churchill played the role of kingmaker in Britain's new Levantine fiefs, the Cabinet decided that the function of the Iraq Levies was to relieve British and Indian troops of the Imperial Garrison in Iraq by taking over outposts in the villayet of Mosul and in Kurdistan, and to fill the gap until the new Iraqi National Army was trained up.

The Indian Army was supported by numerous units beyond its own strength. The Army in India, as more technically precise writers once chose to call it, constituted regular British forces, regular Indian forces, the Auxiliary Force, the Indian Territorial Force, and the Indian Army Reserve. In addition to these forces there were the Indian State Forces (also known as Imperial Service Troops) 'when placed at the disposal of the Government of India'.[21] In 1914,

---

[21] The structure and composition of the inter-war Indian Army, following the changes brought by the First World War, is captured in *The Army in India and its Evolution, Including an Account of the Establishment of the Royal Air Force in India* (Calcutta: Superintendent, Government Printing India, 1924). Between 1600 and 1708 'the forces of the East India

29 Indian states maintained troops in this category totalling 22,479 men. As a narrator of the Army's history writing in the 1920s put it, 'this is the Army in India as it is known today, but it is only in recent times that the categories above enumerated have been completed and their several designations have crystallised. The Auxiliary Force and the Indian Territorial Force were established in 1920'.[22] Even the term 'the Army in India' 'only became a stereotyped and officially recognised title after 1903.

Even India's peripheral military formations could perform an important role. In one of the innumerable minor but dramatic episodes of the Second World War, for instance, four Axis merchant ships interned in the neutral Portuguese harbour of Goa on India's west coast were attacked by superannuated members of the Calcutta Light Horse and the Calcutta Scottish.[23] These were Indian Auxiliary Force units that had not seen active service since the Anglo-Boer War. Their escapade was the brainchild of SOE's India Mission, which had been charged by London with the destruction of a secret wireless transmitter aboard the German ship *Ehrenfels*, which was relaying intelligence on the movement of Allied ships leaving Indian ports to U-boats that would surface in the Indian Ocean at a prearranged time in order to receive messages. It was considered essential that the mission be absolutely clandestine and unofficial, for the Government of India and the British government could not risk the political ramifications that would attend a breach of Portuguese neutrality. This was why the Calcutta Light Horse was chosen by SOE as the unlikely and therefore unsuspected instrument of destruction, making a roundabout trip from east to west India by rail and ship.

Company were isolated and unorganized entities'. The second period, 1709–1857, the Army in India was defined by 'the Presidency Armies under the Company'; during the third period, 1858–94, by the Presidency armies 'under the British Crown'; the fourth period, 1895–1920, was the 'period of union, after the abolition of the Presidency armies'; and the 'period of consolidation' began in 1921. The Army in India 'is now regarded as comprising three categories of troops': Covering Troops (for minor frontier outbreaks), the Field Army, and Internal Security Troops.

[22] Ibid., p. 1.

[23] See James Leasor, *Boarding Party* (London: Corgi, 1980).

The Indian and Colonial Empire Contribution during the Second World War

During the Second World War the military forces of the Raj and the colonial empire experienced great expansion. The following table presents figures for the colonial empire:

	1939	**1945**
East Africa	11,000	228,000
West Africa	8,000	146,000
Caribbean/Bermuda	4,000	10,000
Falklands	250	200
St Helena	–	250
Gibraltar	–	700
Malta	1,400	8,200
Cyprus	–	9,000
Palestine/Transjordan	1,500	25,000
Aden	700	1,800
Mauritius	250	3,500
Seychelles	–	1,500
Ceylon	3,500	26,000
Malaya/Borneo	10,000	–
Sarawak	–	–
Hong Kong	1,500	–
Fiji	650	7,000
Tonga	–	2,000
New Hebrides	–	100
Gilbert/Ellice/Ocean	50	2,000
Solomons	–	2,000
Total:	**42,800**	**473,250**[24]

NB: This excludes the 36,000 men recruited from Basutoland, Bechuanaland, and Swaziland (because, though run like colonies and staffed by the Colonial Administrative Service, they formally came under the Dominions Office and not the Colonial Office). It also excludes the many thousands of men recruited into home guard-style units and colonial civil labour units such as the Mauritius Civil Labour Corps, the Ceylon Essential Services Labour Corps, and the Ceylon Agriculture Corps. It also omits colonial personnel serving in *non colonial* services, thus the thousand-plus Mauritian women in the Auxiliary Territorial Service (the women's branch of the British Army), or the 6,800 Mauritians in the Royal Pioneer Corps.

24 Official Papers, Bodleian Library, Oxford. Command 7167, *The Colonial Empire (1939–1947)* (London: HMSO, 1947). Appendix III 'Comparative Strengths of Military Forces in Various Colonial Territories, 1939 and 1945'.

India provided by far the largest number of service personnel in the British Empire, second only to Britain itself. On 1 March 1943 the Secretary of State for India, Leo Amery, circulated a paper to the War Cabinet entitled 'India's War Effort'.[25] The paper reviewed the war effort since March 1942. The Indian Army in India in December 1941 numbered 600,000 British and Indian soldiers. In addition, there were 300,000 men in overseas theatres, including two divisions in the Middle East, three divisions in Iraq, two weak divisions in Malaya, and two infantry brigade groups in Burma, as well as a large number of base and lines of communications units for maintenance of these formations and the protection of lines of communication. 'India's overseas forces were in fact at this time larger than those of any other country of the British Empire.'[26] Of the 600,000 in India, over half were recent recruits still undergoing training, whilst some 150,000 were occupied in their peace-time duties of watch and ward on the North West Frontier and Internal Security duties within India. The only field formations in India itself were three divisions undergoing training and three further divisions in the process of formation, but consisting of little more than the three infantry battalions and entirely lacking artillery and practically all administrative units. Of the three more or less complete divisions only the 17th Division had anything like completed its training and had been offered to the War Office. Two of its battalions were soon dispatched to Malaya and one to Burma.

In 1941 India had dispatched all its administrative units overseas in response to urgent demands, so that at that time there were literally no base and line of communication units available to maintain any field army divisions in the field in India. Further heavy calls for administrative units for Malaya were complied with during December, and over 2,000 infantry reinforcements were also sent there for the two Indian divisions. The total number of AA guns in India was eight, of which four were sent to Rangoon in January. The equipment situation was equally as serious. None of the divisions other than the 17th had anything more than a training scale of weapons except rifles, and heavy guns and signals equipment were almost entirely lacking.

By March 1942 Singapore and Rangoon had fallen, but not before two extra Indian battalions (from 14th Division) had been sent as reinforcements to Burma along with most of the administrative units raised in India during January and February. The 34th Division minus one brigade group had been sent to Ceylon. The divisions in India at the start of March were: 14th (less one brigade group); 23rd; 7th and 19th forming. 'With the fall of Rangoon and shortly afterwards

[25] The National Archives, Kew. CAB 66/34/39. 'India's War Effort', War Cabinet, 1 March 1943.

[26] Ibid., p. 1.

of the Andaman Islands, Ceylon and the whole East and North-East coasts of India were open to Japanese attack, a coastline as long as from Hamburg to Gibraltar. It was obvious that the available troops were insufficient to protect the whole of this vast coastline, and it was, therefore, decided to concentrate what troops there were available for the defence of the two most vital areas, Ceylon and Bengal.'[27] The situation was similar to Britain after Dunkirk; well trained troops were scarce and equipment scarcer still. In the air the situation was equally bad owing to demands of an even higher priority elsewhere on the still limited RAF resources and to the length of time which it takes to move reinforcements to India. Ceylon indeed had two and a third fighter squadrons equipped with Hurricanes, but for the defence of Eastern India there were only two fighter squadrons, equipped with obsolete Audax aircraft. AA guns and reinforcements of AA regiments were beginning to arrive from the UK, and the ground defences of Ceylon were now beginning to take shape. The Calcutta area, however, was still practically defenceless.

By denuding the defences of the North West Frontier of all reserves a force was concentrated in the East of India consisting of 23rd Indian Division, 14th Indian Division less one brigade group, and three independent brigade groups. Sufficient administrative units were scraped together to give this force limited mobility which it was hoped would be sufficient for defensive operations. During March 1942 reinforcements arrived in the shape of the 70th British Division, less one brigade group, from the Middle East, and this was added to the Eastern Army. At the same time the defences of Ceylon were increased by the addition of the third brigade of the 70th Division, one East African brigade, and two Australian brigades, giving a total force in Ceylon comparable to two full divisions.

By the end of May 1942 this time the Japanese had completed the conquest of Burma. Most of the indigenous units of the army had ceased to exist. The 17th Indian Divisions and the 2nd Burma Division (mostly British and Indian units) with battalions in many cases reduced almost to cadres and lacking all vehicles and 90 per cent of their equipment had crossed over into Assam, where they were being collected under the cover of the 23rd Indian Division holding an outpost line of the Assam-Burma frontier. The 17th Indian and 2nd Burma (later renamed the 39th Indian) Divisions required long rest and complete refitting. On the other hand substantial reinforcements had begun to arrive from Britain, while a steady stream of equipment had commenced to arrive from Britain, Canada, and America. The 5th British Division, less a brigade left in Madagascar, arrived in May and was sent to the Eastern Army at Ranchi. Reinforcements of

[27] Ibid., p. 2.

field, anti-tank, and AA artillery had arrived while redoubled efforts had been made to increase the numbers and rate of raising new Indian artillery units. New equipment also meant that the 14th, 23rd, and 26th Indian divisions (Eastern Army), 19th and 20th Divisions (Southern Army), and 34th Division, 16th British Infantry Brigade (from 70th Division), 21st East African Brigade, and two Australian brigades (Ceylon) were up to a stage nearing completion. The anti-aircraft defences of Ceylon had been further strengthened and some anti-air and ground defences provided for Calcutta and the Assam oilfields.

By September 1942 considerable progress was made with the arming, equipping, and training of field formations in India and the raising of additional administrative units for their maintenance. The Eastern Army now consisted of one British and five Indian divisions plus a tank brigade equipped with Valentines, and sufficient administrative troops to make it mobile for active operations. In the Southern Army, the 19th Division was approaching readiness for war, whilst the 25th Indian Division, which had replaced the 20th when it was sent to Ceylon following the departure of the Australian division, had been nearly completed. In addition, the 2nd British Division arrived and was concentrated for GHQ reserve at Poona, the 5th British Division having moved to Iraq. The RAF had received reinforcements and in conjunction with the 10th US Air Force had commenced offensive operations against the Japanese in Burma. The demand for Indian service personnel had significantly altered traditional patterns of recruitment:

> Recruiting from the 'Martial classes' recruited in the pre-war Indian Army is now gradually drying up, and the monthly intake of these classes in only just sufficient to maintain existing units. All further expansion has now to be carried out with Madrassis (Southern Indian classes), who were only recruited to a very small extent before the war.[28]

By December 1942, in India and Ceylon (and in addition to the forces on the NWF, internal security, and training units etc), two British and six Indian divisions were ready for service. Four more Indian divisions were expected to be ready within the following three months, and two Indian Armoured Divisions and two independent tank brigades were to be ready between May and July 1943. There was still one Indian Armoured Division and five Indian divisions in the Middle East and Persia and Iraq Command. There number of anti-aircraft guns in India had increased to 548 heavy and 892 light guns. Owing to the setback in the Middle East in June 1942 the RAF build up in India had been delayed owing

---

28 Ibid., p. 4.

to the diversion of units that had been on their way to India. The construction of 200 aerodromes, which was given the highest priority, 'has strained to the utmost India's exiguous engineering resources' and 'delayed the construction of roads, factories, storage for ammunition etc'.[29]

During the period covered by this report, from September 1939 to December 1942, the total numbers recruited for the Indian Army stood at 1,348,000. The strength of Indian Army in India Command (including Ceylon) in December 1942 stood at 1,226,000, and the strength of the Indian Army overseas stood at 270,000 (these figures include British service personnel serving with Indian Army units and formations, but excluding British Army formations and units).

Post-imperial Imperial Defence

So the British Empire and British military and security posture throughout the world has for hundreds of years heavily influenced the utilisation of indigenous military formations – as recruits into British forces and as less formal allies. Despite the end of empire, this remains substantially true today. Britain, usually through the medium of the armed forces, still pursues its defence and security interests by allying with overseas military formations such as the Northern Alliance in Afghanistan and the armed forces of the Five Powers Defence Agreement in South-east Asia, and by training indigenous forces such as the Republic of Sierra Leone Armed Forces, the Iraqi Navy, 20 Parachute Battalion Kenya Army, the Jaji Infantry Training School in Nigeria, and Chilean sailors responsible for ex-Royal Navy warships.[30] It continues to utilise colonial base infrastructure and to deploy its forces for military tasks related to the defence of Britain's global interests and the international system that it was at the forefront of creating. Some of Britain's old 'imperial' interests now masquerade as NATO, UN, or even EU initiatives and policies.[31] Whilst Britain continues to pursue

---

[29] Ibid., p. 5. Air forces in India December 1942: 1 heavy bomber squadron; 2 medium bomber squadrons; 5 light bomber squadrons;14 day fighter squadrons; 8 GR flying boat squadrons; 3 GRMR landplane squadrons; 1 long-range fighter squadron; 5 bomber and fighter recce squadrons; and 2 transport squadrons.

[30] For an interesting example of the work of British forces in founding a new national army, see Tone Kvernbekk, Harold Simpson and Michael Peters (eds), *Military Pedagogies and Why They Matter* (London: Sense Publishers, 2008).

[31] For the development of these ideas, see Ashley Jackson, 'Empire and Beyond: The Pursuit of Overseas National Interests in the Late Twentieth Century', review article, *English Historical Review*, cxxii, 499 (2007) and Jackson, 'Imperial Defence in the Post Imperial Era', in Greg Kennedy (ed.), *Imperial Defence: The Old World Order, 1856–1956* (London: Routledge, 2008).

its interests in the world by operating alongside the military formations of other nations and seeks to influence the military and security policy of less powerful states, it also continues to employ soldiers from the former Empire in its own armed forces. South Africans and Zimbabweans are present in some strength, as are Fijians. And of course, in the Brigade of Gurkhas, the old Indian Army continues to live on in the very ranks of the British Army.

Chapter 2

Indian Army Command Culture and the North West Frontier, 1919–1939

Patrick Rose

Introduction

Policing the North West Frontier was the primary task of the British Indian Army between the two World Wars. It formed a principle influence on the inter-war Indian Army as an institution, and on the mindset and professional practices of its soldiers and officer corps. This chapter examines the understanding, philosophy and practice of command within the Indian Army, its command culture, during this time. It shows how organisational characteristics unique to the Indian Army combined with the persistent experience of frontier operations to shape a philosophy of command broadly, but informally, based on the principles of what is now termed mission command. This formed a key distinguishing feature of the Indian Army from its British Army counterpart during the period, despite the common doctrine and professional education for command shared between the two services. The Indian Army's operational experience on the North West Frontier between 1919 and 1939 demonstrated many benefits derived from the mission command approach, but also certain shortcomings that highlighted an immature understanding of key aspects intrinsic to its effective and proper operation; clarity of higher direction and effective command organisation. These positive and negative aspects of Indian Army command culture were reflected in the battles and campaigns fought by Indian Army formations and its senior officers during the Second World War. By examining the sources and nature of the Indian Army's pre-war approach to command, this chapter seeks to enhance understanding of how it performed the core task of securing and pacifying the frontier during the inter-war years, and to contextualise the later challenges faced and successes achieved as it adapted to the demands of global war between 1939 and 1945.

The dominant characteristics of any military organisation's system of command, and those of its underlying philosophy, can be referred to as its command culture (sometimes also referred to as command climate). The command culture of every organisation lies in practice between two theoretical extremes, those of restrictive control and directive (or mission) command. Restrictive control emphasises detailed planning and strict obedience to precise orders in order to achieve a given military task, whilst mission command provides instead a framework of objectives to coordinate the activities of subordinates, working under their own initiative and authority, to deliver the required effect. Restrictive control and mission command both represent ways of dealing with the complexity and dynamism of battle. The former does so by creating a structured decision-making environment to constrain the impact of uncertainty upon its operation; the latter by decentralising the very function of decision making itself to mitigate and exploit it.[1] Military practitioners, theorists and historians typically express a clear preference for mission command as the most effective way to control and coordinate military power in battle.[2] In reality, both methods can be appropriate dependent upon the circumstances, nature of the operation and environment at hand.[3] Command culture itself is informed and shaped by many sources, ranging from overt and easily identifiable factors such as formal doctrine, to the more nebulous influence of organisational structure and collective experience, tempered in practice by the personalities and preferences of individual commanders themselves. In its examination of the Indian Army's command culture between 1919 and 1939, this chapter first describes the role and organisation of the service within the Army in India during the inter-war years. It then identifies the key structural differences of the Indian service and their influence on its organisational mindset and practices of command. It then describes the nature of the professional education and training with which the Army informed its inter-war officer corps, before examining the manifestation of its command culture in active operational service on the North West Frontier.

---

[1] Snyder, F.M., *Command and Control: The Literature and Commentaries* (Washington D.C., National Defence University Press, 1993), pp. 106, 152; Kolenda, C.D., 'Discipline: Creating the Foundation for an Initiative-Based Organisation' in Kolenda, C.D. (ed.), *Leadership: The Warrior's Art* (Carlisle, Army War College Foundation Press, 2001), pp. 88–92.

[2] See for example von Lossow, W., 'Mission-Type Tactics versus Order-Type Tactics', *Military Review*, No. 57, June 1977, pp. 87–8; Van Creveld, M., *Command in War* (Harvard University Press, 1985); Lind, W.S. and Wyly, M.D., *Maneuver Warfare Handbook* (Boulder, Westview, 1985). And for a somewhat controversial case study justification see Fitz-Gibbon, S.S., *Not Mentioned in Despatches: The History and Mythology of Goose Green* (Cambridge, Lutterworth, 1995).

[3] Leonhard, R., *The Art of Maneuver: Maneuver-Warfare Theory and AirLand Battle* (New York, Ballantine, 1994) affords a nuanced treatment of this issue.

Structure and Organisation of the Inter-War Indian Army

In the early 1920s, the British Army maintained a permanent force of almost 70,000 troops in India, a number that dropped to just over 40,000 by the eve of the Second World War. Led primarily by British Officers and manned entirely by Indian soldiers, the Indian Army coexisted with its British counterpart under joint administrative control from the Indian Government, and known collectively as the Army in India. The inter-war Indian Army was maintained at approximately two hundred thousand men, delivering a roughly three to one ratio of Indian to British soldiers sustained as an insurance measure since the Indian Mutiny of 1857. The role of the Indian Army throughout the inter-war years was threefold: to ensure the security of the Raj; police the various Indian frontiers; and provide expeditionary troops for the needs of the British Empire.[4] In theory, the tasks of internal security and frontier defence were split equally between British and Indian formations. In practice, and in part reflecting largely baseless concerns over the reliability of Indian soldiers for domestic policing, the British Army provided the majority of garrison troops for internal security duties, whilst the Indian Army performed the bulk of frontier tasks. By the 1930s, this meant that British Army units invariably languished in the garrisons of central India for long and often miserable six year tours of duty, infrequently enlivened by short spells of active service alongside their Indian counterparts on the North West Frontier. In stark contrast, for officers and soldiers of the latter, frontier service formed the core of their military activity and experience.[5]

At the start of the twentieth century, India was split into four administrative military districts: Bombay, Madras, Bengal and the Punjab; each under command of a Lieutenant-General. As part of his modernising reforms during 1904–1905, Lord Kitchener as Commander-in-Chief (C-in-C) overturned this system, decentralising regional command to permanent divisional structures monitored by two roving 'Inspector Generals'.[6] This arrangement lasted throughout the

[4] Moreman, T.R., 'Small Wars and Imperial Policing: The British Army and the Theory and Practice of Colonial Warfare in the British Empire, 1919–1939' in Reid, B.H. (ed.), *Military Power: Land Warfare in Theory and Practice* (London, Frank Cass, 1997), p. 112; Barua, P., 'Strategies and Doctrines of Imperial Defence: Britain and India, 1919–1947'. *The Journal of Imperial and Commonwealth History* 25, No. 2, 1997, p. 241; Omissi, D., *The Sepoy and the Raj: The Indian Army, 1860–1940* (London, Macmillan, 1994), p. 237.

[5] British troops were also generally confined to barracks between 9am and 4pm in the summer months due to the risk of heat-stroke: Omissi, p. 210; Masters, J., *Bugles and a Tiger: My Life in the Gurkhas* (London, Cassell, 2002), pp. 23–4, 164; Prendergast, J., *Prender's Progress: A Soldier in India, 1931–47* (London, Cassell, 1979), p. 42.

[6] Heathcote, T.A., 'The Army of British India' in Chandler, D.G and Beckett, I.F.W. (eds), *The Oxford History of the British Army* (Oxford University Press, 2003), pp. 379–80;

First World War, but confronted divisional commanders with such large administrative responsibility that they lacked any time to train and exercise their formations. Following the recommendations of the Esher Committee in the early 1920s, the district command system was reinstated, with Northern, Eastern, Southern and Western Commands under the administrative control of Army Headquarters (AHQ) India and comprising the Indian General Staff and four key figures of Commander-in Chief, Quartermaster-General, Adjutant-General and Chief of the General Staff. In normal circumstances, the post of C-in-C alternated between British and Indian service officers, each sitting on the Governor General's Executive Council, the supreme Indian military authority under control of the Secretary of State for India.[7]

Like their British Army counterparts, Indian Army units contained roughly 800 men and 30 officers, commanded by a lieutenant-colonel and centrally administered by a parent regiment that had no command authority. For garrison and frontier duties brigade groups were formed, comprising one British Army battalion and either two Indian or one Gurkha and one Indian battalion, permanently supported on frontier service by a battery of (3.7" pack howitzer) mountain artillery. Opposite to the regiment, brigade groups served only a command function and their commanders enjoyed no non-operational administrative control over the units placed in their charge.[8]

The fundamental organisational difference between the British and Indian Army was the position and role of the Viceroy's Commissioned Officer (VCO). In the British Army all officers held the Sovereign's (King's) commission, but the Indian Army maintained the VCO as an intermediate layer of command. Greater in status and responsibility than a British Army warrant officer, VCOs were appointed from the ranks after a long period of meritorious service as senior non-commissioned officers. They played an essential role in maintaining good relations between British Officers and native Indian troops, and greatly set the tone and efficiency of a unit. As such, of the 30 officers within an Indian Army unit only about 12 were British. The remainder were VCOs primarily responsible for the day to day running of the unit, ranging in rank from jemedar

---

Omissi, pp. 206–7.

[7] MacMunn, G.F., *Behind the Scenes in Many Wars: Being the Reminiscences of Lieutenant-General Sir George MacMunn, KCB, KCSI, DSO* (London, John Murray, 1930), pp. 321–2; Bond, B., *British Military Policy between the Two World Wars* (Oxford University Press, 1980), p. 99; Jacobsen, M. (ed.), *Rawlinson in India* (Publications of the Army Records Society, Vol. 19 (Stroud, Sutton, 2002), p. xx.

[8] Mostyn-Owen, H.L., *India Remembered*, ch. 4, p. 1 (Unpublished Memoir, 1965), Mostyn-Owen Mss., *The Papers of Colonel H.L. Mostyn Owen*, Liddell Hart Centre for Military Archives (LHCMA), King's College London, UK; Heathcote, p. 40.

at platoon command level, to infantry subadar or cavalry risaldar, equivalent to a captain and second-in-command of an infantry company or cavalry squadron. The highest VCO rank was the subadar-major, the Commanding Officer's right hand man and chief advisor on troop welfare, discipline, and religious practices.[9] The VCO system gave a very real command function and enhanced responsibility to the Indian Army's long service professionals and was a primary influence on its culture of command. It gave long serving VCOs a considerably greater role than senior British Army NCOs, and most significantly removed the need for junior British Officers in the Indian service to assume command at the lowest formed unit level of the platoon.

The Characteristics of Indian Army Service, 1919–1939

Following a post-First World War slump, the recruitment of British Officers into the Indian Army improved steadily throughout the late 1920s. Competition for Indian Army commissions was usually strong, and by the early 1930s 'only the top thirty-five or so of those who passed out of Sandhurst were considered fit for it'.[10] In part, this reflected the tainted popular image of the British Army after the First World War which, despite ultimate victory in 1918, remained inextricably linked to the slaughter of the Western Front. In contrast, the romantic image of colonial warfare, typified by tales of derring-do on the iconoclastic North West Frontier, was so firmly ingrained in British culture that it 'survived the horrors of the First World War'.[11] Actions in the remote outposts of empire could still capture the British public imagination, and popular mythical constructions of imperial soldiering also proved attractive to seasoned military veterans. Having

[9] Cohen, S.P., *The Indian Army: Its Contribution to the Development of a Nation* (Berkeley, University of California Press, 1971), pp. 42–3; Mostyn-Owen, ch. 3, p. 2; Prendergast, pp. 58–60.

[10] Coleridge to Montgomery, 8/3/1926, *Montgomery-Massingberd Mss., The Papers of Field Marshal Sir Archibald Armar Montgomery-Massingberd*, 9/3/6, LHCMA; Freeland, Colonel J.C., 'The Indian Army Since the Great War', *Journal of the Royal United Services Institute* (*JRUSI*), Vol. 73, No. 492, November 1928, p. 767; Hayter, A., *The Second Step* (London, Hodder & Stoughton, 1962), pp. 20–21. A maximum of 60 Indian Army commissions were usually available each year from a total of 300.

[11] Bond, B. and Murray, W., 'The British Armed Forces, 1918–1939', in Millett, A.R. and Murray, W. (eds), *Military Effectiveness Vol. II: The Interwar Period* (London, Allen & Unwin, 1988), pp. 98, 104–7; Stainforth, G.H., 'Officer Material', *Army Quarterly and Defence Journal* (*AQDJ*), Vol. 104, No. 3, April 1974, p. 325; MacKenzie, J.M., 'Introduction: Popular Imperialism and the Military', in MacKenzie, J.M. (ed.), *Popular Imperialism and the Military, 1850–1950* (Manchester University Press, 1992), p. 19.

previously served for over two years on the Western Front during the First World War, one British officer new to India in 1921 noted he was 'thrilled at the thought of seeing some action … against the wild tribesmen [of the North West Frontier]'.[12] Such opportunities were very much possible in the inter-war British Army, but the Indian Army alone guaranteed recurrent exposure to the unique challenges of imperial soldiering away from 'England's leaden skies and dripping landscape'.[13] It also offered a lesser decrease in excitement and responsibility to the many young men of the 1920s who had served within Britain's swollen armed forces during the First World War. As Field Marshal Sir Claud Jacob, Military Secretary at the India Office, stated in 1928: 'The Indian Army is still a very fine career for any man who wants to show initiative and possesses strength of character and will … It is not a moribund army by any means'.[14] Following the end of the First World War, many British Army officers, including Slim of Fourteenth Army fame, accordingly applied for transfer into the Indian Army with its promise of a more active career. Such transfers remained possible throughout the inter-war period, but were increasingly difficult to obtain and frequently subject to conditions of rank, age, and satisfactory service record.[15]

As a result of its more proletarian roots in the East India Company, the Indian Army also suffered from a lesser degree of social snobbery than the inter-war British Army, and 'many officers [chose it] as a means of enjoying a standard of living and status which they could not have aspired to socially, or afforded financially, at home'.[16] Indian Army officers of relatively junior rank could enjoy large and comfortable living quarters, and as a married captain or major often employed ten or more servants. Due to the benefits of local knowledge and continuous establishment, the standard of living within an Indian regiment was generally higher and cheaper than its British counterpart, even when the latter was in India. Nonetheless, in certain regiments, especially of Indian cavalry, 'for reasons of prestige the standard of living … was kept high and was correspondingly expensive', and junior British Officers who lacked external financial means

---

12 'Arrival in Waziristan to Rejoin 2/3rd (Queen Anne's Own) Gurkha Rifles, 1921', p. 1, *Langlands Mss., The Papers of Brigadier E.W. Langlands*, LHCMA.

13 Prendergast, p. 250.

14 Freeland, p. 769.

15 Coleridge to Montgomery, 8/3/1926, *Montgomery-Massingberd Papers* 9/3/6; Lewin, R., *Slim, The Standardbearer: A Biography of Field Marshal the Viscount Slim* (Ware, Wordsworth, 1999), pp. 35–6.

16 Stanley, P., *White Mutiny: British Military Culture in India* (New York, New York University Press, 1998), p. 281; Cohen, p. 115.

found debt difficult to avoid, especially if they had families to support.[17] Living conditions in frontier stations however differed starkly from the comfortably established cantonments of the Indian interior. Permanent accommodation, even for officers, could be very poor, ranging from tents to 'home-made mud cell[s]', with privation most severe during special duty with locally raised irregular forces, such as the Tochi Scouts.[18] Sport, especially the hunting of local wildlife, and heavy drinking typically provided the only distractions from interminable boredom that could manifest during inactive spells. Memoir accounts of frontier service recount frequent bouts of heavy drinking, often accompanied by alcohol fuelled 'high jinks' in which injuries, sometimes fatal, were not uncommon. Field Marshal Montgomery, who famously failed to gain an Indian Army commission from Sandhurst in 1907, pointedly characterised Indian Army officers as 'good mixers ... [men] who never refused a drink'.[19]

On arrival in India, all newly commissioned British Officers destined for the Indian Army spent one year serving with a British infantry regiment, regardless of whether they were to be posted to the infantry or not. Known as ULIAs (Unattached List Indian Army officers), they led rifle platoons and in theory 'it was the responsibility of the British regiment involved to teach [them] something of practical soldiering'.[20] This period also enabled them to learn Urdu, the essential language of their trade, and gave opportunity for appraisal by the Indian regiments they hoped to join the following year. Placement was by no means guaranteed and following assessment visits of up to a week in duration, a vote by junior regimental officers often decided acceptance of a candidate.[21] On joining Indian Army units, British Officers faced a swift escalation in the demands made of them, finding 'as a sharp contrast to the British Army, an Indian Army officer was given plenty of responsibility'.[22] Having led 30 men as ULIAs, Indian Army subalterns were placed in charge of companies of three to four rifle platoons (or squadrons of four cavalry troops), and more than 120 Indian soldiers. Commanded by a major, a British infantry company contained a captain as 2 i/c and four subalterns commanding platoons, whereas its Indian

---

[17] See especially Mostyn-Owen, ch. 3; ch. 4. One married officer remembered his early career as 'fifteen years of poverty and debt': 'Waziristan', pp. 4–5, *Langlands Papers*.

[18] Prendergast, pp. 88, 94; Lydall, E., *Enough of Action* (London, Jonathan Cape, 1949), pp. 159–62.

[19] Heathcote, *Indian Army*, p. 121, Mackenzie, 'Popular Imperialism', p. 10; Roberts, O.L., 'Memoir', p. 60, *Roberts Mss., The Papers of Lieutenant-General Sir Ouvry Lindfield Roberts*, LHCMA.

[20] Hayter, p. 25.

[21] Mostyn-Owen, ch. 3, p. 1.

[22] Prendergast, p. 55.

equivalent was officered by a single British second-lieutenant, with a subadar and four jemadars under command. This structure immediately advanced the command responsibility of British subalterns in the Indian service to a much higher level and at a much earlier age than their British Army contemporaries, achieved within the security of the close partnership between British Officers and their highly experienced VCOs, whose tutelage formed the foundation of their professional education.[23]

Indian Army officers were entitled to two months of yearly leave, always taken during the summer to avoid soldiering during the hottest season. Every four years, six months extended leave was granted on half pay to enable travel home to England. British Officers also frequently detached to undertake professional training courses and as a result the full compliment of 12 British Officers per unit was usually only achieved during the winter training period. In the summer months, it was commonplace for only four or five British Officers to run the entire unit. Of necessity, even the most junior British Officers became conditioned to acting several steps up the chain of command to fill vacant posts, often performing multiple roles at one time. It was not uncommon for unit command to fall to captains for short term periods, and in one extreme case during the 1920s the 2/3rd Gurkhas were led by a 24-year-old captain for six months. This stood in stark contrast to the British Home Army, within which 'in 1922 200 officers, half of whom had already commanded brigades in war, were awaiting vacancies to command battalions'.[24]

This shaped a command culture in which experience and rank mattered less than the practical ability to cope with the pressures of multiple or more senior commands, and new officers were often flung in at the deep end. One new second-lieutenant posted to 2/4th (Prince of Wales's Own) Gurkha Rifles found himself immediately in temporary command of two rifle companies, responsibility far in advance of his one year ULIA experience. Under such conditions, 'it can be appreciated that all officers, young ones especially, had the opportunity of gaining wide experience and confidence by holding appointments of much responsibility'.[25] This was an acknowledged advantage of the shorthanded situation caused by long summer leave periods, and the peculiarities of Indian Army routine created a body of British Officers with a degree of confidence and regimental command experience greatly surpassing their counterparts of the British service. Also instructive was the confidence demonstrated by senior

---

23 Masters, *Bugles*, pp. 95–130; Mostyn-Owen, ch. 3, p. 3.

24 'Waziristan', pp. 9, 28, *Langlands Papers*; Mostyn-Owen, ch. 3, pp. 1–6; Masters, *Bugles*, pp. 168, 134, 241–2; Drewry, C.F., 'The Lessons of the 1920s and Modern Experience', in Reid, B.H. (ed.), *The Science of War* (London, Routledge, 1993), p. 20.

25 Masters, *Bugles*, p. 109; Mostyn-Owen, ch. 5, p. 6.

officers habitually leaving their units in the care of relatively junior officers for extended periods of time.[26]

With significant or multiple command responsibilities, Indian Army officers often lacked the time to focus on the 'spit and polish' minutiae of soldiering, a much criticised feature of contemporaneous British Army practice.[27] More pertinently, their limited numbers shaped acceptance of a greater reliance on the abilities of all men under their command, not just the VCOs. Unfavourable perceptions propagated of the British Army that, 'with its large numbers of officers, tended to wet nurse the men mentally, with the result that the rank and file never thought for themselves and all, including warrant officers and NCOs, lacked initiative'.[28] Development of initiative in the Indian Army was not confined to the commissioned ranks, but pervaded the entire structure of the unit. One former Indian cavalry officer recalled the dual purpose of hunting trips:

> It was taken very seriously by everyone and discipline in the jungle was strict ... Often a couple of men were sent off for several days at a time with their horses to get *khabbar* (news) of a tiger, and so they might become self reliant – This undoubtedly stood them in good stead when sent out on reconnaissance on active service.[29]

Whilst Indian Army officers enjoyed significantly advanced seniority of command over their British Army counterparts, they did not necessarily enjoy swifter promotion. In 1926, the Military Secretary, AHQ India, noted that many junior officers remained subalterns for an undesirably long time, leading eventually to problems in the selection of COs. Promotion for regimental grade officers was gained by seniority, as in the British Army, and by passing certain exams held regularly within units themselves. Command responsibility did not always increase with rank and officers could hold similar jobs, or even previously held positions, after promotion. Lieutenants who had joined the Indian Army commanding companies could find themselves doing the same job a decade

---

26 Hayter, pp. 87–8.

27 Fuller, J.F.C., *The Army in My Time* (London, Rich & Cowan, 1935), pp. 6–8, 63–7, 220–22 provides rich commentary on this facet of British Army life; Kier, E., *Imagining War: French and British Military Doctrine Between the Wars* (Princeton University Press, 1997), pp. 125–6.

28 Prendergast, p. 56. French, D., *Raising Churchill's Army: The British Army and the War Against Germany 1919–45* (Oxford University Press, 2000), pp. 55–60 asserts that the inter-war British Army 'habitually placed obedience over initiative'.

29 Mostyn-Owen, ch. 4, p. 15.

later whilst acting or substantive majors. This was not unusual by the standards of the time, and facing even more stagnant promotion prospects some British Army officers transferred to the Indian service with the hope of gaining faster and more certain advancement. Called the 'hungry hundred' in reaction to their overt careerism, most were, if competent, ultimately well received.[30]

Despite such opportunities, the daily routine of garrison life could be monotonous, if not interminably boring. One British Indian Army Officer remembered:

> There were daily morning parades when we took our platoons for P.T. [physical training] and weapons training, the hot hours after breakfast on the dry, dusty plain taking arms drill, minor tactical exercises, or classification on the rifle range. About mid-morning the troops went off to education or some indoor parade, while we inspected barrack rooms, company cook-houses and latrines, and then retired to the company office to waste time in simulated paper activity.[31]

The working day ended in theory at 1pm, in practice often before, with platoon and company sport in the evenings followed by dinner and socialising in the Officer's Mess. Under such conditions, it became habitually difficult for some officers to maintain their professional enthusiasm.[32] Service in the most isolated frontier stations during routine garrison duties enhanced this deadening effect with an often very limited exposure to normal everyday life. The inhospitable surroundings could become 'very draining [and] officers tended to become a bit mad'.[33] This was most prevalent within certain Gurkha Regiments whose home depots were permanently located in the foothills of the frontier, catering to the Himalayan origins of their Nepalese soldiers. The result was the curious phenomenon of 'Gurkhaitis', combining the overriding affection of British Officers for all things Gurkha with the effects of an extremely parochial outlook engendered by living within a closed society for long months, even years, at a

---

30 Coleridge to Montgomery, 8/3/1926, *Montgomery-Massingberd Papers* 9/3/6; 'A Gurkha in Rajputana' p. 2, *Langlands Papers*; Prendergast, pp. 54, 107; French, D., *Military Identities: The Regimental System, the British Army, and the British People c.1870–2000* (Oxford University Press, 2005), pp. 149–52, 340. For a US Army perspective on promotion and advancement, see Ossad, S.L., 'Major General John P. Lucas at Anzio: Prudence or Boldness?', *Global War Studies*, Vol. 8, No. 1 (2011), p. 39.

31 Hayter, p. 25.

32 'Address by His Excellency the Commander-in-Chief, Sir P.W. Chetwode, at the Staff College, Quetta, 8th October 1934', *Journal of the United Services Institute of India*, Vol. 65, No. 278, January 1935, p. 8; Hayter, pp. 25–6.

33 'Rajputana', p. 4, *Langlands Papers*.

time. Manifestations included the unhealthy 'worship' of the troops themselves, and in the 1st and 3rd Gurkha Rifles, the bizarre habit of only speaking Gurkhali in the Officer's Mess. Although generally less extreme, individual oddities were not rare in other regiments; an excessive and near exclusive devotion to a particular sport was particularly commonplace.[34]

Education and Training for Command

The core of higher professional military education in the Indian Army between the two world wars was the Indian Staff College in Quetta (originally established in Deolali in 1905, moving to Quetta in 1907), running two year courses almost identical to those at the British Army Staff College in Camberley. Officers from both British and Indian services took a common entrance exam and if successful could be allocated a place at either college. Although it took until the late 1920s for change to occur, it became increasingly important for officers of the Indian Army to become p.s.c. (passed staff college) in order to have serious prospect of promotion above battalion command. The unwelcome effects on advancement amongst those without this qualification caused growing resentment against the 'trade union' of staff-trained officers, 'for whose members all the higher ranks were reserved'.[35]

The inter-war Staff College syllabus included in its first year of study consideration of doctrinal principles and command and staff duties at brigade and division level, including the use of artillery and air support. The second year concentrated on these same subjects, but applicable to corps and the cavalry division, and also examined staff work at Army and G.H.Q. level.[36] Practical command training employed Tactical Exercises Without Troops, or TEWTs, plus various map-based exercises and wargames. Working 'in syndicates of three, four or more officers, in which one might be anything from an army commander to a staff captain',[37] these exercises typically required students to examine a scenario and undertake an appreciation of tasks, enemy situation, resources and ground, producing a viable plan of action and corresponding orders within a set

[34] 'Waziristan', pp. 23–4, *Langlands Papers*; Hayter, p. 37; Prendergast, p. 53.

[35] Major-General J.D. Coleridge, Military Secretary, AHQ India, to Montgomery, 8/3/1926, *Montgomery-Massingberd Papers* 9/3/6; 'Address by ... Sir P.W. Chetwode', p. 15; MacMunn, p. 61; Barua, 'Imperial Defence', p. 249; Masters, p. 36.

[36] War Office, *Staff College Regulations* (London, H.M.S.O, 1921), The National Archives, Kew, London, UK (TNA): WO 32/3098, pp. 11–16 details the full syllabus.

[37] Barclay, C.N. 'Four Generations of Staff College Students, Part III: "1930"', *Army Quarterly*, Vol. 65, No. 1, October 1952, p. 50.

timeframe. Several larger exercises conducted as 'telephone battles' also featured, lasting several days. Although they could not replicate the true pressures of command in war, one student observed that without the inherent delays imposed during live field manoeuvres by troops marching or conducting actions, the pace of some war games unconstrained by practical reality could be unremitting and far beyond the level expected, or indeed previously experienced, in combat.[38]

Although comprehensive, a key complaint was that the training was of too high a level, not at all commensurate with the appointments officers could attain on graduation. Some participants and observers alike held in particular that 'the second year of study was a waste of time'.[39] Such lofty instructional aspirations so early in an officers' career could be inherently risky, and Lieutenant-General Kenneth Wigram, QMG Northern Command, noted of the training regime in 1925 that 'we try to turn out Napoleons and Moltkes. Instead we find ... men who are guaranteed to destroy any army in less than a month.'[40] Other less tangible influences tempered the effectiveness of formal command training. Although in many respects the Indian Army was highly professional by this time, the demands and distractions of active soldiering in India also created a body of British Officers in the Indian Army who prided themselves on being 'real practical fighting soldier[s] devoted to regimental soldiering as opposed to staff duties'.[41] The distinctly different human fabric of the Indian Army itself encouraged such an attitude. Even in 1941, written orders were rarely used within infantry battalions, almost totally unnecessary from company level down since 'the majority of soldiers couldn't even read or write. 'It was a delightful Army', wrote one former officer, 'there was no "bumf."'[42]

Unit and formation command training similarly employed the TEWT as a primary means to develop the professional skills and mental abilities required for command in active operations. In contrast to Home Army training programmes, with the clear and recurrent operational task of policing the frontier facing Indian Army units in particular, TEWTs in India were often

38 'Staff conference at the Staff College, January 1933', pp. 26–7, TNA: WO 279/74; Memoir, p. 151, *Roberts Papers*; pp. 46–7; Masters, J., *The Road Past Mandalay* (London, Cassell, 2002), pp. 104–5.

39 Carver, M., *Harding of Petherton: Field-Marshal* (London, Weidenfeld and Nicolson, 1978), p. 39; Barclay, 'Four Generations', p. 50.

40 Wigram to Montgomery, 12/12/1925, *Montgomery-Massingberd Papers* 9/3/2.

41 Matthews, M.M., 'An Ever Present Danger: A Concise History of British Military Operations on the North-West Frontier, 1849–1947', *US Army Combat Studies Institute Occasional Paper*, No. 33, June 2011, p. 69; 'Waziristan', p. 21, *Langlands Papers*.

42 Quoted in Thompson, J., *The War in Burma 1942–45* (London, Sidgewick and Jackson, 2002), pp. 404–5.

specifically integrated into unit preparations for frontier deployments. Whilst no substitute for practical experience, such techniques held considerable value in illustrating the proper use and function of the chain of command, as well as testing planning ability and developing tactical thought.[43] These skills were built upon during tactical manoeuvres, held yearly in India during the cooler winter months. The largest scale inter-war manoeuvres were conducted by the four regional commands involving forces up to infantry division size, supported by cavalry, artillery, engineers and a full supply echelon. A typical manoeuvre involved two such forces operating against each other in simulated combat for up to three days, adjudicated and stage-managed by a system of umpires and directing staff.[44] Despite the inherent artificiality of such schemes, a considerable degree of realism could be achieved. One member of the directing staff for the 1925 Northern Command manoeuvres, with four years of wartime experience between 1914 and 1918, commented that they were 'from 1800 hours on the 26th [November] to 1600 hours on the 29th ... an exact replica of war ... Quite the most realistic thing I have seen.' A high degree of imagination shown at all levels of command was also noted, although without any clear institutional approach to the higher direction of war, senior Indian Army commanders had little else on which to rely.[45]

Both the British and Indian Army elements of the Army in India formally adopted the Home British Army's main training and doctrinal publications in 1911. This included the capstone volumes of *Field Service Regulations* (FSR), and the official prescriptions therein on command. By the mid-1930s, based on the Home Army's ongoing examination of its First World War experience, certain elements of mission command thinking were creeping into formal British doctrine. Most notably, *FSR Volume III – Operations, Higher Formations* of early 1936, designed for brigade commanders and above, contained a description of command that captured all the fundamental elements of this approach:

> In dealing with his subordinates, a commander will allot them definite tasks, clearly explaining his intentions, and will then allow them liberty of action in arranging the methods by which they will carry out these tasks. Undue centralization and interference with subordinates is harmful, since they are apt either to chafe at excessive control or to become afraid of taking responsibility. Besides clear and definite orders, personal touch is an essential factor in conveying a commander's

43 Hayter, p. 98. Such TEWTs could last several days: Memoir, p. 68, *Roberts Papers.*

44 Wigram to Montgomery, 12/12/1925, *Montgomery-Massingberd Papers* 9/3/2; Bristow, R.C.B., *Memories of the British Raj: A Soldier in India* (London, Johnson, 1974), p. 80.

45 Wigram to Montgomery, 12/12/1925, *Montgomery-Massingberd Papers* 9/3/2.

> intentions to his subordinates and in inspiring them with confidence and determination.[46]

This was however the very first iteration of a specific doctrinal publication intended for higher commanders, and neither previous doctrine nor the companion *FSR Volume II – Operations*, published in 1935, contained such sentiment. More significantly, the Indian Army also shared the reluctance of its British counterpart, persistent throughout the inter-war period and only addressed in the midst of the Second World War, to impose any single approach to command upon its senior officers; an issue exacerbated in India by the geographical remoteness of garrison stations that made formal efforts to cohere the force around a commonly understood approach inherently challenging both intellectually and practically.[47] The lack of a uniformly adopted understanding of what command meant and conferred, and how its responsibilities were to be discharged, opened the way for great individual variation in the approach to higher command. This reflected most interestingly, although very anecdotally, in the command styles described of the major participants in the Northern Command manoeuvres of 1925, laden with regimental and other service stereotypes: On one side was

> [Major-General A.E.] Wardrop, the dashing horse artilleryman, full of energy, untiring, and with the gleam of the hunt in his eye … . [On the other, Lieutenant-General L.R.] Vaughan, the student, who preferred to work from the map than on the ground.[48]

Such exercises did however uncover key weaknesses in the ability of Indian Army formations to operate effectively as a coherent force, and after witnessing the 1926 Western Command manoeuvres, Major-General J.D. Coleridge stated:

---

46 British Army General Staff, *Field Service Regulations, Volume III: Operations- Higher Formations* (London, H.M.S.O, 1936), p. 9.

47 Skeen to Montgomery, 9/11/1926, *Montgomery-Massingberd Papers* 9/3/1; Moreman, 'Lord Kitchener', p. 71. The Indian Army did however develop formal tactical doctrine for frontier warfare, *The Manual of Operations on the North-West Frontier of India*, first published in 1924: Moreman, 'Small Wars', pp. 113–16. A more detailed discussion on command doctrine can be found in Rose, P., 'British Army Command Culture, 1939–1945', Unpublished PhD Thesis, King's College London, 2009.

48 Wigram to Montgomery, 12/12/1925, *Montgomery-Massingberd Papers* 9/3/2. Commandant of the Staff College, Quetta from 1919–23, Vaughan transferred into the Indian Staff Corps from the British Army in 1896: http://armystaffcollege.gov.pk/, Pakistan Armed Forces Command and Staff College, Quetta, accessed 06/08/2008.

> I think the show may well be termed a success; the troops who were hard and keen worked very well when in small formations, but were not so good when brigaded, and it appears that the brigade commanders had very little opportunity of exercising their commands ... before the manoeuvres began.[49]

This situation did improve into the 1930s, but lack of finance and the shortages of British Officers within Indian Army units during the summer period continually reduced higher formation training to a level considerably below that of the better led commands in the Home British Army. The only time Indian Army brigadiers could reasonably hope to independently field their commands outside of active service remained the brief yearly shakedown period immediately before regional manoeuvres.[50] At regimental level, the reduced numbers and cost involved enabled more frequent collective training opportunities. COs often exercised their companies against one another, more rarely conducting informally arranged manoeuvres against other battalions from different garrisons. Creating realism remained a different challenge altogether, and at the tactical level, complete dissociation from even the most basic realities of warfare could occur. It was at this level that umpires were most stretched to provide the necessary authenticity, through competent and strict tactical judgement. Unfortunately, many lacked the ruthless qualities required to stamp realism over truculent participants, and as one officer noted 'the errors denounced by the umpire on manoeuvres could be excused verbally, because a human umpire lacks the cold impartiality of bullets'.[51] Although universal, this problem was generally perceived as most severe within British Army units at home and in India. And it was for this reason that the Indian Army proudly regarded the North West Frontier as its primary training ground, its 'tribesmen ... the best tactical "umpires" in the world', providing a continual impetus to maintain a serious attitude toward realism in training and conditioning the methods of command utilised and reinforced when these programmes were carried out.[52]

---

49 Coleridge to Montgomery, 14/10/1926, *Montgomery-Massingberd Papers* 9/3/6.

50 Masters, *Bugles*, pp. 110, 115.

51 Bristow, p. 80; Hayter, p. 27.

52 Mackenzie, 'Popular Imperialism', p. 10; Moreman, T.R., *The Army in India and the Development of Frontier Warfare, 1849–1947* (London, Macmillan, 1998), pp. 139–40; Fuller, *Army in My Time*, pp. 67–70; Masters, *Bugles*, p. 226.

Command and Control on the Frontier

Policing the frontier was the core activity of the Indian Army between the two world wars, its battalions spending two years out of every six serving there. This rotation dated back to the Kitchener reforms of the early 1900s and over time created within 'Indian Army battalions a large cadre of officers, NCOs and other ranks with practical experience and training in frontier warfare'.[53] It also encouraged the constant review and feedback of tactical lessons back into the training cycle, because Indian units knew they would again see active frontier service within a few short years.[54] This was a fundamental difference to British Army units which, stretched between widespread global commitments and prioritised to internal garrison duties within India, simply did not gain the same institutional experience of frontier operations. In 1931 there were for example just five British Army infantry battalions stationed on the frontier, compared to 37 of the Indian Army, and they conducted 12 rather than 24 month tours.[55]

With this limited exposure, the British Army was not shaped in any comparable way by the experience of soldiering on the North West Frontier. Although falling far short of the criteria of major warfare throughout the period in question, the demands of inter-war frontier operations were by turns unique, considerable, and very different to those experienced between 1914–18. One Indian Army officer considered commanding an infantry company on the North West Frontier a greater challenge than commanding a battalion on the Western Front, noting

> In France you were always near other troops, and usually could see the enemy. Here in this wild mountainous country a company commander was on his own, in very difficult country. [He] never knew from which direction the tribesmen would attack. It is not surprising that in the Second World War some of the best commanders and regiments had their early training in Waziristan.[56]

Conduct of any activity within the North West Frontier Province demanded utmost tactical vigilance, and training excursions frequently merged into real operations. Violence was never far from the surface in even the most apparently serene surroundings, with the tribal foe experts at concealed movement, surprise and ambush. The brutal reality of frontier warfare stood in stark contrast to

---

[53] Moreman, 'Small Wars', p. 116, Heathcote, 'Army of British India', p. 379; Moreman, *Army in India*, p. 146.

[54] Langlands, 'Waziristan', pp. 11–12.

[55] Marston, *Phoenix*, p. 38; Moreman, 'Small Wars', p. 116.

[56] 'Waziristan', p. 2, *Langlands Papers*.

its romantic image, and although tactical engagements often involved small numbers, significant casualties were a frequent result. The 'Battle of Spinchilla' in 1921, in which one Gurkha company suffered over 80 killed and wounded, was not atypical, and British and Indian casualties from individual engagements in the larger inter-war campaigns often totalled several hundreds.[57] The killing and torture of prisoners and horrific mutilation of British and Indian dead and wounded at tribal hands was commonplace. Such brutality could cause reciprocal action by Indian Army units, not uncommonly with the participation or acquiescence of their British Officers. To give one example, in retaliation to heavy losses incurred at the hands of Pathan tribesmen, 'one day in 1936 the 2/4th Gurkhas brought 23 [severed Pathan] heads back to camp', bringing a jocular reprimand from their officers.[58] Frontier warfare was definitely not cricket, and demanded distinctly different attributes to 'civilised' European conflict. To be successful and avoid unnecessary casualties, officers had to replicate the cunning and ruthlessness of their enemy:

> Techniques like scouting, bluffs, drawing the enemy into premature attacks, feints, surprise assaults [and] scorched earth policies were all at a premium. Craftiness and cunning [and] the ability to confuse the enemy ... were the mark of the successful colonial officer.[59]

The staple of frontier operations was the column. Undertaken to open roads or perform 'flag marches' and punitive raids into tribal territory, columns were typically conducted by an infantry brigade group, including a battery of mountain artillery and engineers. The artillery commander accompanied the brigadier who, 'according to his temperament, went with the Advanced Guard or the Main Body', whilst individual artillery troops leap-frogged along the column, one always deployed ready to fire as the others moved to new positions.[60] The principle tactic of the column was the picketing of key peaks and ridges flanking the route of advance, preventing their use by hostile tribesmen to secure the passage of the main body. Always remote, pickets were usually commanded

---

57 Moreman, *Army in India*, p. 139; Lowry, pp. 30–31; Prendergast, pp. 72–3; MacKenzie, 'Popular Imperialism', pp. 8–9; 'Waziristan', p. 8, *Langlands Papers*. On 14 January 1920 for example, 450 British and Indian casualties were taken during a single engagement in Waziristan: Matthews, p. 42.

58 'Some notes on Gurkhas', p. 7, *Stevenson-Hamilton Mss., The Papers of Lieutenant-Colonel V.E.O. Stevenson-Hamilton*, LHCMA. See also Masters, *Bugles*, pp. 197–9.

59 MacKenzie, 'Popular Imperialism', p. 7; Masters, *Bugles*, p. 213.

60 Henniker, M.C.A., *Memoirs of a Junior Officer* (London, Blackwood & Sons, 1951), p. 201; Prendergast, pp. 70–72.

by a subaltern or VCO, ranging in size from section to company strength. The placement of pickets was the responsibility of the vanguard battalion, whose CO typically gathered his officers at the start of the day's march to decide, often directly from the ground, where to position them. Once assigned, pickets were the individual responsibility of company commanders to occupy, administer and maintain during the day. If an essential height was held by the enemy, it fell to the company commander involved to organise and carry out an assault, coordinating supporting fire from artillery and machine-guns. Even if a picket was suspected unoccupied, no unnecessary risks were taken and the last yards before the summit were always rushed in extended line, with bayonets fixed. The most reliable method of communication with the picket was by signal flag, even in 1940. But whilst they might be in sight of the main column, there was no chance of a picket position receiving immediate or even timely help in the event of unforeseen emergency, and command rested firmly with the officer on the spot. Pickets were at their most vulnerable when withdrawing, and to avoid ambush all possible speed and considerable tactical skill was required during the return to the column, overwatched by its rearguard company, with all dead ground covered by artillery and infantry support weapons.[61]

Column operations thus made substantial and specific demands upon the most junior of British Officers in Indian Army units. They required not only 'a very skilled eye for country and ... great physical fitness', but the ability to operate effectively and confidently independent of higher direction.[62] Whilst control of the all-arms battle centred in inter-war British doctrine on the division, Indian Army subalterns as company commanders could find themselves coordinating infantry, artillery and machine-guns against a live enemy. It was further commonplace for relatively junior officers to hold multiple command appointments simultaneously during active operations, and in the heat of the moment the burden (and chain) of command could weigh heavily on those unable to take quick, decisive action.[63] Routine regimental command practices helped foster the flexible mindset this operational environment demanded toward the assumption of this greater responsibility by junior officers and the acceptance of it by their superiors. Flexibility of approach and the mental courage to make firm decisions without recourse to higher authority were essential to even the most

61 'Notes on Mountain Warfare Course, April 1940', *Donlea Mss., The Papers of Captain B.J.F. Donlea*, LHCMA; Lowry, M., *Fighting Through to Kohima: A Memoir of War in India and Burma* (London, Leo Cooper, 2003), pp. 31–2; Henniker, p. 201; Prendergast, p. 72; Masters, *Bugles*, p. 217; and see photograph of 'Picket Orders Group', Fordyce Mss., *The Papers of Captain C.E. Fordyce*, LHCMA.

62 Prendergast, p. 72.

63 Masters, *Bugles*, pp. 241–2; Henniker, p. 206.

junior Indian Army officer engaged in frontier operations, and the importance of nurturing and developing these qualities was not lost on the Army in India's high command.[64] During his tenure as C-in-C India, Field Marshal Sir Philip Chetwode stressed the need for wartime commanders to have imagination and develop the confidence to take bold, well calculated risks. These were precisely the attributes routinely practised and developed by the Indian Army's regimental officers on the North West Frontier between the two world wars and became the defining characteristics of its culture of command.[65]

Many aspects of the frontier command experience thus fit comfortably within the framework expected of a decentralised, mission command culture. The common occurrence for company and battalion commanders to be entirely responsible for the execution of their given task, within the column commander's overall scheme, provides clear manifestation of this approach in action.[66] In the absence of a formally approved doctrinal conception of command within the Army, the practice of command in each unit and formation was highly susceptible to the proclivities and personality of its commander. However, the incidence of commanders using restrictive and autocratic methods of control was rare, and discernibly out of step with the methods of command to which Indian Army officers were accustomed. This was strikingly different to the British Home Army at the time, whose exercise reports of the period are littered with concerns over the production of unrealistic and highly detailed orders that gave no room for subordinate initiative or the contingencies of battle.[67] Within the Indian Army, it was commonplace even for unit commanders to encourage their subordinates to solve their own tactical problems and develop true command responsibility. Certain senior officers further publicised the benefits of fostering the independence of subordinates from detailed and continual higher direction, clearly reflection of the dominant approach to command employed during, and conditioned by, operations on the North West Frontier.[68]

---

64 Bradshaw-Smith, B., 'Protection on the March in Mountain Warfare', *JUSII*, Vol. 55, No. 240, July 1925, pp. 49–50, Prendergast, p. 71.

65 Chetwode, 'Address by His Excellency', pp. 10–14.

66 See for example the very close similarity between Hayter's description of command and control on the North West Frontier (p. 139) and the definition of mission tactics in von Lossow, pp. 88–9.

67 See for example the report on 'Cavalry Staff Exercise, 1927', p. 13, TNA: WO 279/58.

68 See especially Hayter, pp. 139–44; Prendergast, p. 70 and Major-General Sir W.H. Anderson's 'Some Thoughts on Advanced Guards and their Command', *JUSII*, Vol. 55, No. 238, January 1925, pp. 11–14.

At the level of higher command, the complexities of coordinating the action of a fighting column of several thousand men, plus artillery, engineers and supply train, were considerable. The methods by which this was achieved were similar to those of the advanced guard, involving the face to face dissemination of brief verbal instructions by the brigade commander to his subordinates during a daily orders group. Detailed briefings or further instructions required were usually given by the Brigade Major or Intelligence Officer. Brigade commanders thus gained valuable experience in the operational control and administration of a sizeable all-arms force, but because columns were a highly stylised and well practised form of activity, with generally limited objectives and opposition, opportunities for practising 'constructive command' with a formation of this size were modest and rare. The notable exceptions to this rule were larger scale frontier campaigns, of which several were mounted between the two world wars. These provided sterner test of the abilities of higher commanders drawn from the Indian and British services, and also gave fuller scope for the use of modern military technology. Major General John Burnett-Stuart, GOC Madras District, during suppression of the Moplah rebellion of 1921–22 for example, employed 'highly mobile columns of infantry, armoured cars and pack artillery'.[69] By the end of the following decade aircraft added additional capability and complexity, forming a common adjunct to ground forces and often under control of the ranking Army commander present.[70]

In the 1930s, the two major frontier campaigns were the Mohmand campaign of 1935, and Waziristan campaign of 1936–37. Conducted under the overall direction of a regional administrative HQ, Northern Command India, the Mohmand campaign perfectly illustrates the higher command organisation typical of larger scale colonial operations. Operational command was assigned to Major-General Sir Sydney Muspratt, Indian Army officer and commander of Peshawar Military District, who had previously spent six years in senior staff positions since commanding a brigade between 1925–27. His command, 'Mohforce', reflected precisely the sort of *ad hoc* tactical grouping employed in such campaigns. Essentially a reinforced division, it numbered ten regular infantry battalions in three brigades, one with an attached cavalry regiment, a further infantry brigade of irregular frontier forces, two sections of light tanks and three artillery batteries: a total of 14,687 officers and men. Certain officers destined to become senior Second World War commanders cut their professional teeth in such operations, the then Brigadiers C.J.E. Auchinleck and H.R.L.G.

69 Henniker, M.C.A., *Memoirs of a Junior Officer* (London, Blackwood & Sons, 1951), p. 203; Barua, 'Imperial Defence', p. 250.

70 See for example 'The Afridi Blockade 1939', *Rees Papers., Mss Eur. F274, The Papers of Major-General Thomas Wynford Rees*, British Library India Office Collection (BLIOC).

Alexander commanding infantry brigades in Mohforce. Leading a battalion in the latter's brigade was Lieutenant-Colonel J.G. Smyth, future commander of 17 Indian Infantry Division during the retreat from Burma in 1942. Similarly improvised forces were also organised for smaller offensive operations, typical of which being Kajuri Force of 1939, comprising three infantry battalions with supporting arms based around the Landi Kotal Infantry Brigade. Its commander was Lieutenant-Colonel T.W. Rees, later to lead 19 Indian Infantry Division during the final years of the Burma Campaign.[71]

Of the conduct of Mohforce, Tim Moreman has noted that:

> Perhaps the most striking feature of the campaign was the willingness of Indian commanders and units to undertake large operations at night, enabling them to seize the initiative, disconcert tribal plans, and avoid the delay inherent in mounting deliberate attacks against strongly defended positions.[72]

The main tenets of this statement fit easily into any modern exposition of the manoeuvrist approach, placing utmost emphasis on the use of surprise and momentum in attaining the mental and physical destruction of one's enemy. Enabled by a decentralised approach to command, and confidence in its use, these operations traded physical security for speed and surprise in most difficult terrain, creating an impact upon the enemy out of proportion to the forces employed. Such methods, including night attacks in force, had been part of large scale frontier operations since the Waziristan Campaign of 1919–20. Their advantages were readily understood by Indian Army officers, even those relatively junior, imbued with the mental creativity and courage required to utilise them from constant exposure to active service on the North West Frontier and these necessary habits of command this experience engendered.[73] Such boldly conceived operations also stand in stark contrast to higher level training exercises in the British Home Army during the same period, in which

---

71 Wigram, GOC-in-C Northern Command (India), to Bartholomew, CGS Indian Army, 1/12/1935, *Bartholomew Papers* 2/2/5; 'Order of Battle-Mohmand Force', and 'Frontier Operations: Operations in the Mohmand Country (August–October, 1935)', BLIOC: L/MIL/7/16968; 'The Afridi Blockade 1939', *Rees Papers*; Warner, P., 'Auchinleck: Field Marshal Sir Claude Auchinleck' in Keegan, J. (ed.), *Churchill's Generals* (London, Abacus, 1999), p. 133.

72 Moreman, *Army in India*, p. 150.

73 'Operations in Mohmand Country', pp. 6–8, OIOC L/MIL/7/16968; Smyth, J.G., *Milestones* (London, Sidgwick and Jackson, 1979), pp. 67–73; Hayter, p. 128. Kiszely, J., 'The British Army and Approaches to Warfare Since 1945', in Reid, B.H. (ed.), *Military Power: Land Warfare in Theory and Practice* (London, Frank Cass, 1997), pp. 180–81 outlines the manouevrist approach.

many senior commanders proved unwilling to undertake any manoeuvres at all at night, let alone offensive operations under active service conditions.[74]

Despite the overall success of the Mohmand campaign, the experience of Mohforce illustrated a key potential drawback concerning the use of a highly devolved approach to command and control in a fluid battle of manoeuvre and exploitation. Whilst moving forward on the night of 29 September 1935, lead elements of 5/12th Frontier Force Regiment (Queen Victoria's Own Corps of Guides) were ambushed, resulting in over 80 casualties, including 33 killed. The severity of the incident was exacerbated by the Guide's customary practice whereby the CO and his command group, including artillery FOO and signallers, led the main battalion advance at night. When the ambush was initiated, all members of the command party became casualties or were pinned down by enemy fire, resulting in complete loss of control over the battalion and its immediate fire support, as well as all contact with higher command. Denied detailed information concerning their tactical situation, it was impossible for the Guide's parent brigade to give effective reinforcement or provide artillery support before the two lead platoons were overrun.[75]

This incident further demonstrated a central dilemma of operational command in such operations. Although commanders could maintain effective touch with the battlefield situation by placing themselves well forward, this was often only achieved by exposing them to its inherent and often hidden dangers. Maintaining a forward command posture was however common amongst battalion and brigade commanders during frontier operations. Rees for example commanded Kajuri Force with just two staff officers from a hastily established tactical headquarters in line with his forward pickets, but sensible restrictions had to apply. During the Mohmand incident, the Guide's CO demonstrated a lack of responsibility by placing himself and his command team at unnecessary risk. By 'putting all his eggs in one basket', in Chetwode's words, in a vulnerable position during a night advance in enemy territory, the Guide's CO courted the total loss of control and communications in any subsequent engagement, resulting in a catastrophic outcome for his battalion when action was joined.[76]

---

[74] War Office, *Army Training Manual No. 4A, Guide for Commanders of Regular Troops at Home* (London, 1932) TNA: WO 32/3115, p. 6, WO 32/3115; Pile, F., 'Liddell Hart and the British Army, 1919–1939', in Howard, M. (ed.), *The Theory and Practice of War* (London, Indiana University Press, 1975), p. 164.

[75] 'Operations in Mohmand Country', pp. 19–20, OIOC L/MIL/7/16968; Moreman, *Army in India*, p. 150.

[76] Chetwode to Wigram, 22/10/1935, *Bartholomew Papers* 2/2/2; 'Afridi Blockade', *Rees Papers*.

The problems of commanding dispersed and fast moving frontier operations were increased by a paucity of wireless equipment and operators, and shortages of trained and available HQ personnel within the Army in India's field formations. For the Kajuri Force campaign, Landi Kotal Brigade lacked both the staff officers and signal personnel necessary to facilitate control of its own forces. Rees was forced to enable the most basic communications forward of his HQ by stripping men and equipment from his infantry battalions for the duration of the operation. Even in the early 1940s there existed no standing establishment for wireless communication between battalion and brigade.[77] Placing this issue in a broader perspective, it was noted on the eve of the Second World War that the Indian Army's basic hardware of command and control consisted of 'semaphore flags, lamps and heliographs [that] would have been familiar to Lord Roberts as he marched in 1880 from Kabul to Kandahar, and the field telephone equipment dated back to 1918'.[78]

Technology was however only one part of the problem. Following the Guides ambush in 1935, a general opinion amongst the higher echelons of the Army in India held that not enough had been done by the senior commanders involved to compensate for this known lack of intercommunication. Wigram, who oversaw the operation as GOC Northern Command, considered that the catastrophe had been unnecessarily exacerbated by an overly relaxed attitude within Mohforce to the control of subordinate formations. Decentralisation of command is never synonymous with relinquishing effective control of subordinate units. Appreciation of this essential point cannot be readily discerned from the conduct of the Mohmand campaign, reflecting the *ad hoc* nature of the command organisation for the operation and the conceptual immaturity of the fundamentals of mission command in the Army more broadly at this time. Inherent and in some respects intuitive practice of an experientially and structurally defined command culture that prioritised distributed activity and initiative did not necessarily lead senior Indian Army officers to recognise the paradoxical necessity of ensuring coherent and constant top down guidance, if not control, over the activities of their subordinates. This is an intrinsic requirement for the effective use of mission command, and in this light the catastrophe that befell the Guides becomes more easily explained by reference to the Indian Army's command culture, rather than the personal failings of a specific individual at a point in space and time. This argument becomes even more persuasive when it is considered that Mohforce had no true operational

[77] 'Afridi Blockade', *Rees Papers*; Hayter, p. 128.

[78] Lunt, J., 'Prelude: The Imperial Commitment and Threat in the Far East and Pacific, 1918–1941', in Smurthwaite, D. (ed.), *The Forgotten War: The British Army in the Far East, 1941–45* (London, National Army Museum, 1992), p. 9.

HQ at its head. In essence, it was a division without a divisional HQ, led by an improvised headquarters formed hastily from the commander and staff of a regional district command. Whilst certain senior officers within the Army in India railed against Muspratt's apparent willingness to continue the operation regardless following loss of precise details on the state and location of the Guides battalion, what they universally failed to recognise was the extent to which rudimentary higher command organisation made effective forward contact and higher direction so hard to achieve.[79] These very same issues would live on and haunt the effectiveness of British higher command more widely during the early years of the Second World War.

Conclusion

In his recent study of British generalship during the Second World War, Raymond Callahan posed the pertinent question of how relevant the Indian Army's inter-war experience was in preparing it for modern warfare between 1939 and 1945.[80] In terms of command, much of its experience was very relevant indeed. The future Field Marshall Wavell noted in 1936 that in order to provide the best higher commanders for the future, it was essential that junior officers regularly trained to act at least one level above their rank.[81] Due to the unique organisational characteristics and service conditions of the Indian Army, this was one of the defining facets of its officers' professional experience between the two world wars. As this chapter has demonstrated, the Army's peacetime routine further encouraged a flexible, confident attitude towards assumption and delegation of command responsibility among junior and senior officers. This was ingrained on active service in the North West Frontier Province, and the persistent, repetitive nature by which Indian Army units performed this task informed a uniform and coherent, yet informal, adoption of a decentralised, mission command-oriented culture at both higher command and regimental level. Although effective in operation and widespread, this existed as a *de facto* construct conditioned by the Army's structure, environment and operational experience, and was never explicitly codified, endorsed or enforced by the Army's high command.

Nonetheless, the conduct of the larger frontier operations during the inter-war years demonstrated that senior Indian Army officers were willing and

[79] Wigram to Bartholomew, 1/12/1935, *Bartholomew Papers* 2/2/5; Chetwode to Wigram, 4/11/1935, *Bartholomew Papers* 2/2/4.

[80] Callahan, R., *Churchill and his Generals* (Kansas University Press, 2007), p. 65.

[81] Wavell, A.P., 'The Higher Commander', *JRUSI*, Vol. 81, 1936, p. 28.

able to effectively utilise a decentralised approach to command in prosecuting campaigns often imaginatively conceived and aggressively executed. The mindset and experience this developed proved highly valuable to a generation of Indian Army officers destined to lead large formations in the major British campaigns fought between 1940 and 1945. The immaturity, and in many respects absence, of formal Indian Army conceptions of command also led to certain negative practices which were also exposed by operations on the North West Frontier. Chief among these shortcomings was the use of improvised tactical formations such as Mohforce to wage frontier campaigns. The habitual and unreflective employment of *ad-hoc* higher tactical organisations and geographically defined but essentially administrative regional HQs to control major operations was repeated throughout the period. This arrangement proved adequate for the purposes of offensive action against a tribal enemy on the North West Frontier, but the experience gained should have identified a requirement to adopt more formal executive command structures as subsequent operations demonstrated their shortcomings. Instead, the inadequacy of this practice remained equally ingrained in the inter-war Indian Army's command culture as the positive elements of devolved responsibility and independent subordinate initiative. The inherent weaknesses of this approach were ruthlessly exposed fighting against the well trained, well equipped and highly motivated opponents Indian Army formations faced on the battlefield during the early years of the Second World War.[82]

---

[82] The views expressed in this chapter are those of the author alone and do not in any way reflect or imply the official policy or position of the Ministry of Defence or any other UK government department.

Chapter 3

Did Winston Matter? Churchill and the Indian Army, 1940–1945

Raymond Callahan

Over 40 years ago A.J.P. Taylor, writing about the ponderous Cabinet Office official histories, quipped that their practice of applying anonymity wherever possible to decision makers broke down when it came to Churchill, thus creating the 'perhaps misleading impression that he ran the war on his own'.[1] an impression reinforced by Churchill's own memoirs and a number of quasi-hagiographic biographies. This version of Churchill's war leadership is unlikely to be significantly affected by more nuanced scholarship anytime soon. There is however one area where the popular sense of Churchill as utterly dominant over the British war effort intersects with the historians' understanding of the huge complexities – political, economic, bureaucratic and imperial – of that astounding final chapter in Britain's long Great Power history (a chapter whose imperial dimension Ashley Jackson has done so much to illuminate[2]). In 1940–41 Churchill drove through decisions and made choices that shaped the war effort of Britain and its Commonwealth/Empire for the next five years. Since no part of that vast imperial structure was more important than India, Churchill's choices in 1940–41 therefore shaped the war India's army fought.

The questions about those choices asked in this essay are two: what did he actually know about India's army, whose war he shaped; and to what degree did he involve himself in the great transformation that the war and his decisions wrought in what he, in one of his rare moments of attention to (and even rarer benignity about) the Indian Army, called 'the splendid old time Indian units'.[3] To alleviate suspense, the brief answers are: very little; and rarely, and then usually unhelpfully. Working these questions out in detail offers an indication both of how autonomous much of the Indian war effort really was and how much of the

---

1 A.J.P. Taylor, *English History, 1914–1945* (Oxford 1965), p. 635.

2 Ashley Jackson, *The British Empire and the Second World War* (London, 2006).

3 Churchill to Amery, 10 August 1943. Public Records Office (now The National Archives): PREM 3, 232/9.

mighty endeavour that was the British Empire at war occurred quite without reference to the remarkable man who led it.

Churchill's experience of India was slight. He went there in 1896, a subaltern in a British cavalry regiment. British regular officers, almost without exception, could expect a tour of duty in India, sometimes several, during their careers. Being in India, however, did not necessarily mean learning much about it or about its army, which was a separate institution and one moreover with which the British Army had had a distant and edgy relationship since the days of John Company (or, as Geoffrey Best has put it: the British Army had consistently displayed 'endemic snobbery and dismissiveness towards the Indian Army'[4]). Churchill, in a letter to his mother, shortly after landing in India, remarked on how easily he had adjusted to his new surroundings but, as subsequent letters recorded at great length, that adjustment did not involve investigating those new surroundings or even the civil and military structures of the Raj. At this point in his life, he was a self-centred, polo-playing young man who was also frighteningly ambitious, busy with self-education and obsessively laying plans for a future political career to which India was a stepping stone. There is no evidence that the extensive reading programme he had embarked on to fill the long, languid afternoons in his regiment's cantonment at Bangalore included anything about the country in which he found himself (and quite enough in his letters to conclude that he had a lofty disdain for even the British who staffed the Raj). He certainly saw the Indian Army in action on the Northwest Frontier (and took part in several small-unit actions), but neither his dispatches to the *Daily Telegraph* during the Malakand campaign nor the book he subsequently built upon them says much about the Indian Army. What little one does find is simply the reassuring commonplaces of late Victorian thinking about the Indian Empire: 'Nothing is so remarkable as the ascendancy which the British officer maintains over the native soldier. The dark sowars follow the young English subaltern who commands them with a strange devotion ... The military history of England – a long and diverse volume – does not record an instance of their confidence being misplaced.'[5] He certainly absorbed the 'martial races' ideology, but the only Indian Army units he spends any ink on are the Sikhs: 'The Sikh is the guardian of the Marches. He was originally invented to combat the Pathan.'[6] Even though he had not seen Gurkha units in action, he felt compelled to

[4] Geoffrey Best, from a review of the author's *Churchill and His Generals* in *The Journal of Cold War Studies*, 9:4 (Fall 2007), p. 158.

[5] Frederick K. Woods (ed.), *Young Winston's Wars: The Original Despatches of Winston S. Churchill War Correspondent, 1897–1900* (New York 1972), p. 16.

[6] Winston S. Churchill, *The Story of the Malakand Field Force* (London 1898; reprint edn New York 1990), p. 198.

include praise for these imperial icons: '... it is impossible to consider Indian fighting races without alluding to these wicked little men .... Small, active and fierce, ever with a cheery grin on their broad faces ....'[7]

Now there is nothing particularly unusual about this – many British cavalry subalterns of the era probably passed through India learning less about it than Churchill. (British units in India were very self-contained worlds – in Churchill's time and later.[8]) What is interesting is that little happened thereafter to change the picture of India and its army that took shape in Churchill's mind late in Victoria's reign. Perhaps it was simply that Churchill never held a position before 1940 in which he had to confront Indian civil and military realities, because one of the hallmarks of his career was the speed with which he could absorb information relevant to any office he held. Had the Tories been returned to office in 1929 and had Baldwin made him Secretary of State for India – apparently a real possibility – the story of Churchill, the Indian Army and the end game of the Raj might now read very differently, although for better or worse I will leave to others. As it was, Churchill took into his bitter, five-year fight against what ultimately became the 1935 Government of India Act many of the ideas about the Indian Army (and much else) that one finds in his letters and dispatches from India 30 years before – the 'warrior races' would never stand for the rule of the 'Hindu priesthood' (a curious description of the lawyers, journalists, landowners and businessmen who ran the Congress Party) and much more in the same vein. The two brief chapters on India in his *History of the English Speaking Peoples*, drafted in the late 1930s, are the textbook verities of the time – and the Indian Army is noticed only when part of it mutinies in 1857.

On the eve of the Second World War then Churchill's knowledge of India and of the Indian Army in particular was in fact very weak, and none of his many military acquaintances were Indian Army officers. (Certainly among his associates in fighting the India Act were retired Indian Army officers; some, like Field Marshal Sir Claude Jacob, of considerable distinction. But it would seem that they were sources of reinforcement for views already formed, rather than suppliers of more recent and nuanced information.) By 1940 when he became Prime Minister there was no time for a crash course on the subject, so the bottom line throughout the war remained this: the Prime Minister and Minister of Defence knew relatively little about the army that would make a bigger contribution to the imperial war effort on land than all the self-governing

7 Churchill, *Malakand Field Force*, p. 194.

8 Michael Lowry's *Fighting Through to Kohima: A Memoir of War in India and Burma* (Barnsley, UK, 2008) is by a British regular officer of the Queen's Royal Regiment who served in India 1939–44. There is virtually nothing in it about either India or the Indian Army. By comparison Churchill looks observant.

Dominions taken together. (Hastings Ismay, his wartime chief of staff, was an Indian Army officer, but his career had been a very unusual one and he had been long away from Indian service. There is no indication he tried to enlighten Churchill, always assuming that Ismay, who had joined the Indian Army during the Edwardian era, had something new to add. In his position he had to pick his fights carefully, and he may have simply accepted that this one was already lost.)

India of course had always had its own civil and military administration, which operated with considerable autonomy and was moreover heavily staffed by people whose families had served in India for generations. Most Britons – at least most Britons from the class that still supplied most of the nation's leadership – knew something about India, but the day-to-day working of the Raj was left to those who made their careers there. Churchill's weak grasp of the realities of the Raj and its army in 1940 is not, perhaps, so very surprising – but unfortunately he believed he knew a great deal. This was a problem with which his Secretary of State for India and Burma, Leo Amery, had to cope with indifferent success throughout the war.

But even if Churchill had known as much about India as he thought he did, the dominating fact in 1940 was the existential threat to Britain itself and, whatever controversy there may be over this or that aspect of Winston Churchill's career, there is virtual unanimity about the single-minded ruthlessness with which he went about meeting that challenge. In doing so, he and his cabinet took two decisions that shaped India's war: those dealt with the size of the Indian Army and where – at least initially – it would fight.

The decision to fight on – and the companion decision to maintain Britain's position in the Middle East – drove an expansion of the Indian Army that not only outstripped previous plans but available equipment as well, a point continually raised with London and just as continually ignored. (An Indian Army officer, whose family had served in India for generations, noted during the 1941 Iraq campaign that the weaponry of the Iraqi Army, supplied from Britain, was more up-to-date than that of the Indian Army units which defeated it.[9]) One example can illustrate how dire the equipment situation in India was. In January 1941 a new unit, the Mazhbi and Ramdasia Sikhs (later the 1st Sikh Light Infantry) was raised at Jullundur in the Punjab, the heavily recruited province that, on the eve of war, supplied nearly half of the Indian Army's intake. 'Unit transport' consisted of the adjutant's car, supplemented eventually by bicycles, camels, and

[9] John Masters, *The Road Past Mandalay* (New York, paper edn, 1963), p. 17. The 1930 Anglo-Iraqi Treaty, which made Iraq (mostly) independent, stipulated that the British weaponry supplied to the Iraqi Army should be the same as that used by the British Army. Equivalency in weapons, however, could do nothing to change the low combat value of the Iraqi Army.

requisitioned civilian buses. The first consignment of weapons included ten rifles adapted to use buckshot and a vast quantity of .22 caliber ammunition – but no rifles capable of using it. Sniper training was carried out with six air rifles purchased in the local bazaar. In an early exercise the entire battalion was 'armed' with bamboo mosquito net poles. This unit, intended as first line combat infantry (a role it would fill with distinction in Burma), was less well equipped as it began its training than some British Home Guard formations.[10] The expansion programme also focused the Indian Army's training and doctrinal development almost exclusively on the requirements of the Middle East theatre. All this is very well known, as is the resulting and precipitous drop in quality and cohesion that accompanied breakneck expansion (the development of India as a huge supply base for the imperial war effort east of Suez and the steadily rising indebtedness of Britain to India were other results of 1940 – with consequences that would extend well beyond 1945). There is little evidence in Churchill's papers that he tracked the detail of any of this – although by 1943 he had become aware of (and very unhappy about) Britain's indebtedness to India. As in 1914, India had been mobilised to support the imperial war effort, and the vast machine of the Raj could be left to get on with it. (When details of Indian Army expansion were brought to his attention, his reaction was unhelpful. General Sir Claude Auchinleck raised with him in August 1941 the Indian Army's lack of modern equipment only to be asked whether he was sure that, given updated weaponry, the Indian soldiers would point their guns in the right direction.[11]) One of the consequences, however, if the Prime Minister had taken note of it, would almost certainly have caused him pronounced distress and doubtless led to the composition of some pungent minutes. The open-ended expansion of the Indian Army drove a dramatic acceleration in the 'Indianisation' of its officer corps, shredding the cautious pre-war plans for slowly increasing over a period of decades the number of Indians holding the King's Commission. That, in turn, would fundamentally change the nature of the Army in ways difficult, if not impossible, to reverse – with considerable implications for the future of the Raj.[12]

[10] Obituary of Lieutenant Colonel John Maling, *Daily Telegraph* (London), 7 April 2009. Maling won a DSO while in command of the 1st Sikh Light Infantry in Burma in 1945.

[11] John Connell, *Auchinleck – A Critical Biography* (London 1959), p. 274, n. 1. Auchinleck, an Indian Army officer, was then Commander-in-Chief, Middle East. He had come to that appointment from being Commander-in-Chief, India, where he had presided over the first stages of the Indian Army's expansion.

[12] In 1939 there were about 2,500 officers in the Indian Army, then about 190,000 strong. Only some 350 of the officers were Indians, and those were either subalterns or

Churchill made another decision in the late summer of 1940 that would produce devastating results for the Indian Army – he decided that the necessary focus on the war in the West, especially the Mediterranean and Middle East, meant gambling that the growing menace of Japan would be contained by the Americans and that reinforcements for Malaya could therefore be held to minimum. It was a ruling he maintained until the eve of the Pacific War. The result was the Malayan debacle, which consumed two raw Indian divisions (neither complete in men nor equipment) plus several additional brigades, made up of recruits with little beyond basic training, if that, rushed in when it was far too late, a fate that also befell the entire British 18th Division.[13] The Prime Minister's judgement on Indian Army performance in Malaya was characteristically both uncomprehending of the state of the units involved and ungenerous: 'the Japanese have only had two white battalions and some gunners against them, the rest being Indian soldiers',[14] he told the Australian Prime Minister in January

medical officers. By 1945 the 2.5 million strong Indian Army had 43,000 officers, 14,000 of them Indians – and some of those were field grade officers commanding British subordinates.

[13] The volume of the British official history covering the Malayan campaign – S.W. Kirby et al., *The War Against Japan. Vol. I: The Loss of Singapore* (HMSO, 1957) prints a note (Appendix 19, p. 528) by Brigadier G.C. Ballentine, whose 44th Indian Infantry Brigade arrived in Singapore far too late to do anything but swell the total of prisoners in Japanese hands. Nearly half the *jawans* (the term that by the Second World War had replaced the older usage 'sepoys') were raw recruits, some under 18; there were only three pre-war regular officers per battalion, and the remaining officers, recently commissioned, had on average less than a year's Indian Army experience. This meant, among other things, that their language skills were rudimentary. 'What is surprising', the official historian noted, is 'that they fought as well as they did' (p. 515) – a fact that few noted then or later, especially Winston Churchill.

[14] Churchill to Curtin, 14 January 1942. Churchill Archive Center, Churchill Papers, CHUR 4/235A, f. 128. When printing this note in his memoirs, Churchill dropped without ellipsis the phrase 'the rest being Indian soldiers' on the advice of his syndicate of assistants, who argued that the complete wording would be offensive to the Indian Army. Churchill's note to Curtin raises as well the seldom visited question of Churchill's views on race. Clearly, as Geoffrey Best has noted, the young Churchill 'accepted unquestioningly ... the then prevalent notion of white superiority. He seems never subsequently to have thought differently', *Churchill: A Study in Greatness* (London, 2001), p. 24. Ronald Hyam, in a trenchant essay on 'Churchill and the Colonial Empire' in his *Understanding the British Empire* (Cambridge, 2010) makes the point that 'adverse judgment on his attitudes has focused too much on what he *said*, relaxing in private, rather than what he *did*' (p. 335). Hyam, however, excluded consideration of Churchill and India from that essay. Another careful study of Churchill's relationship to Britain's empire notes 'many observers felt that the mere mention of India brought out a streak of unpleasantness or even irrationality in Churchill.' See,Richard Toye, *Churchill's Empire* (London, 2010), p. 236. A study of Churchill and the Indian Army seems to support the views of Best and Toye rather than those of Hyam.

1942 about the fighting in northern Malaya, which had decimated the recently raised, inexperienced 11th Indian Division.

Out of the catastrophe in the Far East came a renewed focus on the area by the Prime Minister because British military performance there had a significant impact on his relationship with his all-important American allies, who disapproved of the Raj on principle while entertaining a delusionary enthusiasm for the regime of Generalissimo Chiang Kai Shek. Churchill precipitated a major argument with the Australians (not all that difficult for him to do) when, in an effort to salvage American access to China via the Burma Road, he tried to send to Rangoon two Australian divisions returning home from the Middle East.[15] After the loss of Burma, it was plain that any counteroffensive to reclaim it – or anything else that had been lost to Japan – would have to depend upon the Indian Army. (In the course of the war only four British divisions would serve East of Suez: the 18th, lost at Singapore; the 70th, eventually broken up in late 1943 for use by Major General Orde Wingate in his 'Special Force'; the 2nd, which fought at Kohima; and the 36th, formed in theatre and understrength – as were nearly all British units in South East Asia Command (SEAC) by 1944, with little prospect of the shortfalls being made good.) Indian Army performance became briefly important to Churchill because a road to China across Burma was important to the Americans.

Unfortunately Churchill's renewed attention coincided with the Indian Army's absolute nadir – the first Arakan campaign in the winter of 1942–43, a campaign driven in large part by Churchill's pressure on General Sir Archibald Wavell, then Commander-in-Chief, India, to mount a counterattack into Burma. A liaison officer from Lieutenant General William Slim's XV Corps (which was not used in the operation until the situation was out of hand because Lieutenant General Noel Irwin, a British regular in charge of the Arakan attack, disliked Slim, an Indian Army officer) reported back from the Arakan that the troops – the end result of the frenetic expansion policy – were in many cases little better than 'a rather unwilling band of raw levies'.[16] As the campaign collapsed, the

---

15 The argument over the defence of Rangoon is fully discussed in the Australian official history: Lionel Wigmore, *The Japanese Thrust* (Canberra, 1957), pp. 442–65. It seems clear that the Prime Minister wanted 'white soldiers' rather than Indian Army units to defend this (politically) crucial point.

16 The report from which the quotation is taken – 'Report on a Visit to the Maugdaw Front, 4–9 May 1943' – is in the Irwin Papers 2/1, Imperial War Museum, Department of Documents. The relationship of regular British Army officers to British officers of the Indian Army is an underexamined subject. The tension had been present since the first British Army units arrived in India during the Seven Years War, and the King's officers found a large 'local' army officered by men whose commissions came from a company of merchants. That

Prime Minister exploded. Called back to London for consultations (prior to being kicked upstairs to the Viceroyalty), Wavell was on the receiving end of a diatribe about the failures of the Indian Army going back to the 1857 mutiny in the East India Company's Bengal Army. India Command, and the whole of the Raj for that matter, were dismissed as a 'welter of lassitude and inefficiency'.[17] The result of the Arakan disaster, as far as the Prime Minister was concerned, was to trigger a search for a strategy that would satisfy the Americans (with whom he was simultaneously struggling to defend his Mediterranean priorities) – and not depend upon the Indian Army. As that army began in the aftermath of the Arakan fiasco a process of rejuvenation that would produce the great Fourteenth Army of 1944–45, in one of his most remarkable policy initiatives of the war, the Prime Minister set out to marginalise the Indian Army's future role in the Burma campaign.

One of the most curious facts about all this is that the Prime Minister ignored a striking testimonial to the Indian Army's institutional strength that was right before his eyes. While worrying aloud to Auchinleck about the loyalty of Indian soldiers and reminding Wavell of the 1857 Mutiny, he missed the fact that Gandhi's 'Quit India' movement and the resulting 'Congress Revolt' of August 1942 did not produce a tremor in the Army, although it now included growing numbers of both Indian officers and soldiers drawn from outside the family circle of the martial races – a striking case of a dog that failed to bark in the night. On the eve of the August 1942 upheaval, the Director of Military Intelligence at Army Headquarters admitted in a 'most secret' memorandum that most soldiers looked forward to postwar independence, yet the event passed without either trouble in the Army or note of that fact being taken in Downing Street. On the Indian Army, it seems Churchill's prejudices were quite simply unshakeable.

Those prejudices had much to do with the solution to the conundrum of Burma for which he opted in the late summer of 1943. The new SEAC would remove control of the war against Japan from Army Headquarters, India, now under Auchinleck. SEAC's orientation would be maritime and amphibious

tension remained until 1947. See my *The East India Company and Army Reform, 1783–1798* (Cambridge, MA, 1972) for the early stages of the story, and *Churchill and His Generals* (Lawrence, KS, 2007) for its manifestations during the Second World War. One of those manifestations was Irwin's hostility to Slim. Only Irwin's removal from command prevented him from sacking Slim, who had just successfully halted the rout from the Arakan that Irwin had done almost as much as the Japanese to precipitate. The whole subject of the relationship between British and Indian Army officers deserves a book to itself.

17 Churchill to Ismay, 24 July 1943, in W.S. Churchill, *Closing the Ring* (Boston 1951), p. 656.

with the goal of restoring imperial prestige by carrying the Union Jack back to Singapore. As to Burma, Churchill thought he had found the answer in a man who was perhaps the strangest figure thrown up by the British Army in the twentieth century: Orde Wingate. This is not the place for an extended assessment of Wingate, his career and his ideas (regular soldiers operating behind enemy lines in independent 'columns' supplied by air and coordinated by radio, their mission being to disrupt Japanese communications).[18] What does need to be highlighted, however, is that he and the Prime Minister were agreed on the low quality of the Indian Army, which Wingate dismissively referred to as a 'system of outdoor relief', a phrase Churchill would be repeating to Amery as late as April 1945.[19] Wingate's ideas offered a way both to satisfy the Americans that at least enough of Burma would be conquered to restore their ability to pour supplies into the black hole of Nationalist China and, moreover, to do so without depending upon the Indian Army (whose units, Gurkhas apart, Wingate refused to use in his columns). The changes Churchill imposed in August and September 1943 on theatre organisation and strategy in South Asia were in many ways more sweeping than the results of his better known descent on Cairo in August 1942 (where, incidentally, a high percentage of the victims of the purge that followed the Eighth Army's May–June defeat at Rommel's hands were Indian Army officers). But if the Prime Minister thought he had substantially removed the Indian Army from the equation, he was – as was so often the case where India was concerned – wrong.

The revitalisation of the Indian Army that began after the withdrawal from Burma and accelerated dramatically with Auchinleck's arrival in mid 1943 as Commander-in-Chief, Major General Reginald Savory's appointment as Director of Infantry, and of course Slim's appointment as Fourteenth Army commander, occurred simultaneously with the fading of Churchill's brief flare of interest in the Indian Army and the war in Burma. American pressure on

[18] Recently there has been an effort to situate Wingate within the mainstream of British Army thinking, a finding that would have surprised most, it not all, of those who had to work with him, especially in India (Simon Anglim, *Orde Wingate and the British Army* [London, 2010], a thoroughly researched study which future students of Wingate's career will have to weigh carefully. It should be noted, however, that Anglim does not address Wingate's views of the Indian Army). The consensus view on Wingate has been that his ideas, based on his experience with small raiding parties, when scaled up to corps size as they were once he had Churchill's patronage, were an unworkable and unnecessary diversion of men, resources and attention from Fourteenth Army's campaign.

[19] Christopher Sykes, *Orde Wingate: A Biography* (Cleveland, Ohio, 1959), p. 455; John Barnes and David Nicolson (eds), *The Empire at Bay: The Leo Amery Dairies 1929–1945* (London 1988), 1039, diary entry for 27 April 1945. 'Outdoor relief' is an early nineteenth-century term for welfare payments.

that subject relaxed in 1944 as the acceleration of their advance across the Pacific made China less important as a platform for the final assault on Japan (and perhaps as well because the events of that year in Burma – Fourteenth Army's great victory at Imphal-Kohima – meant the road to China would be completed). Churchill's major argument in 1944 about the war against Japan was not with the Americans about Burma but with his own Chiefs of Staff about his preference for an Indian Ocean-centred strategy to be executed by SEAC versus their desire to join the Americans (who did not want them) in the Pacific – an unreal argument over strategies for neither of which did the necessary resources exist. Meanwhile the business of rebuilding the Indian Army, which Daniel Marston has so very ably described, and reshaping its doctrine, a process analysed by Tim Moreman, could go on under the radar.[20] This was of course the work of Army Headquarters, India, and Fourteenth Army, not of Whitehall. It is however striking how very little India, Burma or Fourteenth Army figures in Churchill's papers (or Brooke's diaries) between the September 1943 Quadrant Conference and the war's end. Slim got on with winning the war in Burma, with an army that, by the end, was largely Indian, without much of London's attention – probably a blessing in disguise. About the time Rangoon fell to Slim in May 1945, Auchinleck remarked that every Indian officer worth his salt was a nationalist[21] – a remark that sums up a long-term consequence of the Indian Army's wartime transformation, and one that would have made it impossible, whatever the result of the 1945 general election, to 'keep a bit of India,'[22] as Churchill, by then (fortunately) a bystander, urged the beleaguered Viceroy, Wavell, to do in the late summer of 1945.

But Churchill was not yet finished with the Indian Army and its war. There is the matter of his enormously influential memoirs. The striking thing about them is how absent the Indian Army, as such, is. There is never any acknowledgement of how important the Indian Army was in sustaining the imperial war effort in the Middle East theatre, especially in 1940–41 (although Wavell, when Viceroy, had pointedly reminded Churchill of this), or of the fact that by war's end, the British Eighth Army in Italy depended heavily on Indian manpower. But it was in relation to Burma that Churchill's prejudices were really on display. The chapter on the 1942 withdrawal from Burma (drafted by his military assistant Lieutenant General Sir Henry Pownall) is lavish in praise of the overall commander there, Lieutenant General Sir Harold Alexander – Churchill's favourite general and a

20 Daniel Marston, *Phoenix from the Ashes: The Indian Army in the Burma Campaign* (Westport, CT, 2003); T.R. Moreman, *The Jungle, the Japanese and the Commonwealth Armies at War 1941–45* (London, 2005).

21 David Omissi, *The Sepoy and the Raj* (Basingstoke, UK, 1994), p. 242.

22 Penderel Moon (ed.), *Wavell: The Viceroy's Journal* (London 1973), p. 168.

Guardsman – but never mentions Slim, the real architect of the longest fighting withdrawal in British military history. In *Closing the Ring* the Fourteenth Army's first success, the February 1944 victory in the Arakan, gets a paragraph, Imphal a page. Neither Slim nor Fourteenth Army is mentioned by name. When *Closing the Ring* was published, the Fourteenth Army (British) veterans group, the Burma Star Association, noticed these omissions and their unhappiness was conveyed to Churchill by Slim, by then Chief of the Imperial General Staff. The result, in Churchill's final volume, *Triumph and Tragedy*, was two chapters on 'the famous Fourteenth Army' (again by Pownall) and an acknowledgement of Slim's leadership – but none of the fact that Indian (and African) troops made up about 85 per cent of that army. Nowhere does Churchill display any recognition of what the British war effort owed to the Indian Army (or to the massive mobilisation of Indian resources described by Graham Dunlop in a pioneering study[23]).

It is a sad story. Nowhere else in his public life did Winston Churchill display such a depressing lack of generosity of spirit – or refusal to accommodate realities – as he did on this subject. Why this should be so remains hard to explain. Saying 'Victorian racial attitudes' is insufficient, although that is clearly part of it. Some of it was probably class – an institutional condescension towards the Indian Army he absorbed in the cavalry messes of his youth. Some of it is clearly due to Churchill's personal vision of Britain and its place in the world. De Gaulle famously began his war memoirs by confessing to a 'certain vision' of France, a vision from which glory was inseparable. Churchill had a comparable vision of his country: 'my ideal is narrow and limited', he wrote to the Viceroy, Lord Linlithgow, in 1937. 'I want to see the British Empire preserved for a few more generations in its strength and splendour.'[24] India was crucial to Churchill's vision of a beneficent, globe-girdling empire, and so the Raj somehow had to be maintained, even if that meant refusing to face the evidence that its condition might be terminal – or that the cost of national survival might well be an imperial sunset. But whatever the roots of Churchill's attitudes, this much is clear: the remarkable war effort of the Indian Army took place in spite of lack of support from the top at the time – or appreciation (or even acknowledgement) in retrospect.

---

[23] Graham Dunlop, *Military Economics, Culture and Logistics in the Burma Campaign, 1942–45* (London, 2009). Like the monographs by Marston and Moreman, this is a crucial study, indispensible for a rounded understanding of the Indian Army's achievement.

[24] Churchill to Linlithgow, 3 November 1937, in Martin Gilbert, *Winston S. Churchill, V 1922–1939* (London 1976), p. 886.

Chapter 4
Training the Indian Army, 1939–1945

Alan Jeffreys

This chapter will examine the development of training in the Indian Army from the 1930s until the end of the Second World War. It will concentrate on the training manuals produced by the Indian Army before and during the war as well as the officers who were responsible for training in the Indian Army. In comparison to the British Army, there were far fewer officers in the Indian Army but nearly all the regular officers spent a period of time at a training establishment.[1]

The two main roles of the Indian Army in the inter-war period were internal security and policing the frontiers. By the mid-1930's, the Indian Army was proficient in fighting on the North West Frontier with a developing doctrine and *esprit de corps* developed by the 'endless round of regimental sport'.[2] However as Mark Jacobsen has indicated the Indian Army had shown little interest in modernisation from within even without the financial restraints of the period.[3] The Indian Army Modernisation Committee report was drawn up by the Deputy Chief of the General Staff, Major General Sir Claude Auchinleck, the Director of Staff Duties, General Sir G.N. Molesworth and the Director of Military Training (DMT) Colonel Eric Dorman-Smith known as the Auchinleck Committee. The resulting report noted that the Indian Army's most likely fight was an Asiatic war and needed to be ready for the five roles of frontier defence, coastal defence, external defence, internal security and a reserve force and modernise accordingly, the report was then adopted by the Chatfield Committee.[4] It was not ready to fight an army equipped with up-to-date weapons, British Army units going out to India had to be retrained in

---

1 See Alan Jeffreys, *Training the Indian Army, 1939–45* (Farnham: Ashgate, forthcoming).

2 Alan Warren, *Waziristan, The Faqir of Ipi, and the Indian Army* (Karachi: Oxford University Press, 2000), p. 110.

3 See Mark H. Jacobsen, *The Modernization of the Indian Army, 1925–39* (Irvine: University of California, Phd thesis, 1976), p. 387.

4 See Jacobsen, *Modernization of the Indian Army*, pp. 388–95. See also Sri Nandan Prasad, *Official History of the Indian Armed Forces in the Second World War: Expansion of*

obsolete weapons and outdated tactics.[5] The Indian Army was much smaller at this stage than perhaps generally imagined, numbering 194,373 men, with just 1,912 British officers and 344 Indian officers before 1939.[6]

Pre-war Training

The pre-war training structure consisted of four training centres or schools for the Artillery, three for the Engineers, two for signals and the Veterinary Corps, one each for the Royal Indian Army Service Corps, and the Indian Army Ordnance Corps.[7] Training was quite relaxed as Spike Mays found out when he transferred from the 1st King's Dragoon Guards to the Signal Training Centre at Jubbulpore during the 1930s and was immediately put in the picture by a fellow trooper, who commented on the training centre:

> Queer bloody lot here, mate. The horses are a dead loss and everybody is sports mad. Football, hockey, swimming, boxing, the lot! There's no parades for the sports wallahs ... no fatigues, guards or picquets. A bit of training twice a day and every bloody weekend off ... Special diets, too. Bleedin' great steaks and as many eggs as they can bolt, and that's only for breakfast![8]

Following the recommendations of the 1920 Esher Committee, infantry training was carried out by the 10th battalion of each regiment from 1922 onwards. The battalion's main role was the training of recruits for the reinforcement of the active battalions in the regiment. Training lasted eight months in peacetime and six during war, the *Training Battalion Manual* regarded the battalion as the nursery of the regiment and essential 'for its efficiency and *esprit de corps*, and for its traditions'. The regiment depended 'largely on the success with which the training battalion carries out its role'.[9] Instructors needed to have

---

the Armed Forces and Defence Organisation 1939–45 (India and Pakistan: Combined Inter-Services Historical Section, 1956), pp. 20–26.

5 See Typescript of Historical Section (India)'s history 'India at War 1939–1945', pp. 10–11, *Corbett Mss.*, Papers of Lieutenant General Thomas Corbett, Churchill Archives Centre (CAC), CORB 2/28.

6 See Chris Kempton, *'Loyalty & Honour': The Indian Army September 1939–August 1947: Part III* (Milton Keynes: The Military Press, 2003), p. 104 and Establishment of the Indian Army Officer Cadre, Annexure A, OIOC, L/WS/1/924.

7 See Prasad, *Expansion*, pp. 27–8.

8 Spike Mays, *Fall Out the Officers* (London: Eyre & Spottiswoode, 1969), p. 198.

9 Training Battalion Manual, 1931, p. 1, OIOC, L/MIL/17/5/2216.

recently undertaken courses at an army school of instruction even though units were loath to part with their best personnel.[10] The syllabus consisted mainly of physical education, drill, handling weapons and general education. In the case of cavalry, from 1937 three regiments were set apart as training regiments, namely Sam Browne's Cavalry, 15th Lancers and the 20th Lancers.[11] The Field Artillery Training Centre at Muttra was established in 1935.[12] Other training schools included ones for equitation, weapon training, small arms, physical training, education, chemical warfare and cookery.[13]

Training was divided up into collective and individual. Collective training was from company up to brigade level with exercises in the Plains and columns on the North-West Frontier. It took place in the cold weather and all battalion officers were meant to be present. Whereas individual training took place in the hot weather where all ranks could concentrate on such matters as weapon training and drill. A series of *Training Memorandum* were produced by Army Headquarters during the 1930s. Two were issued per year, one for individual training and one for the collective period. The manual for the individual training period had sections on officer training, historical campaigns to study, Staff College entrance examinations, sections on the various arms of cavalry, artillery, tanks, signals; sections on Internal Security duties, weapon training, anti-gas, field works, physical training, educational, language study, co-operation with RAF, riding instruction, Indian Army officers attending demonstrations in Britain, available manuals, vocational and reservist training. At the end of the pamphlet were sections on the individual schools such as the Senior Officer's School and the Small Arms School (Ahmednagar and Pachmarhi wings). Copies of the manual were also produced in Roman Urdu.[14] The manual for the collective training period during 1930–31 concentrated on more tactical matters such as internal security, mountain warfare and co-operation with the RAF. The pamphlet also stated the training policy for the Indian Army which

10 See Courses of Instruction (India) 1932, p. 1, OIOC, L/MIL/17/5/2200. See also Army Headquarters (AHQ) Training Memorandum No. 1: Individual Training Period, 1930, p. 23, OIOC L/MIL/17/5/2199.

11 See F.W. Perry, *The Commonwealth Armies: Manpower and Organisation in Two World Wars* (Manchester: Manchester University Press, 1988), p. 98. See also John Gaylor, *Sons of John Company: The Indian and Pakistan Armies 1903–91* (Tunbridge Wells: Parapress, 1996), p. 13.

12 See Lieutenant General S.L. Menezes, *Fidelity and Honour: The Indian Army from the Seventeenth to the Twenty-first Century* (New Delhi: Oxford University Press, 1999), p. 325.

13 See Prasad, *Expansion*, p. 28.

14 See AHQ Training Memorandum No. 1: Individual Training Period 1930, OIOC, L/MIL/17/5/2199.

was to train for expeditions against frontier tribes, maintain internal peace but also for larger operations against a 'moderately well equipped army'. This was in contrast to the British Army in India who would need to be prepared to defend the Empire in any part of the world.[15] As the number of British officers in the Indian Army was much less than in an equivalent British Army regiment, initiative was encouraged:

> The aim of training must, in the first instance be directed to the production of a body of junior officers imbued with initiative and self-reliance. They must know how to use ground by day and night, and have confidence in their ability to gain ground with their own weapons. Skill in handling of fighting patrols has been found to form a useful basis for teaching the elements of infiltration tactics.[16]

Training developed during the 1930's as lessons were drawn from the Mohmand operations of 1935 and Waziristan 1935–36 which were then assimilated.[17] At the same time the role of the Army in India slightly changed as did the resulting policy. The Army in India would now need to be able to face an enemy with more up to date weapons than those used by the Frontier tribes, and future exercises needed to assume that the enemy used aircraft, artillery and machine guns. Thus the updated training policy stated:

> The primary duty of the Army in India is to train for war against an enemy whose armed forces are inferior to those of the leading military powers in respect of organization, training and equipment. At the same time officers must be kept in touch with the most up-to-date equipment and armament, and the latest doctrines evolved for their employment.[18]

The manual warned against boredom as the enemy of training, suggesting that schemes should develop initiative and rapid decisions with an element of

---

15 See AHQ Training Memorandum No. 2: Collective Training Period 1930–31, OIOC, L/MIL/17/5/2199.

16 AHQ Training Memorandum No. 6: Collective Training Period 1932–33, p. 8, OIOC, L/MIL/17/5/2199.

17 See AHQ India Training Memorandum No. 12, pp. 2–8 and AHQ India Training Memorandum No. 14, pp. 8–12, OIOC L/MIL/17/5/2199. See also Tim Moreman, *The Army in India and the Development of Frontier Warfare, 1849–1947* (Basingstoke: Macmillan, 1998), pp. 150–72 and Alan Warren, *Waziristan, The Faqir of Ipi and the Indian Army: The North West Frontier Revolt of 1936–37* (Karachi: Oxford University Press, 2000).

18 AHQ India Training Memorandum No. 12: Notes on Collective Training Period 1935–36, p. 8, OIOC, L/MIL/17/5/2199.

surprise during exercises, although the troops needed to be clearly in the picture before the exercise began and during it to keep their interest.[19] In 1938 the policy was slightly amended again, the main tasks were still the defence of the frontiers and coasts of India as well as internal security stating that the Indian Army was mainly concerned with extensive warfare of small forces operating with strict economy rather than the intensive warfare of western armies. However, the threat of other Asiatic armies was noted, remarking:

> It must be recognized that the armies of many Asiatic powers are re-arming with modern weapons and becoming increasingly mechanized. The possibility of meeting enemies who are better armed and more highly mechanized must not be overlooked, and it is no longer sufficient for the Army in India to train solely for warfare with an inferior enemy.[20]

Indian Army officers now needed to understand the organisation, equipment, armament and tactics of the British Army at home as well as other European and Asiatic armies and thus War Office training memoranda were to be more widely distributed in India with AHQ training memoranda to deal with issues that directly affected India. For instance, infantry training in India was to follow the War Office pamphlet *Infantry Training 1937* except with the absence of equipment such as mortars, machine guns and other supporting arms and weapons. Thus the Indian Army had to develop their firepower and tactics in both day and night operations to make up for this lack of equipment. Lessons from Waziristan continued to be learnt showing that fighting in thick scrub and jungle 'was just as unfavourable to the enemy, as it was to our own troops. The thick cover enable our troops to get to close quarters with the enemy, to envelop his flanks and to threaten his lines of withdrawal.'[21]

Most British officer cadets for the Indian Army attended the Royal Military College at Sandhurst for 18 months. Prestige for the Indian Army was very high during this period. As Alan Warren has succinctly noted that there was no shortage of volunteers for the Indian Army as 'The adventure, higher responsibilities and economical lifestyle of India assured there was no shortage of applications'.[22] Competition was fierce, only the top 60 officers who passed out of Sandhurst could apply for the Indian Army. One cadet who did so called a British Army officer a 'failed Indian Army officer' with the result that much distrust and envy developed between officers of the British and Indian Armies.

19 See AHQ India Training Memorandum No. 12, OIOC, L/MIL/17/5/2199.

20 See AHQ India Training Memorandum No. 16, p. 2, OIOC, L/MIL/17/5/2199.

21 AHQ India Training Memorandum No. 16, p. 6, OIOC L/MIL/17/5/2199.

22 Warren, *Waziristan*, p. 109.

The Indian Army was more popular with many of the cadets due to the quicker promotion and more responsibility and 'was also much admired because of the glamour and prospects of seeing active service on the North West Frontier'.[23]

Indian officer cadets had been attending the Indian Military Academy (IMA) at Dehra Dun since 1932. They spent 30 months at the IMA, with the course mirroring Sandhurst except in the length.[24] General Musa who later became C-in-C Pakistan Army was one of the first batch of cadets. He remembered how hard they worked and that very high standards were demanded.[25] According to evidence proffered to the Indianisation committee, Indian officers graduating from the IMA were considered to better trained than their contemporaries at Sandhurst with very thorough tactical training by first class British officers such as Brigadier Lionel Collins, Major Reginald Savory, Major David 'Punch' Cowan and Major Le Fleming.[26] As Lieutenant General Harbakhsh Singh commented in his memoirs:

> The staff for the newly started Academy were the pick of the Indian Army, and included those who were sympathetic to the Indians for there is no doubt that the British wanted to make this experiment of Indianisation, however small, a success.[27]

Both Indian and British officer recruits would then spend a year with a British unit in India before joining their Indian regiment, although often little was learnt in the year and prowess in sport seemed to predominate.[28] By 1939 60 Indian officers and 120 British officers were commissioned each year into the Indian Army.

---

23 John Archibald Hislop, *A Soldier's Story: From the Khyber Pass to the Jungles of Burma: The Memoir of a British Officer in the Indian Army 1933–1947* (Newhaven: Newhaven Publishing, 2010), pp. 26–7.

24 See Pradeep Barua, *The Army Officer Corps and Military Modernistion in Later Colonial India* (Hull: University of Hull Press, 1999), p. 49.

25 See General Mohammad Musa, *Jawan to General: Recollections of a Pakistani Soldier* (Karachi: East & West Publishing Company, 1984), p. 25.

26 See Prasad, *Expansion*, p. 179 and Daniel Marston, *Phoenix from the Ashes: The Indian Army in the Burma Campaign* (Wesport: Praeger, 2003), pp. 20–21. See also Cohen, *The Indian Army: Its Contribution to the Development of a Nation* (Delhi: Oxford University Press, 1990), pp. 118–19, 121, 131 and Musa, *Jawan to General*, pp. 25–6.

27 Lieutenant General Harbakhsh Singh, *In the Line of Duty: A Soldier Remembers* (Delhi: Lancer Publishers, 2000), p. 31.

28 See Musa, *Jawan to General*, p. 29. See also Papers of Major B.E. Barrow, *Barrow Mss.*, IWM.

For more senior officers, there was the Senior Officers School at Belgaum and the Staff College at Quetta. Belgaum was for majors before getting command of their battalions.[29] The course lasted three months with the tactical aim to ensure 'uniformity of method in their application throughout the Army'.[30] The Staff College was established in 1907. During the interwar period, it was on the same level with the Staff College in Camberley teaching a similar syllabus and advocating the mobilisation of the army.[31]

During the late 1930's, some Indian Army officers took training very seriously such as Lieutenant Colonel Francis 'Gertie' Tuker and Lieutenant Colonel Thomas Corbett. Tuker took over command of the 1st Battalion, 2nd Goorkha Rifles and immediately instigated a new training regime for the battalion, as the regimental historian commented 'His contribution to his regiment and to the Indian Army was in effect the replacement of offensive for defensive thinking.'[32] In a paper on training infantry written in 1934 Tuker remarked that 'All is most certainly not well with the training of our infantryman.'[33] Within the battalion he issued training circulars, orders and instructions and some of his ideas were absorbed into Indian Army doctrine and published in *AHQ India Training Memorandum No. 17* (1938).[34] The battalion trained for night work, patrolling and forest fighting. As a result of his thorough training of the battalion, Tuker came to the attention of GHQ India and was made Deputy Director of Staff Duties, GSO1 in 1939.[35] He was moved to the training directorate in October 1939. Similarly, Corbett issued training memoranda when he commanded the 2nd Lancers (Gardner's Horse), his *Collective Training Report for 1934–35* was based on AHQ *Training Memorandum No. 8* and Northern Command's *Training Instruction No. 3*. He advocated raising the standards of junior leadership and made sure his regiment trained for night operations and river

---

[29] See Prasad, *Expansion*, pp. 16, 27–8. See also Colonel H.R.C. Pettigrew, '"It seems very ordinary": Memoirs of Sixteen Years in the Indian Army 1932–1947' (Unpublished memoir), p. 115, IWM 84/29/1.

[30] Courses of Instruction (India) 1932, p. 11, OIOC, L/MIL/17/5/2200

[31] See Patrick Rose, 'British Army Command Culture 1939–1945: A Comparative Study of British Eighth and Fourteenth Armies' (PhD thesis, KCL University, 2009), p. 67 and Raymond Callahan, *Churchill and his Generals* (Lawrence, Kansas: University Press of Kansas, 2007), p. 65.

[32] Lieutenant Colonel G.R. Stevens, *History of the 2nd King Edward VII's Own Goorkha Rifles (The Sirmoor Rifles) Volume III 1921–1948* (Aldershot: Gale & Polden, 1952), p. 27.

[33] The Training of Infantry 1934, *Tuker Mss.*, Papers of Lieutenant General Sir Francis Tuker, IWM 71/21/2.

[34] See AHQ Training Memorandum No. 17: Notes on Individual training period 1938, pp. 15–17, *Tuker Mss.*, IWM 71/21/5.

[35] See Stevens, 2nd Goorkha Rifles, p. 34.

crossings concluding that 'Troop commanders have realised the importance of studying their profession and are vastly improved instructors.'[36] Corbett was an advocate of mechanisation and went on to become an instructor at Quetta. In his opening address to the Senior Division in the Spring term of 1937 Corbett addressed the issue of training commenting that it lacked inspiration and that modernisation of the Indian Army would be accelerated by first class training based on manuals, that could also be developed by the new generation of officers attending the course.[37] In January 1940 Corbett was appointed Brigadier Cavalry to oversee mechanisation within the Indian Army cavalry regiments. Thus, most pre-war regular Indian Army officers spent a period of time at one of the training establishments in India or as in instructor at one.

Second World War Training

With the outbreak of the Second World War, after an initial hiatus, the Indian Army embarked on a massive expansion programme in May 1940 to meet the requests for increased manpower.[38] In 18 months the Indian Army doubled in size, although it was very short of equipment. To accomplish this experienced NCOs, Viceroy-commissioned officers and officers were 'milked' from their units in order to bolster new and raw units. Expansion meant that a large number of the new Indian troops had little basic training, in direct contrast to the professional Indian Army of the pre-1939 period.

In October 1940, Tuker was appointed Director of Military Training with Lieutenant Colonel David 'Punch' Cowan as Deputy Director, who later commanded 17th Indian Division. The Military Training Directorate consisted of 12 officers at the beginning of the war divided into three sections. MT1 was responsible for the military training schools and establishments, MT2 dealt with higher training and training publications and MT3 looked after individual training and exercised executive control of the training schools.[39] The Directorate slowly grew with another ten officers by the end of 1941 as well as the upgrade of the Director and his deputy to Major General and Brigadier. In this period the directorate produced a huge number of manuals. Much was based on existing experience, for example, a doctrine was finally produced for internal security

[36] Collective Training Report 1934–35 for 2nd Lancers (Gardner's Horse), 5 March 1935, *Corbett* Mss., CAC CORB 1/17.

[37] See Notes for Opening Address Spring Term Senior Division 1937, *Corbett Mss.*, CAC CORB 2/29.

[38] See 'India at War', p. 27, *Corbett Mss.*, CAC CORB 3/28.

[39] See Prasad, *Expansion*, pp. 305–6.

with the publication of Military Training Pamphlet (MTP) No. 11 (India), *Notes on training for duties in aid of the civil power, 1941*.[40] The directorate also produced new training manuals relevant to Indian Army formations stationed in various parts of the Empire at the beginning of the Second World War, such as the first edition of MTP No. 9 (India) on *Forest Warfare* which was produced in 1940 based on Tuker's experience in Assam in 1919 and training with the 2nd Goorkhas in 1933.[41] Likewise, a second edition of MTP No. 7 (India) *Extensive warfare (notes on warfare in mountainous country between modern forces in Eastern theatres)* was produced in June 1941.[42] As Tuker noted in the DMT's address of 23 September 1941:

> It has always been our object on the training side to try and get everybody under one hat. We do not wish this so as to control them but to get their help in order to devise our various tactical doctrines, and in order that they may be able to spread the news abroad whenever we have built up new methods and produced new ideas.[43]

These training pamphlets were not meant to be the last word and were revised in light of further experience. In the same address Tuker advocated the importance of all arms co-operation providing Iraq as an example and stating '... we are not only up with other people but well ahead in tactical doctrine and training'.[44] As Tuker continued, the Indian Army had had to accept the equipment it was given but there was no reason why the army had to be organised in the same way as everybody else stating that: 'There is no manner of doubt that the doctrine of warfare comes before anything else in the Army's make-up.'[45]

Tuker and GHQ India decided to concentrate all the training schools in Southern Command. OTS Belgaum was set up in October 1939 replacing the Senior Officers' School which was closed. OTS Mhow and Bangalore were

---

40 See Military Training pamphlet No. 11 (India), Notes on training for duties in aid of the civil power, 1941 (Delhi: GSI, 1942), OIOC L/MIL/17/2252. See also Srinath Raghaven, 'Protecting the Raj: The Army in India and Internal Security c. 1919–1939' in *Small Wars and Insurgencies*, Vol. 16, No. 3, December 2005.

41 See Military Training Pamphlet No. 9 (India), IWM. See also Attack on Aihang village, Assam, May 1918, *Tuker Mss*, IWM, 71/21/2/1.

42 See Military Training Pamphlet No. 7 (India). Extensive warfare (notes on warfare in mountainous country between modern forces in Eastern theatres (Delhi: GSI, 2nd ed., June 1941), OIOC L/MIL/17/5/2248.

43 DMT's Address, 23 September 1941, p. 1, *Tuker Mss.*, IWM 71/21/2/5.

44 Ibid., p. 4.

45 Ibid., p. 9.

formed in September 1940.[46] Returning officers from North Africa taught desert warfare to the newly formed divisions, who were also trained by two training teams, consisting of two or three GHQ officers. No. 1 Training Team was based at Poona and No. 2 at Secunderabad. The teams continued to be used until 1942, as the evacuated Argyll and Sutherland officers from Malaya taught jungle warfare to formations. Southern Command was at the heart of training for the Indian Army until Central Command was formed in April 1942 which took over responsibility for some of the training areas.[47]

Tuker conducted a tour of the Middle East in 1941 as DMT and learned some valuable lessons as well as how useful the material produced by the directorate had proved in theatre. The Indian troops were regarded as well-trained. However, Tuker noted during his tour that: 'Training is the main thing that wins battles, for it is the only thing that makes soldiers out of common citizens. GHQ India as a whole has yet to realise this and to realise that we will never reach a standard that is high enough for today.'[48] MTPs (India) were seen to be very useful in the Middle East with the Commandant of the Staff School at Haifa stating: '... he believed Indian Infantry to be the best soldiers in the Empire. He also stated that he constantly reminded all his students to try and get hold of every GHQ India Training Memorandum and Pamphlets they could lay hands on.'[49] MTP's Nos 13 and 14 on *Navigation by Stars* and *Infantry Section Leading* respectively proved very popular and Tuker promised to send out more training pamphlets across the theatre.[50]

The directorate produced *Army in India Training Memorandum* (AITMs), a development of the pre-war *AHQ Training Memorandum*, with the first one appearing in May 1940. They were originally meant to complement the War Office's *Army Training Memorandum* (ATM) but in order to cut down the amount of material that officers were meant to read important lessons from the

---

46 See Alan Jeffreys, 'The Officer Corps and the training of the Indian Army with special reference to Lieutenant General Sir Francis Tuker', in Kaushik Roy (ed.) *The Indian Army in Two World Wars* (Leiden: Brill, 2011), pp. 285–310.

47 See Lieutenant Colonel R.S.M. Calder, 'From Sloth Belt to Springboard: Being an Account of activities of Southern Command India in the Second World War' (Unpublished Account), pp. 10, 13, 19–20, 25–51, 33, NAM 8209–14. See also DMT's Address, 23 September 1941, p. 9, *Tuker Mss.*, IWM 71/21/2/5 and Alan Jeffreys, *British Army in the Far East 1941–45* (Oxford: Osprey, 2005), pp. 71, 86.

48 DMT's tour of the Middle East, Note C, *Tuker Mss.* IWM 71/21/2/6.

49 DMT's tour of the Middle East, Note F, *Tuker Mss.* IWM 71/21/2/6.

50 See Military training pamphlet No. 13 (India). Navigation by the stars (Delhi: GSI, 1941), OIOC L/MIL/17/5/2255 and Military training pamphlet No. 14 (India). Infantry section leading, 1941 (Calcutta: GSI, 1941), OIOC L/MIL/17/5/2256.

ATMs were copied in AITMs.[51] Both dealt 'with all aspects of military training carried out by all arms of service'.[52] The second AITM, published in November 1940, clearly shows the importance of patrolling and 'infiltration' for infantry a lesson that had repeatedly to be learnt in most theatres of war throughout the Second World War. It also showed why training was proving difficult at this early stage of the war due to the large number of inexperienced officers, warrant officers and NCOs in the Indian Army together with the reorganisation, mechanisation and change of tactical methods within it and the added problem of the further expansion of the army.[53] AITM No. 3 listed all the various training material available in 1940 which came to 21 War Office MTPs and eight Indian MTPs stating that MTPs (India) 'cover special subjects and forms of war, on which no other guidance is readily available'.[54] In contrast, the British army had different series of training pamphlets including *Current Reports from Overseas*, *Notes from Theatres of War* and *Army Training Instructions*. None of these seem to have been distributed in India or even mentioned in the Indian training material, although lessons learnt from all theatres including North West Europe were mentioned in the AITMs.

British Army formations were forbidden to issue training instructions whereas Indian formations in all theatres produced them.[55] One of the first Indian Divisions to produce training directives and instructions was 5th Indian Division in Summer 1941 when it was training for desert warfare. Training instruction No. 2 commented that, like mountain warfare, training for the desert 'is a specialist job but it is a job that can be learnt, if not mastered, by well trained troops quickly, if training is practical and intense'.[56] The Division moved to Iraq in late 1942 and began training for a new role as a 'mixed infantry and armour division'. 5th Indian Division issued over ten training instructions and revisions, together with General Briggs's GOC's training directives for this new role.[57] 4th Indian Division issued training instructions when Tuker took over command in December 1941 and he, of course, sent copies back to the DMT India. Training

[51] AITM No. 3, p. 1, OIOC L/MIL/17/5/2240.

[52] List of GS Training publications 1945, p. 1, OIOC L/MIL/17/5/2197.

[53] See AITM No. 2, pp. 17, 25, OIOC L/MIL/17/5/2240.

[54] AITM No. 3, p. 22, OIOC L/MIL/17/5/2240.

[55] See ATM No. 25, p. 16, IWM.

[56] 5th Indian Division Training Instruction No. 2, TNA WO 169/3301. See also 9th Indian Division in Malaya who produced two training Instructions in April 1941 in Tim Moreman, *The Jungle, the Japanese and the British Commonwealth Armies at War, 1941–45: Fighting Methods, Doctrine and Training for Jungle Warfare* (London: Frank Cass, 2005), p. 21.

[57] See TNA WO 169/7541 and WO 172/1936. See also Antony Brett-James, *Ball of Fire* (Aldershot: Gale & Polden, 1951), pp. 244–7.

Instruction No. 3 was clearly founded upon Tuker's experience with sections on mountain warfare, based on MTP (India) No. 7, infantry tank co-operation and night training – all subjects that he had been studying since the 1930s. The Division produced over 40 training instructions in North Africa and Italy and were continually learning new lessons and then integrating it into their training.

The Indian Army was well versed in mountain warfare due to the experience of fighting on the North West Frontier. This experience was drawn upon during the war with twenty Indian Army officers being loaned as mountain warfare advisors for the Norwegian Campaign in 1940.[58] During the East African campaign, 4th and 5th Indian Divisions fought at the Battle of Keren which was largely fought in the mountains. In the month long lull in between the battles of Keren, training in mountain warfare was undertaken by the individual brigades, for example 29th trained at Tessani and 9th Brigade at Agordat.[59] 5th Indian Division had a month in Sudan spent training and learning the lessons that 4th Indian Divison had learnt from the Battle of Sidi Barrani.[60] At Kassala, officers of both Indian Divisions had briefings around a model of the Keren stronghold.[61] Brigadier Frank Messervy commanding 9th Brigade issued training instructions stating that: 'It is the problem of the last 400 yards when our men are tired, when our fire support problem becomes more difficult, and when the enemy will put in everything he can to stop us, which has to be satisfactorily solved.'[62] The Battle of Keren showed the importance of the pre-war training of the Indian Army particularly in mountain warfare and night attacks, that helped defeat a numerically superior force even though it was equipped as a mechanised force rather than for mountain warfare. It meant that a company within each battalion had to act as carriers. The battle was an important link between 'a classic adventure of the British Empire' and the modern Indian Army of 1945, as Compton Mackenzie asked: 'Has any campaign in history lasting two months produced from two divisions a fighting army commander, two fighting corps

---

58 See Loan of Indian Army officers experienced in mountain warfare, 1940, OIOC L/WS/1/377. See also John Prenderghast, *Prender's Progress: A Soldier in India 1931–1947* (London: Cassell, 1979), pp. 115–40.

59 See A.J. Barker, *Eritrea 1941* (London: Faber & Faber, 1966), pp. 117, 127; Henry Maule, *Spearhead General: The Epic Story of General Sir Frank Messervy and his Men in Eritrea, North Africa and Burma* (London: Odhams Press, 1961), p. 69.

60 See Major General J.G. Elliott, Unpublished volume on the Battle of Keren (1974), p. 54, IWM, Misc 952. See also Lieutenant Colonel Sir Geoffrey Betham and Major H.V.R. Geary, *The Golden Galley: The Story of the Second Punjab Regiment 1761–1947* (Oxford: 2nd Punjab Regiment Officers' Association, 1956), p. 186.

61 See Maule, *Spearhead General*, p. 75. See also Elliott, Keren, p. 104.

62 Quoted in Maule, *Spearhead General*, p. 75.

commanders and seven fighting divisional commanders within four years?'[63] For example, Brigadier William 'Bill' Slim who had commanded 10th Indian Brigade went on to command 14th Army in Burma; Major General Lewis 'Piggy' Heath, Commanding Officer (CO) 5th Indian Divison commanded III Corps in Malaya; Brigadier Frank Messervy, CO Gazelle Force and 9th Indian Brigade, commanded 4th Indian Division, 7th Armoured Division in North Africa and 7th Indian Division and IV Corps in Burma; Brigadier Harold Briggs, CO 11th Indian Brigade commanded 5th Indian Division in the Middle East and Burma; Brigadier Lloyd, CO 5th Indian Brigade became commander of 14th Indian Division during the disastrous First Battle of Arakan; Major Donald Bateman, Brigade Major in 5th Indian Brigade commanded 5th Indian Brigade from 1942–43 and became DMT in 1945; Lieutenant Colonel Dudley 'Pasha' Russell, GSO1 with 5th Indian Division became commander of 8th Indian Division; Brigadier Thomas 'Pete' Rees, CO 10th Indian Brigade commanded 19th Indian Division; Brigadier Reginald Savory, CO 11th Indian Brigade commanded 23th Indian Division and then became Inspector of Infantry at GHQ India and Lieutenant Colonel Denys Reid, Battalion Commander of the 3rd Mahratta Light Infantry became Divisional Commander of 10th Indian Division in Italy. All these Indian Army officers used training instructions once they commanded divisions and Bateman and Savory held important positions in the Military Training Directorate.

During the Italian campaign, 4th, 8th and 10th Indian divisions together with the 43rd Gurkha Lorried Brigade all mounted successful operations on the mountainous Gothic Line underpinned by their training in mountain warfare. 4th Indian Division Training Instruction No. 40 on mountain warfare, issued in 1943, noted: 'For this we have trained and will continue to train, – as our recent visit confirms this as the right policy.'[64] Mountain warfare continued to be of importance in both Britain and India. The War Office set up the Mountain Warfare Committee in 1944 where two of the three man committee were Indian Army officers, namely Colonel Le Marchand, who had been commandant of the Mountain Warfare school in India and had helped train British formations in the Middle East and Mediterranean theatre, and Brigadier Donald Bateman, who had commanded 5th Indian Infantry Brigade in Italy. It was responsible for the ensuing doctrine that was produced in MTP No. 34 on *Snow and Mountain*

[63] Andrew Stewart, '"Speed and dash": The British Commonwealth's Campaign in East Africa, 1940–41' in Ashley Jackson (ed.), 'New Research on the British Empire and the Second World War: Part II', *Global War* Studies, Vol. 7, No. 2 (2010); Compton Mackenzie, *Eastern Epic* (London: Chatto & Windus, 1951), p. 63.

[64] 4th Indian Division Training Instruction No. 40, 10 December 1943, TNA WO 169/14735.

Warfare in December 1944.[65] In India, training teams from 8th and 10th Indian Divisions were sent to the North West Frontier to lecture about fighting with modern equipment in mountainous terrain.[66] The Frontier Warfare Committee was set up in 1944 under the chairmanship of General Tuker who thought traditional forms of 'frontier warfare' were now outdated and lessons from the experience of mountain warfare in the Italian campaign should be instigated. However, the proposals of the Committee were not acted upon due to Partition when responsibility for the region went to Pakistan.[67]

Experience of fighting in the jungles of South East Asia was lacking in the Indian Army together with the rapid expansion of the Indian Armed Forces was largely responsible for the disastrous defeats in Malaya, Burma and First Arakan in the Far Eastern theatre.[68] As a result, GHQ India made some important changes in senior staff officers and frontline commanders to improve military effectiveness. Field Marshal Wavell was appointed Viceroy of India and was replaced by General Claude Auchinleck as C-in-C India in June 1943 and operational control for campaigns was now to be conducted by the newly appointed Supreme Allied Commander in South East Asia, Lord Louis Mountbatten. General Slim was appointed as 14th Army Commander and a range of experienced divisional commanders were also appointed such as Major Generals Frank Messervy and 'Pete' Rees, commanding 7th and 19th Indian Divisions respectively, both of whom had not fared well in North Africa but became very distinguished commanders in the Burma campaign.[69] At the same time there were changes in the training structure as Major-General Reginald Savory was appointed Inspector of Infantry, he had commanded 23rd Indian Division in Assam. In his own words: 'I spent most of my time, not only visiting the training establishments, but also infantry units throughout India. I also

---

[65] See Alan Jeffreys, 'Indian Army training for the Italian campaign and the lessons learnt' in Patrick Rose et al., *Allied Fighting Effectiveness in North Africa and Italy 1942–1945* (Leiden: Brill, forthcoming 2012).

[66] See Report by General Sir Claude J.E. Auchinleck, Commander-in-Chief India covering the period 1 January to 31 December 1945, 30 June 1947, p. 22, TNA WO 203/2670.

[67] See Tim Moreman, *The Army in India and the Development of Frontier Warfare, 1849–1947* (Basingstoke: Macmillan, 1998), pp. 182–5.

[68] See 'India at War', p. 144, *Corbett Mss.*, CAC CORB 3/28.

[69] See Callahan, *Churchill and his Generals*, p. 270, note 90. See also Alan Jeffreys, 'Slim's Welsh General: Major General 'Pete' Rees in the Burma Campaign' in *Transactions of the Honourable Society of Cymmrodorion*, Vol. 12, 2006, pp. 147–60.

made regular trips to the front, so as to acquaint myself with conditions at the time and apply the lessons learnt.'[70]

Wavell convened the Infantry Committee in June 1943 with a brief to improve the standard of British and Indian infantry in theatre. The committee was chaired by Major General Roland Richardson, Deputy Chief of the General Staff, with Major General Roland Inskip who was later appointed Inspector of Training Centres; Major General Cecil Toovey; Major General John Grover, GOC 2nd Division; Major General H.L. 'Taffy' Davies who had been chief of staff to Generals Hutton and Slim during the retreat from Burma and had recently been appointed GOC 25th Indian Division; Brigadier Arthur Hammond who had served in the First Arakan and went on to command Lucknow District and Brigadier W.B. Thomas. The committee's proposed solution was the thorough basic training of recruits which would be followed by a period of jungle training. The committee accepted the DMT's proposal that training divisions should be set up in order to teach jungle warfare after basic training. All Indian and British reinforcements would now undergo two months jungle training under designated training divisions.[71]

The need for a comprehensive Jungle Warfare doctrine had been highlighted by the Infantry Committee. This came with the publication of the fourth edition of MTP No. 9 (India), *The Jungle Book*, in September 1943. Its clearly stated purpose was to help commanding officers train their units in the specialised fighting methods needed to beat the Imperial Japanese Army (IJA) in the jungle. It gave the examples of the importance of jungle craft, physical fitness, good marksmanship and decentralised control as the necessary attributes that needed addressing in jungle warfare training. The training manual was used by the Indian Army for the remainder of the Second World War. Indeed, it later formed the basis for two War Office manuals on jungle warfare in 1944–45.[72]

The new C-in-C India ensured that jungle warfare training formed the main focus of all training carried out by units, formations and at training establishments throughout India. 14th and 39th Indian Divisions were chosen as the training divisions and were withdrawn from front line duty to reorganise. 14th Division which had served on the North East Frontier during 1942 and in the First Battle of Arakan was now based at Chhindwara. It was surrounded by jungle and the climate was comparatively mild, which meant that training

---

70 Letter from R. Savory to Professor Callahan, 24 October, 1976, *Savory Mss.*, NAM, 7603-93-71A. See also Prasad, *Expansion*, p. 307.

71 See Report of Infantry Committee 1943, 1–14 June, OIOC L/WS/1/1371.

72 See Military Training Pamphlet No. 51: Preparation for Warfare in the Far East (War Office, June 1945) and Military Training Pamphlet No. 52: Warfare in the Far East (War Office, December 1944), IWM.

continued all year round. Not only infantry, but all arms underwent jungle training as it was such an alien environment to all soldiers. The emphasis was on individual and section training for the infantry, whereas the other arms concentrated on weapons training.[73] Officers were given practice in command and control, medical officers and administrative units were also trained in jungle warfare.[74] These training divisions were seen as 'a revolution in training policy and practice and proved their worth in the successes that followed',[75] Although it can also be seen as a continuation of the Indian Army practice of using training battalions in a particular regiment but for a specific terrain and type of warfare.

After two months in the training divisions the recruits were sent to the reinforcement camps, where training was continued until they could join their battalions. The rest and reinforcement camps were reorganised under Colonel Gradige. They had been set up in April 1943 on the example of those in the Middle East and were designed to hold and train 3,000 troops. The instructors were from India, often with little experience of frontline conditions, and ratios of instructors to troops were very low with little direction for training, all resulting in poor morale and cases of ill discipline. After August 1943, each camp was allocated to a particular division, with 12 Reinforcement Camps for 14th Army each with two British and eight Indian sections, realistic training was undertaken and discipline restored.[76]

Formations also underwent jungle training, 5th Indian Division started training in June 1943 in Bihar, and then moved to Ranchi, where it reorganised as a combined animal and motor transport division and retrained for fighting in the jungles of Burma. The Division, under the command of Major General Harold Briggs, was already battle-hardened after its experiences in the Middle East, but had to adapt to jungle warfare conditions. A new series of Training Instructions starting again at No. 1 (India) were produced. The first one stated: 'This division has now to train for operations of a character different to which it has been accustomed and to train quickly, hence every lesson must have a specific object and be practical.'[77] As they were training before the issue of *The Jungle Book*, the division was relying on the earlier edition of MTP No. 9 published

---

[73] See Report 14th Indian Division July 1943–November 1945, *Curtis Mss*., Papers of Major General Alfred Curtis, IWM P140.

[74] See 'India at War', p. 235, *Corbett Mss*., CAC CORB 3/28.

[75] 'India at War', p. 139, *Corbett Mss*., CAC CORB 3/28.

[76] See Brigadier J.H. Gradige, 'How the Fourteenth Army was Reinforced', *Journal of the Indian United Services Institution*, Vol. LXXV, No. 321 (October 1945), pp. 452–3. See also 'India at War', p. 226. *Corbett Mss*., CAC CORB 3/28.

[77] 5th Indian Division Training Instruction No. 1 (India), 16 July 1943, TNA WO 172/1936.

in August 1942 calling it 'our Bible for jungle tactics'.[78] A very thorough set of training instructions together with training instructions as a result of GOC's conferences were again produced by the division before going into action in the Arakan. Even after action, weekly newsletters were produced by the division with the aim of informing the reinforcement camp of the division's activities with news of training and the lessons learnt.[79]

Thus, India Command, the training divisions, training within 14th Army's divisions and the new doctrine of jungle warfare encapsulated in *The Jungle Book*, provided a basis for uniformly jungle trained troops ready to defeat the enemy, as well as the terrain, the climate and the diseases. 5th Indian Division together with 7th fought in the Second Arakan campaign where the Battle of the Admin Box and defence of similar defensive boxes were successfully defended from repeated Japanese attacks, whilst supplied from the air. This heralded the turning point of the Burma Campaign.

India was also the base for combined operations training. A Combined Training Centre at Kharakvasla set up in 1941, coming under the direction of 36th Indian Division in 1942 which was the foundation for the Combined Training Centres at Madh Island and Cocanada.[80] In 1943 training was organised under the newly formed Directorate of Combined Operations and was responsible for the training of two Indian infantry divisions, an Indian Beach Group and an Indian brigade. In addition a Combined Operations mobile staff school toured and instructed staff at 11th Army Group.[81] Thirty-eight Combined Operations Pamphlets, including some specifically produced for India, were issued to units at the Combined Training Centres.[82] By 1945 combined operations training of 34th Corps was top priority for the planned reconquest of Singapore and Malaya which was successfully undertaken although Operation Zipper did not take place.

In training terms, after the initial fighting in the jungle formations and units underwent retraining for the plains of Burma. In 1944–45 new training pamphlets were still being produced such as the *Battle Bulletins* whose object was 'to publish first hand reports received from troops in the forward areas'.[83] *Battle Bulletin* No. 5, for example, was published in October 1944 with sections on the attacks on Jail Hill at Kohima and crossing the Gargliano in Italy, lessons

78 Ibid.

79 See 5th Indian Division weekly news letter No. 1, 3 January 1944, TNA WO 172/4278. See also Brett-James, pp. 249–3.

80 See Calder, 'From Sloth Belt to Springboard', p. 19.

81 See 'India at War', pp. 139–40, 235–6, *Corbett Mss.*, CAC CORB 3/28.

82 See List of GS Training publications 1945, pp. 20–22, OIOC L/MIL/17/5/2199.

83 See List of GS Training publications 1945, p. 5, OIOC L/MIL/17/5/2199.

learned in the problems of infantry–tank co-operation and the experiences of other Allied Armies such as the Australians in New Guinea.[84] The Military Training Directorate staff more than doubled between 1944 and 1945 and had increased from three sections in 1940 to ten by September 1945.[85] In 1945 the new Director of Military Training was Major General Donald Bateman and the Military Training Directorate was responsible for all training apart from medical training.[86] There were now 920 training pamphlets listed by GHQ India, although those listed included both those produced by GHQ India and War Office manuals reprinted in India and 75 training schools and establishments.[87]

In conclusion, during the Second World War the Indian Army had been transformed from an Imperial Policing force in 1939 to a modern professional army in 1945 making a huge contribution to the Allied cause. This was aided to a large degree by the development of training from the 1930's onwards. Officers such as Generals Bateman, Briggs, Corbett, Cowan, Messervy, Rees, Savory and Tuker either taught in training establishments, worked in the Military Training Directorate or issued training instructions within their formations. This generation of Indian Army officers were instrumental in training the Indian Army during the Second World War and inculcating the importance of training to the next generation of Indian Army officers. At the same time, the training structure and published training manuals grew to unprecedented levels under the direction of the Military Training Directorate with the Indian Army leading the way in training for jungle and mountain warfare. These developments within the Indian Army were instrumental in the crushing defeat of the IJA in Burma and made an important contribution to the Italian Campaign.

84 See *Battle Bulletin No. 5*, October 1944, Gurkha Museum.

85 See Prasad, *Expansion*, pp. 307, 509.

86 See 'India at War', p. 324, *Corbett Mss.*, CAC CORB 3/28.

87 See List of GS Training publications 1945, OIOC L/MIL/17/5/2199. See also *Reorganisation of the Army and Air Force in India, 1945*, Vol. 2, pp. 98–9, OIOC L/WS/2/77.

Chapter 5

The Battle of Wadi Akarit, 6 April 1943: 4th Indian Division and its Place in 8th Army

Chris Mann

> History will probably write this battle by this division up as the most brilliant single operation so far.
>
> Major-General Francis Tuker to General Sir Alan Hartley, Deputy Commander-in-Chief, India, 10 April 1943.[1]

Yet it clearly has not. The Battle of Wadi Akarit of 6 April 1943 was probably 4th Indian Division's finest hour. Using bold and, by 8th Army standards, innovative tactics they smashed the Italian Division in front of them tearing a five-mile hole in Axis line. For moment it looked, at least to 4th Indian Division, that the whole of 1st Italian Army was there for the taking if the 8th Army's exploitation formation, 10th Corps could pass through the gap that they had created. 10th Corps never did and therefore the Italian/German Army withdrew from the Akarit position in good order to fight another day. Thus the battle is little known. In 1958 Francis Tuker, the division's commander at Akarit, scented conspiracy claiming that:

> Various officers have been publicising their experiences in North African campaign and histories have been published covering that period. Certain statements have been made and views expressed that are patently fallacious ... other important factors have been omitted. For instance Montgomery has little

[1] The Imperial War Museum (IWM), The Papers of Lieutenant-General Sir Francis Tuker KCIE, CB, DSO, OBE, FRSA, 71/21/2 Folder 9, Tuker to Hartley, 10 April 1943. Acknowledgments: I am grateful to Brigadier David Allfrey, Major Will Lynch and Major Reay Henstock and the staff of HQ 51st Scottish Brigade for the opportunity to visit the Akarit battlefield in September 2009. I would like to thank my colleagues Dr Peter Lieb and Dr Klaus Schmider for their help in preparing this article.

> to say about Wadi Akarit in either of his books, yet it should have been the cheapest and most shattering victory by 8th Army.[2]

Indeed the battle gets fairly light coverage in any of the accounts of main 8th Army commanders.[3] Yet there was some subsequent engagement with the issue. The Official History published in 1966 gives the battle decent coverage and acknowledged the 8th Army 'had an opportunity to dispose of *AOK 1* [*Armee Oberkommando* 1 or 1st Army] for ever'. However, it rather unhelpfully concluded that this was a question 'the military historian should not presume to settle'.[4]

By studying a single action, the Battle of Wadi Akarit on 6 April 1943, this paper will examine the relationship of 4th Indian Division with its parent formation the 8th Army – the division was the only Indian Army formation of this scale within the Army during the Tunisian Campaign. The main emphasis will be on the battle and thus the culture and fighting style of 4th Indian Division and the differences with its parent Army in their respective approaches to battle. There were also a number of personality clashes between the key figures involved – the divisional commander, Major-General Francis 'Gertie' Tuker at times welded remarkable influence for a man of his rank. Yet he felt somewhat apart from his fellow commanders and held a number of the men senior to him in real distain. So this is very much the story of a rather admirable man, who while having a great number of qualities, viewed what had happened to him and his division with real bitterness.

By the time the 8th Army reached Wadi Akarit in Tunisia in early April 1943, General Bernard Montgomery had been in command about nine months. He had led the Army through its great if painfully won victory at El Alamein in October and November 1942. There followed a somewhat ponderous pursuit of the retreating German and Italian forces across the North African desert. Field Marshal Erwin Rommel, the Axis commander, offered only occasional

---

2 IWM, Tuker Papers, 71/21/1 Folder 6, *History of 4th Indian Division*, notes by Lt. Gen. Francis Tuker, 1958.

3 Montgomery of Alamein, *El Alamein to the Sangro – Normandy to the Baltic* (London: BCA, 1947) pp. 66–7 and *The Memoirs of Field Marshal Montgomery* (London: Collins, 1958), p. 163. See also Brian Horrocks, *A Full Life* (London: Collins, 1960) pp. 159–60 and Francis de Guingard, *Operation Victory* (London: Hodder and Stoughton, 1947), pp. 266–7.

4 I.S.O. Playfair and C.J.C. Molony, *The Mediterranean and Middle East*, Vol. IV, *The Destruction of the Axis Forces in Africa* (London: HMSO, 1966) p. 375. It should be noted that Molony and Tuker corresponded at some length, despite this Tuker thought the Official History's comments on Akarit 'smarmy'.

and fleeting resistance over a retreat of nearly 1,800 miles. He finally turned and stood on the Mareth Line on the Tunisian border in March 1943. Montgomery had transformed the 8th Army from a shaken and dejected force into one with strong cohesion and morale. This was because it had begun to win its battles. Montgomery had achieved this by adopting the methodical set-piece battle, relying on attritional firepower and careful movement rather than dashing manoeuvre.[5] This, more or less, served the 8th Army well, as the string of defeats had ceased for good. Most its formations adopted and adapted to this approach and largely prospered. Indeed one of its divisional commanders, Major-General Douglas Wimberley, noted that prior to Wadi Akarit: 'The morale of the Highland Division was ... very high, and we considered we had never failed in a set-piece attack.'[6] However, Montgomery's approach never really sat well with 4th Indian Division.

According to Tuker, 'Neither I nor any of my division ever had any particular pride in belonging to the 8th Army (nor did we ever feel any particular fellowship for others of that Army).[7] This was in part due to the new army's commander's attitude to the Indian Army. Montgomery is certainly very explicit about his feelings in his Memoirs stating that 'Soldiering in India seemed to me ... to lack something' and that 'the British officers were not all so good.'[8] Tuker reckoned this was 'only "sour grapes". He had not the intelligence to pass into it (he passed low enough into Sandhurst anyhow) so has to disparage it to satisfy his own spite.'[9] Futhermore Montgomery had deliberately snubbed General Claude Auchinleck, his Indian Army predecessor, when he took command of the 8th Army two days early. He then produced an account of the state in which he found Auchinleck and the 8th Army, elements of which were extremely partial or even untrue.[10]

Certainly Montgomery did not seem to rate the 4th Indian Division very highly. Its troops had not been trained by him, but that of course was true of most the Army he inherited. Moreover, its fame stemmed from before his arrival

---

5 See Niall Barr, *Pendulum of War* (London: Jonathan Cape, 2004), p. 410 and for the most detailed examination of Montgomery's operational approach see Stephen Hart, *Montgomery and 'Colossal Cracks'* (Wesport, CT: Praeger, 2000).

6 Douglas Wimberley, *Scottish Soldier*, Vol. II, p. 107. A copy of Wimberley's unpublished memoirs is held at the IWM. See IWM, PP/MCR/182.

7 IWM, Tuker Papers, 71/21/1 Folder 6, *Montgomery Memoirs*, 1958.

8 Montgomery, *Memoirs*, pp. 27–8.

9 IWM, Tuker Papers, 71/21/1 Folder 6, *Montgomery Memoirs*, 1958.

10 The most obvious example is Montgomery's account of his first meeting with Auchinleck. See *Memoirs*, p. 94.

as it had been out in desert from the start.[11] He gave the Division a fairly minor role at Alamein on Ruweisat Ridge because, according to Oliver Leese, its Corps Commander, it was 'only capable of holding the line and could only be relied on provided they were very mined and wired in'.[12] Tuker grumbled that 'Our part is to hold a huge front and make noises to keep the Boche interested. A poor sort of business, but someone has to do it. I don't think he [Montgomery] has moved a man from our front.'[13] However, 5th Indian Infantry Brigade, the only part of the formation deemed ready for offensive operations, was detached to 51st Highland Division and played an important role in the breakthrough during Operation Supercharge.[14] Yet despite 5th Brigade's excellent performance and the fact that the rest of the division, as Tuker later wrote, 'were the only fresh, desertworthy troops now left in the 8th Army' the division was ordered to hand its troop carrying transport over to the Greek Brigade.[15] They were to play no part in the pursuit and were left behind to clear up the Alamein battlefield. The division's Commander Royal Artillery (CRA) Brigadier Kenneth Dimoline considered that:

> The Army Commander's intention is I think to employ the 4th Indian Division in same manner of the rest of the Indian units in Palestine, Cyprus and Egypt, i.e. as garrison troops, useful fatigue parties for salvage, and as police: namely in the manner as Libyan Arab Irregulars and other second line troops employed.[16]

This was immensely galling to a formation with such a fighting pedigree. However, with Auchinleck gone, there was no Indian Army officer of high rank in Middle East Headquarters or on the 8th Army staff and thus no one to fight the division's corner. The winter of 1942 was an alarming time as the division again lost most its transport, this time to the 50th Division. The 5th Brigade found itself on garrison duties in Benghazi. So Tuker trained his division as best he could and fumed that: 'Monty having no use for Indian troops, at once put my division on bottom priority for everything.'[17] He wrote to his corps

---

11 R.W. Thompson, *The Montgomery Legend* (London: Allen and Unwin, 1967), p. 176.

12 Oliver Leese, WAII/I/DA491.2/17, National Archives New Zealand cited by Barr, p. 277.

13 Tuker cited by G.R. Stevens, *4th Indian Division* (Toronto: McLaren and Son, 1948), p. 193.

14 Ibid., pp. 196–8.

15 Francis Tuker, *Approach to Battle* (London: Cassell, 1963), pp. 259–60.

16 Dimoline cited by Compton Mackensie, *Eastern Epic*, Vol. I (London: Chatto and Windus, 1951), p. 603.

17 IWM, Tuker Papers, 71/21/6 Folder 6, Notes, 6 October 1945.

commander, Lieutenant-General Brian Horrocks demanding clarification. Horrocks was 'appalled by Montgomery's behaviour to Tuker's Division'.[18] So he then forwarded Tuker's letter and added his own supportive comment stating that 'this is an experienced Division ... imbued with a fine fighting spirit and in my opinion it would be a tragedy if this fine Division was not given a further opportunity of representing India'.[19] According to Compton Mackenzie's *Eastern Approaches*: 'Neither the letter nor the comment made the slightest impression on General Montgomery.'[20]

The issue came to a head in March 1943, when 4th Indian Division was finally called forward to Medenine near the Mareth Line, where the retreating Italian-German Army had decide to stand. Here Tuker discovered that his division, which had only two Brigades, the 5th and 7th Indian Infantry – the division's third brigade, the 11th, had been destroyed at Tobruk in June 1942 – was to be split between the 8th Army's two corps. The 5th Brigade was to be sent to 10 Corps commanded by Horrocks, the 7th Brigade to 30 Corps under Oliver Leese and the headquarters elements to 8th Army HQ. This somewhat belied Montgomery's famous order from before Alamein that: 'Divisions would fight as Divisions, and they were not to be split up into bits and pieces all over the desert.'[21] Tuker felt, understandably, that there was no point of a divisional commander if there was no division to command and thus he went and offered his resignation to Horrocks, who 'replied that it was the Army's policy and he would ask about it'. Tuker had never thought highly of Horrocks despite his earlier support and was inclined to believe that he 'was trying to grab troops in order to get in on the Mareth battle and so compete with Leese'.[22] However, Horrocks once more took the issue to Montgomery and as the Divisional History records: 'Next day [Tuker] was bidden to tea with the Army Commander. General Montgomery ended all uncertainty. Fourth Indian Division was to be concentrated for battle at once.'[23]

Montgomery makes no mention of this meeting in his writings or papers but Tuker recalled that during tea Montgomery 'told me that he was surprised at this

---

[18] The Liddell Hart Centre for Military Archives (LHCMA), The Papers of R.W. Thompson, Thompson 4/1, Thompson to Wimberley, 2 April 1967.

[19] Horrocks cited by Mackenzie, p. 604.

[20] Ibid., p. 604 and see Thompson, p. 177.

[21] IWM, Montgomery Papers, BLM 27, Review of the situation in 8th Army, 12 August to 23 October 1942.

[22] IWM, Tuker papers, Box 71/21/6, Folder 1, Notes by Maj-Gen FS Tuker, CB, DSO, OBE, 6 October 1945.

[23] G.R. Stevens, *4th Indian*, p. 206 and see also IWM, Tuker Papers, 71/21/2 Folder 9, Tuker to Hartley, 21 February 1944.

splitting up and that it was the doing of Horrocks'. As Tuker characteristically concluded 'I do not yet know which of the two, Horrocks or Monty, was most to be believed (then, or at any other time).'[24] Nonetheless this does not explain why Montgomery acquiesced to Tuker's demands, which rather belies many of Tuker's complaints of his and his division's treatment. Montgomery had no hesitation in sacking or over-ruling his divisional commanders, if he felt it necessary.[25] Yet Tuker was nothing if not determined and the two men knew each other reasonably well. Montgomery had been one of Tuker's instructors at Staff College. Perhaps, Montgomery was convinced by Tuker's, no doubt, well argued case. It also may be that the given the terrain of Tunisia, Montgomery realised that 4th Indian, his only division with any experience of fighting in mountains, might be useful.[26]

All this was happening as the 8th Army moved up against the Mareth Line, a line of pre-war fortifications built by the French to protect Tunisia from the Italians in Libya. Here at last the 1st Italian Army, the remnants of the Afrika Korps and Italian Army from the Western Desert campaign had decided to make a stand. The 8th Army had swatted away a half-hearted Axis counter offensive at Medenine on 6 March, but breaking the Mareth Line raised the prospect of serious fighting for the first time since Alamein. Montgomery's approach to reducing the position was quite interesting. There was a fire power reliant set piece assault up the coastal plain into the heart of the Axis defences by the infantry of 30 Corps, accompanied by a wide left flanking left hook from Lieutenant-General Bernard Freyberg's New Zealand Corps. Montgomery showed considerable flexibility when the main effort by 30 Corps struggled. He shifted emphasis to the left hook from the 2nd New Zealand Division sending another Corps Commander, Horrocks, and 1st Armoured Division round in support. The resulting offensive unlocked the position. Furthermore the 4th Indian Divisional History noted that given the mountainous terrain of the Matmata Hills to the west at Mareth, 'at last a decisive and individual role had been allotted to 4th Indian Division'. This was to secure the high ground on the left flank and facilitate the deployment of 1st Armoured Division. As the history continued, the Division only 'played a minor role in the victory' but it had performed well and impressed the corps commander Oliver Leese. 'Great days were near at hand.'[27]

---

[24] IWM, Tuker Papers, Box 71/21/6, Folder 1, Notes by Maj-Gen FS Tuker, CB, DSO, OBE, 6 October 1945.

[25] See for example, Hart, p. 158.

[26] Thompson, p. 178.

[27] G.R. Stevens, *4th Indian*, pp. 211 and 216.

The Axis forces, as ever, disengaged quickly and fell back on the next defensible line, known to the British as the Akarit line after the Wadi (dry water course) that dominated the centre of the position. It was here Rommel would have preferred to hold rather than on the Mareth Line. There were good reasons for this. Wadi Akarit, or the Gabes or Chott Line as it was sometimes referred to by the Germans was a 15-mile gap between the impassable Fedjadi Chott (or salt marsh) and the sea, about 20 miles north of Gabes. The gap between the Chott and the coast is eloquently described by the divisional history:

> Across two thirds of this gap stands Djebel [from the Arabic for hill or mountain] Zemlet el Beida, a high puckered ridge system which divides the Gabes from the Sfax plain ... a broad deep nullah [from the Hindi for stream of the sea or water course] interposes its moat between the sea and the high ground. Five miles inland and the Roumana saddleback, approximately 500 feet in height and a mile in length, runs into the northwest on a bearing roughly parallel to the coast. To the west of Roumana, the easy contours of a series of rolling hills extend for two miles before ending in the fantastic pile of Fatnassa. This freakish and outlandish agglomeration of high ground is reminiscent of a Disney drawing. A series of transverse crests merge in a labyrinthine tangle of pinnacles, escarpments, counter-escarpments, deep fjord like chimneys and corridors. On the left of this wild tangle a ravine ... carrying a military road ... connects the two plains. Beyond the road the high ground falls away in a series of cones and ridges until five miles to the south-west the barrier ends within a mile of the oozy shore of the salt marshes.[28]

Despite its natural strength both the Axis Commander-in Chief Field Marshal Albrecht Kesselring and Rommel felt that too little had been done to prepare the Akarit position. In retrospect Kesselring lamented that 'The defence measures, which were not taken until too late owing to over-confidence in the strength of the Mareth Line, should have been decided on earlier and carried out more speedily.'[29] Indeed Giovanni Messe, the new commander of 1st Italian Army with Rommel's return to Germany, only ordered work to begin on improving the position on 27 March. All that could be done at this stage was to improve the Wadi's properties as an anti-tank ditch and extend it inland; another ditch was dug between Djebels Roumana and Fatnassa. The Axis engineers put out some wire and laid about 4,000 mines, although the minefields were far from

---

28 Ibid., p. 217.

29 Albert Kesselring, *The Memoirs of Field Marshal Kesselring* (London: Greenhill, 1953), p. 155.

continuous, concentrated mainly between the coastal road and Roumana.[30] Yet the fact remained that it was formidable natural defence line, which unlike Mareth could not be outflanked when attacking from the south – the factor that had drawn Rommel's attention to it in the first place.[31]

Messe placed his 20th Corps next to the sea, with the Italian Young Fascist Division covering the coast to the main coastal road, astride which sat two battalions of the German 90th Light Division. Next to them from east to west were the Italian Trieste and Spezia Divisions covering the bulk of what would become the Akarit battlefield. Messe placed his 21st Corps to their right with Pistoia division covering Fatnassa and the military road and westwards, stiffened by a detachment of 15th Panzer Division. He held the bulk of 15th Panzer Division and 200th Panzer Grenadier Regiment of 90th Light in reserve behind Roumana and 361st Panzer Grenadier Regiment and 190th Anti-tank Battalion, also of 90th Light, behind Fatnassa. The Axis forces had about 200 artillery pieces available, 63 88mm dual role anti-aircraft guns – of which 28 were deployed in the anti-tank role and 15th Panzer could field 22 German and four Italian tanks.[32]

Early on 30 March 1943 the 8th Army, headed by Horrocks' 10 Corps, made contact with Messe's forces on the Akarit Line. Montgomery called his Corps Commanders together at 1400 hours. He ordered Horrocks 'to gain close contact with the enemy to study the form and ascertain whether it was possible with its present resources to overcome the opposition and gain a bridgehead'.[33] Monty hoped that he would be able to bounce Akarit quickly with what was available. It soon became clear this would be extremely difficult. Brigadier Howard Kippenberger, commanding New Zealand 5th Brigade, the lead element of 10 Corps, while keen to press the attack discovered that 'the enemy were standing in strength' and would 'only be turned out by a set piece attack'.[34] Horrocks felt the same, reporting to Montgomery that day 'that he considered NZ Div[ision] could force the crossing but it might involve considerable casualties. I [Montgomery] did not want to cripple NZ Div for the mobile role which lay ahead.' Montgomery ordered Leese's '30 Corps with 4 Ind[ian] Div,

---

[30] Playfair and Molony, Vol. IV, p. 362 and Ronald Lewin, *The Life and Death of the Afrika Korps* (London: Batsford, 1977), p. 194.

[31] B.H. Liddell-Hart (ed), *The Rommel Papers* (New York: De Capo, 1953), p. 392.

[32] Playfair and Molony, Vol. IV, p. 363.

[33] IWM, Montgomery Papers, BLM 33, *The Battle of the Gabes Gap*, 30 March 1943.

[34] Howard Kippenberger, *Infantry Brigadier* (London: Oxford University Press, 1949), p. 294.

51 Div and 201 G[uar]ds Bde to attack the enemy position at the selected point, force the obstacle and secure the bridgehead.'[35]

Montgomery's initial plan for Operation 'Scipio', as the plan was codenamed, was for a two infantry division attack by 30 Corps near the coast. Once the two divisions, namely 4th Indian and 51st Highland, had battered their way through and established a bridgehead, he then would pass 10 Corps' 2nd New Zealand and 1st Armoured Divisions through to exploit northwards and complete the rout.[36] Oliver Leese intended that 51st Highland should attack between the coast road and Djebel Roumana and 4th Indian Division capture Roumana itself, thus protecting the Highlanders' left flank. At midday on 1 April Leese held a conference for his infantry divisional commanders, Tuker, Wimberley of 51st and Major-General J.S. 'Crasher' Nicholls of 50th Division, at Wimberley's Tactical HQ.[37] There he briefed them on Scipio's outline and, after a discussion of the prospect in front of them, his generals dispersed to begin their preparatory work for their own divisional plans. Once they had looked at the ground they were, to say the least, unhappy. Major-General Douglas Wimberley commander of 51st Highland Division explained that:

> Needless to say I was out at dawn and all the morning of the 2nd April studying the ground; and the more I studied it, and compared it with the map, and what we knew of the enemies hidden defences, the less I liked the prospect! ... Then either by accident or design, I forget which, I ran into General Gertie Tuker, commanding the 4th Indian Division also out on a reconnaissance. I found he was even more disquieted than I was, at the outline plan so far indicated ... Steeped as he was ... in mountain warfare ... he pointed out that Roumana Ridge itself, would not only be a tough nut to crack, but in its turn was dangerously overlooked by the still higher ground to the west of it; and further that he felt the frontage of the Corps attack was anyhow much too narrow.[38]

Thus Tuker and Wimberley, agreeing that the plan was unacceptable, met Leese for at a second Corps conference at 1630 hours that afternoon and expressed their concerns to him. Tuker later recalled that 'I told him his plan was wrong because it neglected the Zouai hill on his flank which would sweep his attack away, and I said that however, difficult as it might be to seize the precipitous features, I would take on the task myself rather than see it attempted by someone

---

35 IWM, Montgomery Papers, BLM 33, *The Battle of the Gabe Gaps*, 31 March 1943.

36 IWM, Montgomery Papers, BLM 33, *The Battle of the Gabes Gap*, 31 March 1943.

37 TNA, WO 169/14735, 4th Indian Division HQ War Diary, 1 April 1943 and WO 169/8778, 50th (Northumbrian) Division HQ War Diary, 1 April 1943.

38 Wimberley, II, p. 105.

else.' He also 'asked that a third division, the 50th, should be brought up' to plug the gap that would be created between the 51st and 4th Indian Divisions if the front was extended.[39] Leese was, in Tuker's rather acerbic judgement, 'a man of little real intelligence, but he would listen when one suggested better ways'.[40] So Leese was at least open minded enough to see the merit of Tuker's proposals and after consulting with Montgomery drew up a new plan which was issued at a second conference at 1930 hours that night.[41] The corps frontage was increased to about 12 miles; on the extreme left of the British line 4th Indian would make a silent attack into the Zouai/Fatnassa/El Meida range of hills, in the centre 50th Division would establish a bridgehead across the anti-tank ditch which connected Roumana Ridge to the more westerly high ground. The 51st Highland Division would attack Roumana and also establish a bridgehead over the anti-tank ditch and Wadi Akarit to the east of the ridge. The new plan was, at least in Wimberley's mind, 'a much better one'.[42] Once again Tuker's argument, this time supported by Wimberley, had carried the day. It is a tribute to Montgomery's 8th Army that it could accept a better idea but it is worth noting that, according to one of his staff officers, Montgomery said 'I don't like it when people disagree with me. Nevertheless we will accept Tuker's plan. If he is right we will have won a victory. If he is wrong, I shall know what to do with him.'[43]

The main attack from 50th and 51st Divisions was due to commence at 0430 hours on 6 April behind a barrage provided by Corps and divisional artillery. This was a classic set-piece break-in battle at which 8th Army excelled. However, Tuker had pledged to take the higher ground of the Zouai/Fatnassa/El Meida hills before the two British infantry divisions began their assault. The Indians were going in silently, relying on stealth, aggression and surprise, very much at variance with the firepower laden approach of the rest of the Army. This was facilitated by the fact that the 8th Army had become a little stereotyped in its methods as Messe, the Axis commander at Akarit and Fritz Baylerlein,

---

39 Tuker, *Approach*, p. 320.

40 IWM, Tuker Papers, Box 71/21/6 Folder 1, Notes by Major-General F.S. Tuker, 6 October 1945. Tuker's feelings towards Leese are a little inconsistent, elsewhere in his papers he is quite positive about him, but the above quote may well be coloured by Tuker's discovery that Leese had recommended that he not be given a field command on his return to India in late 1944.

41 Montgomery's papers imply that adding the extra division was his idea. However, while he approved the idea, it is clear the change derives from the lower level commanders. IWM, Montgomery Papers, BLM 33, *The Battle of the Gabes Gap*, 2 April 1943.

42 Wimberley, II, p. 105.

43 G.R. Stevens, *The 9th Gurkha Rifles*, Vol II, 1937–47 (London: Regimental Association 9th Gurkha Rifles, 1953), p. 29 and see also IWM Tuker Papers, 71/21/3 folder 3, Tuker to Cocksedge, 5 September 67.

commanding the Afrika Korps, both believed that the assault would come at full moon, as it had at Alamein.[44] Oliver Leese, for one, was a little nervous. 'There are certain difficulties', he recorded 'It is a pitch black night – and hitherto we have attacked in the moonlight.'[45] Tuker's plan was essentially to use Brigadier Oz Lovett's 7th Brigade to lead the assault and seize the mountain block around Fatnassa and then push Donald Bateman's 5th Brigade through to punch hole out into the Sfax plains behind the position.[46]

The 4th Indian Division assembled at dusk on 5 April. As his battalions filed past his Divisional Headquarters Tuker is reported to have turned to one of his staff officers and said: 'I know my plan is right. But am I asking too much of the men?'[47] As events would show, clearly he was not. He later wrote: 'It is the approach that determines the outcome and we believed that our approach, our designs and our training, the skill of our individual platoon and section commanders in this most telling and skilled form of fighting, this infiltration battle would suffice for the difficult and unusual task that confronted us.'[48] The 7th Indian Infantry Brigade's unusually eloquent War Diary gives a flavour of what followed:

> We are now creeping forward into the foothills where we know the enemy's FDL [forward defence lines] are, suddenly an Italian sentry challenges, immediately a yell of 'pugaroo' goes up and the Gurkhas charge. A fiendish uproar takes place. These positions are held by Italians of Pistoia Division. Some fight as the clatter of exploding grenades and tommy guns shows. Others run screaming away from their positions'[49]

Lovett's brigade made excellent progress. By midnight they were deep into the position. The 1/2nd Gurkhas captured the key heights, including Point 275 where A Company's Subedar Lalbahadur Thapa won a Victoria Cross. The rest of the battalion seized Zouai and Mereb el Alig.[50] The 1st Royal Sussex passed round the right side of the Gurkhas and was able to capture El Meida soon after

---

44 TNA, WO 169/14735, 4th Indian Division Intelligence Summary No 46, 9 April 1943 and Playfair and Moloney, p. 369.

45 IWM, Leese papers, letter to wife, 4 April 1943.

46 TNA, WO 169/14735, 4 Ind Div Op Order 100, Operation Scipio, 4 April 1945 and Stevens, pp. 220–21.

47 Tuker cited by Stevens, *9th Gurkha Rifles*, p. 30.

48 Tuker, *Approach*, pp. 321–2.

49 TNA, WO169/14825, 7th Indian Infantry Brigade War Diary, 6 April 1943.

50 TNA, WO 169/15008, 1/2th Gurkha Rifles War Diary, Note on the capture of the Rass Ei Zouai and El Alig Features by 1/2th Gurkha Rifles on 5/6 April 1943.

0400 hours. The 4/16th Punjab Regiment were loosed against Italian positions to the south and west of the military road at 0500 hours and had cleared them out two hours later.[51] The 7th Brigade had opened the way for their colleagues of the 5th Brigade. So as dawn approached and the barrage proceeding 50th and 51st Divisions' attack began, Bateman's battalions surged forward. The 1/9th Gurkha Rifles pushed on to size the Fatnassa hills towards the back of the position. As Bateman recalled 'In fact, at one stage 1/9 GR were going forward so fast that I had to speak to Ian Roche [the Commanding Officer] severely about getting out of touch!'[52] The 4/6th Rajputana Rifles followed closely behind and thrust between the 1/9th Gurkha and 1st Royal Sussex and by 1130 had captured the Ouidane El Hachana feature deep in the enemy's rear along with some 700 prisoners.[53] The 1/4th Essex Regiment was responsible for bringing forward the division's 6 pounder anti-tank guns. In the process the battalion noticed that 50th Division had failed to secure a bridgehead over the anti-tank ditch in front of them and it was able to clear the positions firing into the flank of their neighbouring division. The Essex Regiment then began help with the crossing over the anti-tank ditch on the boundary of 4th Indian and 50th Divisions.

It had been an extraordinarily successful night. The 1/4th Essex were able to establish contact with 50th Division on their right flank and elements of the battalion along with 4/6th Rajputana Rifles were on the edge of the plain behind the hills. They had taken over two thousand prisoners of war and carved a hole about five miles deep through the enemy line.[54] All that was now needed was the armoured reserve to move through and cut off and destroy the 1st Italian Army. As Tuker put it 'The enemy was so completely surprised by the silent night penetration that he had no conception of what had happened to him and there he sat "on his feet" in his trenches, without M[otor] T[ransport] for escape at the mercy of 10 Corps.'[55] This is the main controversy: why did the 8th Army not turn the tactical achievement of 4th Indian division at Wadi Akarit into operational, even strategic success?

The record becomes a little thinner from this point onwards, placing considerable reliance on the accounts, many written some time after the battle, of Tuker and other members of 4th Indian Division. However, they are more

---

51 TNA, WO 169/15002, 4/16th Punjab Regt War Diary, 6 April 1943.

52 IWM, Bateman Papers, 72/117/1, *5th Indian Infantry Brigade, Tunisia, 1943*, 5 January 1959.

53 TNA, WO 169/149674/6th Rajputana Rifles War Diary, 6 April 1943.

54 In fact the division had taken 2177 POWs made up of 2176 Italians and 1 German. TNA, WO 169/14735, 4th Indian Division Intelligence Summary No 45, 7 April 1943.

55 IWM, Tuker Papers, Box 71/21/1 Folder 1, History of 4th Indian Division, 1958.

detailed than those of any of the other participants and enough of the leadership of 4th Indian Division seem to agree on what happened to give Tuker's interpretation credence. Thus Tuker found his division through the enemy line. According to 4th Indian accounts at 0845 Brian Horrocks, commander of 10 Corps, the 8th Army's exploitation force, came forward to Tuker's HQ to see the situation for himself. Tuker briefed him on how the division had done and 'pointed out to commander 10 Corps that we had broken the enemy, that the way was clear for 10 Corps to go through; that immediate offensive action would finish the campaign in North Africa. Now was the time to get the whips out and spare neither men nor machines.'[56] Horrocks'expressed himself highly pleased' and then phoned Montgomery 'for permission to launch his armour without delay'.[57] He then turned back to Tuker and said that 'his armour was going to go through at once using the 4th Indian Division crossing over the A/Tk [anti-tank] ditch and one on the boundary between 50 and 51 divisions' at the foot of Roumana ridge. Tuker then commented on what was not said: 'Commander 10 Corps did NOT give any indication that their advance forward was restricted by bounds or timings laid down by higher command nor that there were any administrative difficulties.'[58]

The 4th Indian Division then sat there waiting. There was some mopping up to be done, some minor enemy attempts at infiltration to be dealt with and some shelling to be endured. The Division's engineers continued to improve the crossing over the anti-tank ditch. By 0950 hours they could report 'have crossing of anti-tank ditch and going well – wheels of 7 Brigade passing over followed by 5 Brigade'.[59] Even earlier at 0900 the men of 1st Royal Sussex had got their carriers and anti-tank guns forward and by 0930 they had an anti-tank screen in place.[60] It took somewhat longer to get this vital equipment to the 4/6th Rajputana Rifles in the most forward positions but they managed to get their carriers operating out on the plain behind the hills.[61] As their battalion commander, Lieutenant-Colonel R.B. Scott recalled 'we were wondering at the time what was holding the armour up as things seemed fairly quiet and well in

---

56 Tuker, *Approach*, p. 325.

57 IWM, Tuker Papers, Box 71/21/3 Folder 3, Stevens to Tuker, 1 July 1967.

58 Ibid., Notes on a Conversation Between General Horrocks and General Tuker, undated. This is corroborated by the primary evidence as an office note recording this conversation resides in the 4th Indian War Diary see TNA, WO 169/14735, 4th Indian Division War Diary, May, appendix II 'Office Note'.

59 TNA, WO 169/8645, HQ 30 Corps War Diary, 6 April 1943.

60 TNA, WO 169/10303, 1st Royal Sussex Regt, War Diary, 6 April 1943.

61 TNA, WO 169/4967, 4/6th Rajputana Rifles, War Diary, 6 April 1943.

hand'.[62] The 5th Brigade Commander, Donald Bateman's assessment was even more pointed:

> My own view is that the armour could have begun to go through immediately behind 50 Div. From, memory, this would have been about midday, or soon after. I know that about this time I moved Brigade HQ to the wheel axis across the Wadi, and got reports that carriers of 4 Raj Rif were operating down into the plain. In fact, at one stage we tried to shame the armour by offering to lead with carriers![63]

The fact that 4th Indian had brought its anti-guns guns forward and Bateman had moved his HQ over the anti-tank ditch, demonstrated the division's transport route could take wheeled vehicles. Therefore, it would appear that 10 Corps should have been able to bring its armour up without too much difficulty. Yet the 10 Corps attack never developed. The 8th War Diary recorded that 10 Corps headed by 2nd New Zealand Division was to move forward at 1100 hours although this message stated that the gap used would be the crossing on the 50th /51st Division boundary at the foot of Djebel Roumana. By 1220 hours it stated that a regimental group from 8th Armoured Brigade 'may possibly go through 4 Ind[ian] gap'. An hour and half later 'another Regimental Group [from 8th Armoured] was 'trying to pass ... approx 50 Div/4th Ind boundary' and 1st Armoured Division was 'ordered to tag on behind NZ Div and waste no time doing so'. Yet it was clearly slow going as 8th Armoured was only across by 1600 hours.[64] As to what the 10 Corps commander was doing to drive them on is difficult to ascertain. As Tuker pointed out 'Horrocks was confessedly absent from his HQ most the morning of that day and has left no record whatsoever of what he was doing during those hours.'[65] The 10 Corps War Diary is unenlightening, making no mention of the meeting with Tuker and recording only that 'Recce HQ left for the front' at 0710 hours. At 1415 hours it recorded that this HQ in the company of Tuker and Nicolls of 50th Division 'carried out recce of crossings of A/Tk ditch' in the 4th Indian sector.[66] Oddly this meeting

---

62 IWM, Tuker Papers, 71/21/3 folder 6, *Akarit*, 1958.

63 IWM, Bateman Papers, 72/117/1, *5th Indian Infantry Brigade, Tunisia, 1943*, 5 January 1959.

64 TNA, WO 169/8501, Main 8th Army, War Diary Log sheets, From 30 Corps 1100 hours, From Tac Army 1125 hrs, From Tac Army, 1220 hours, From 10 Corps 1350 hours and From Tac Army 1600 hours, 6 April 1943.

65 IWM, Tuker Papers, 71/21/2 Folder 3, Tuker to Stevens, 15 June 1967.

66 TNA, WO 169/8591, Main HQ 10 Corps War Diary, 0710 and 1415 hours, 6 April 1944.

is not mentioned by Tuker or the 4th Indian or even the 50th Division War Diaries.[67]

The frustration felt by 4th Indian Division was mirrored by the men of 51st Highland Division who controlled the other major crossing point which was located at the western foot of Roumana ridge. The divisional war diary noted at 1339 hours that '2 NZ Division had been ordered to move up close behind the Highland Division and the leading tanks of 8 Arm[oure]d Bde were reported to be moving slowly through the 152 Brigade gap'.[68] Yet their attack failed to develop too. For the 5th Camerons and attached engineers who had created the gap, it seemed inexplicable. Their commanding officer, Lieutenant-Colonel Ronnie Miers, had requested tank support as soon as the crossings were open. The Regimental History records: 'This was readily granted, but unfortunately the tanks took the wrong track to B Company's gap and some of them blew up on mines. It proved impossible to convince them that a mine-free track to the vital gap existed, so (exasperating as it was) no more tanks were seen that day.'[69] The divisional commander Wimberley summed up the infantry's bewilderment simply: 'What happened to the tanks of the 10th Corps I never discovered.'[70]

The spearhead of 10 Corps, 8th Armoured Brigade blandly recorded that on 6 April 1943:

> The Staffs Yeo[manry] accordingly moved up to Roumana pass [on the 51st Division crossing] which was still held with anti-tank guns covering the pass. 3 R[oyal] Tanks moved up on the left flank [the 4th Indian crossing] and made considerable progress but could not reach the open country beyond the pass. Staffs Yeo and 3 RTR leaguered for the night in the area that they had reached.'[71]

This quote provides two possible reasons for the failure to get the armour through and into action: enemy action and the poor quality of the routes forward. ... The tanks of the Staffordshire Yeomanry encountered anti-tank fire as they tried to move forward. This is the most common explanation for the stalling of 10 Corps. The 51st Division War Diary recorded that the move forward had 'been hindered by the tanks ... in front who can not make any progress because

67 TNA, WO 169/14735, 4th Indian Division HQ War Diary, 6 April 1943 and WO 169/8778, 50th (Northumbrian) Division HQ War Diary, 6 April 1943.

68 TNA, WO 169/8791, 51st Highland Division HQ, War Diary, 1339 hours, 6 April 1943.

69 Anon, *Historical Records of the Queen's Own Cameron Highlanders, 1932–1948* (Edinburgh: William Blackwood, 1952), p. 64.

70 Wimberley, II, p. 110.

71 TNA, WO 169/8872, 8th Armoured Brigade HQ, War Diary, 6 April 1943.

of 88mm guns'.[72] The British Official History talks of 'the fire of certainly two, and probably more 8.8cm guns, which were concealed on the lower slopes of Roumana and were firing in enfilade'.[73] The New Zealand Official History also mentions 'enemy guns behind the disputed Roumana feature' which 'as well as the commanding positions there, made it impractical to pass 2 NZ through for exploitation'.[74] A couple of secondary sources that have addressed the question also give the presence of 88mm guns at the rear of Roumana as the explanation.[75]

The result was that 'there was a lot of armour sitting about but no serious movement forward ... and 4 Raj[putana] Rif[les] were offering to lead them onto the plain with carriers! However – not unlike the Tuscans – with the armour, itself, there seemed to be: "None who would be foremost to lead such dire attack!"'[76] The issue here is to whether the Axis resistance could be overcome to allow 10 Corps to break-out. Tuker rightly points out that leading the way was 2nd New Zealand, an infantry division. So 'they'd a whole infantry division to clear the way for their armour'.[77] More to the point the best method to suppress the enemy or get the infantry onto the guns was artillery. The offending 88s seem to have been on the backside of Roumana. The 4th Indian Division had brought its guns forward. Bateman's battalions, particularly 4/6th Rajputana Rifles, were positioned with good views to the ridge's rear:

> From first light on, we had in our hands the most perfect observation over the whole Axis position, with the sun behind us. I cannot recall any single use made by 10 Corps of this priceless asset; nor even of anyone coming to look. We used it throughout the morning for sending back frequent artillery and air targets.[78]

Even so the anti-guns were clearly providing more of problem to the 51st Division crossing, as the experience of the Staffordshire Yeomanry showed. The line of sight from the back of Roumana to the 4th Indian crossing from the

72 TNA, WO 169/8791, 51st Highland Division HQ, War Diary, 1339 hours, 6 April 1943. Though it should be noted these tanks were from 4th Country of London Yeomanry from 23rd Armoured Brigade, who were supporting the infantry attack.

73 Playfair and Moloney, p. 373.

74 W.G. Stevens, *The Official History of New Zealand in the Second World War, 1939–1945: Bardia to Enfidaville*, (Wellington: Historical Publications Branch, 1962), p. 264.

75 Kenneth Macksey, *Crucible of Power* (London: Hutchinson, 1969), p. 242 and Shelford Bidwell, *Gunners at War* (London: Arms and Armour Press, 1970), pp. 196–7.

76 IWM, Tuker Papers Box 71/21/6, Folder 1, Notes by Maj-Gen FS Tuker, CB, DSO, OBE, 6 October 1945.

77 Ibid., 71/21/3 folder 6, *Akarit*, 1958.

78 IWM, Bateman Papers, 72/117/1, Bateman to Tuker, 7 July 1960.

rear of Roumana is not great and it is a considerably more distant target. Tuker wondered: 'Can you think of anything that could hinder that great force [10 Corps] from ... if it advanced on our track over the anti-tank ditch and did not wait for 50 Div [actually 51st] to clear theirs at the foot of Roumana (which they did by 12 noon, in any case)?'[79] There was indeed less fighting on the 4th Indian front by then. The Germans concentrated their counter-attacks on Roumana and thus the Highland Division faced continued serious fighting throughout the rest of the day. Yet there was constant shelling and it should be noted that 4th Indian's Commander Royal Engineers, Lieutenant-Colonel John Blundell was killed at their crossing point along with two other sapper officers and an American exchange officer at 1600 hours.[80]

Blundell was working on improving the route across the ditch. The other issue that might explain the difficulties faced by 10 Corps was the quality of the tracks and crossings. The 10 Corps Engineer report on the crossing point reckoned it 'led into country impassable to wheels but passable to tracks'.[81] This is again contradicted by the experience of Donald Bateman:

> In my mind was the wish to join up with our wheels as soon as practicable ... the crossing must have been passable some time before we used it. I would never gone if we had not been assured of a clear run through ... Of the ground leading forward from there: My recollection is of a pretty fair track which improved, and opened out, as one proceeded ... I am quite positive that I was never once told that routes forward were impracticable.[82]

The 3rd RTR Crusader tanks moving through the hills on the 4th Indian front found the track 'single line and difficult going'. Passing large armoured formations through was obviously awkward and the RTR war diary mentions 'endeavouring to push out this bottle neck'.[83] Indeed Bateman noticed 'the mass of armour' on the track and stated that 'I did not go along it in my jeep as there was congestion enough without adding to it'.[84] The advance very quickly began to lose momentum. There were other possible routes through the British left flank. The main thrust of the 7th Brigade attack had come up a track through a gap in the hills to the west. Although it was even worse going than the main track, much of the brigade had come through it and to the eyes of modern British

[79] Ibid., Tuker to Bateman, 21 May 1962.

[80] TNA WO 169/14739, 4th Indian Division, HQ RE, War Diary, 6 April 1943.

[81] TNA, WO 169/8598, CE Branch 10 Corps, War Diary, 6 April 1943.

[82] IWM, Bateman Papers, 72/117/1, Bateman to Tuker, 23 June 1962.

[83] TNA, WO 169/9364, 3rd Royal Tank Regiment, War Diary, 6 April 1943.

[84] IWM, Bateman Papers, 72/117/1, Bateman to Tuker, 23 June 1962.

soldiers at least it seemed to have been capable of taking armour.[85] Yet given the problems elsewhere it is unlikely this would have alleviated the congestion much if at all. However, even further to the west, the 4/16th Punjabis managed to open up the military road and bring up carriers and at least one anti-tank gun.[86] This was something that Peter Hughes, the Punjabi CO, pointed out to Tuker after the war. Donald Bateman agreed but he noted that this might not have solved the congestion either: 'I have some recollection, however, that the going off the road, once you got out the hills, was bad; and may have been difficult for armour in bulk.'[87]

So as the armour backed up behind the position, the staff of 4th Indian Division did their best to encourage the tanks forward. Bateman wandered down and 'chatted to some of the armour to find out why they were not moving'. The Divisional HQ staff were even more frustrated by that time. Lieutenant-Colonel Ken Shepheard, Tuker's GSO 1, recalled 'I remember we were furious at the delay in exploiting our success and were very critical of Corps and Army HQ and I believe I followed up Horrock's visit with a further conversation (telephone) to his BGS [Brigadier General Staff] to find out what they were doing about it.' It appeared to be very little. Part of the problem was that 4th Indian Division was part of 30 Corps and thus was not in 10 Corps' chain of command. Major Alfred Cocksedge, the GSO II, identified the nub of the problem: 'After General H[orrocks] left us, we could presumably have no direct link with his HQ and would have to leave it HQ 30 Corps to urge him on.'[88] This Tuker did claiming that 'I asked Oliver Leese to lay down a barrage <u>behind</u> 10 Corps and blow them through.'[89] So the opportunity drifted away and 4th Indian Division were finally informed by 30 Corps that a set-piece attack by 2nd New Zealand Division was being organised for the following morning at 0930 hours proceeded by an air raid.[90] Over the night of 6/7 April the 1st Italian army rather skilfully disengaged and fell back to their next position. The set piece attack was cancelled and the Battle of Wadi Akarit came to an end. It had

---

[85] See TNA, WO 169/15002, 4/16th Punjab Regt War Diary, 6 April 1943, Appendix B sketch map and discussion with officers of HQ 51st Brigade, Exercise Mareth Lion, 29 September 2009.

[86] TNA, WO 169/15002, 4/16th Punjab Regt War Diary, 6 April.

[87] IWM, Bateman Papers, 72/11/7/1, 6 July 1962 Tuker to Bateman and Bateman to Tuker, 8 July 1963.

[88] Ibid., Bateman to Tuker, 23 June 1962 and Tuker Papers, Box 71/21/3 Folder 3, Shepheard to Drummond, 28 March 1967 and Cocksedge to Tuker, 29 July 1960.

[89] IWM, Bateman papers, 1/1, Tuker to Bateman, 5 January 1959.

[90] TNA, WO 169/8501, Main 8th Army, War Diary Log sheets, From Main 30 Corps, 2345, 6 April and WO 169/14735, 4th Indian Division HQ War Diary, 6 April 1943.

been an impressive Allied victory, breaking the Axis defensive line and taking about 7,000 prisoners, but it was hardly as decisive as Tuker had hoped it might be. He lamented that this failure meant the subsequent battles at Enfidaville and Medjez el Bab had to be fought and this cost the British a further 10,000 casualties in North Africa.[91]

So why was the 1st Italian Army not destroyed at Wadi Akari? On the morning of 6 April when General Horrocks, commanding 10 Corps, came forward to discuss the situation with Tuker, the 8th Army seemed poised for a massive victory. All 10 Corps had to do was get its armour through and cut off the 1st Italian Army which was reeling from the success of the attack by 30 Corps' infantry divisions. Clearly this process began – 3rd RTR was ordered forward at 1200 hours – but 10 Corps very quickly lost momentum and the attack petered out before it even developed. The reasons for this seem to be the presence of anti-tank guns to the rear of Roumana and just the sheer difficulty in passing the armour through the routes available. Yet with a bit of determination and drive, as was shown by the carriers of 4/6th Rajupatana Rifles, breaking out onto the plain beyond was possible. Tuker lamented that 'If I had had a third brigade or even perhaps a recce unit, I could have settled the matter without help from 10 Corps.'[92]

Arguable as Tuker's contention is, it highlights a key difference between division and the rest of Montgomery's 8th Army. Clearly this is a formation that is somewhat different to its fellow units. It is a formation that embraces manoeuvre and innovation. It was well trained – Tuker, like Montgomery, had a reputation as a first rate trainer of men – experienced and its leadership knew each other well. As Tuker, adapting Marshal Suvorov, wrote 'If the approach is good, the battle will be easy.'[93] There is no doubt that Division's approach was 'good'. Tuker, slightly idiosyncratically, put much of this down to his background. He, as a Gurkha officer unlike the rest of the Army, had 'never trained or fought in order to use the bayonet' but rather the Kukri. So he and his men 'fought by sheer individual and collective battle skill – not as a bayonet fronted line'. The Division, under his tutelage, absorbed this attitude and thus Wadi Akarit was 'fought by 4th Indian Division on combined infiltration tactics that no other divisions could use'.[94] This was true enough, no other 8th Army formation could have attempted a silent attack into mountainous country. In contrast the 51st Division, who also fought impressively at Akarit, conducted a very much more

91 IWM, Tuker Papers, 71/21/2 Folder 7, General Tuker's statement on relationship with the Corps during the Akrait and Enfidaville actions, April 1943, undated.

92 Ibid., 71/21/6 Folder 1, Notes by Major-General F.S. Tuker, 6 October 1945.

93 Tuker, *Approach*, p. 6.

94 IWM, Tuker Papers, 71/21/6 Folder 5, Tuker to Caroe, 26 September 1959.

conventional battle, going in behind a barrage. The Highland Division was very much more a product of Montgomery's Army, arriving in the Middle-East at about the same time as the Army commander.

Nonetheless the 8th Army was an army that had begun to win and would continue to do so. Montgomery's approach was to prepare carefully and then fight a firepower reliant set piece battle on a fairly narrow front. It had produced victory at El Alamein and Mareth and, despite Tuker's complaints, also at Akarit. It had not at any of those battles produced a decisive victory. The 8th Army could fight a break-in battle, but it struggled to break-out and exploit the victory. This was for a number of reasons, but much of it was down to Montgomery's caution. The steady process of 8th Army victories was in part due to Montgomery's unwillingness to take risks. It had characterised the pursuit after Alamein and would continue to mark his conduct of operations throughout the war. Yet it was appropriate given his determination to avoid allowing the Axis the opportunity to inflict a reverse on his Army, as had happened so often in the Western Desert prior to his arrival.[95] Tuker himself noted that a commander 'must adapt or change his plans in such a way that his officers and men are not tested beyond their abilities and their best is brought out of them'.[96] Montgomery, it must be said, did exactly that, possibly at the expense of winning more decisively.

Montgomery's approach also included a tendency to control subordinate commanders tightly or 'grip' them to ensure that the battle was conducted in accordance to his wishes. This directly affected the outcome of the battle of Wadi Akarit and certainly Horrock's conduct during it. Again Alfred Cocksedge, Tuker's GSO II, offered a rather insightful assessment of the 10 Corps commander's behaviour and that of Oliver Leese of 30 Corps. Both men were Montgomery protégés and had been appointed his corps commanders at Alamein. Cocksedge reckoned 'the plan was drawn up by General Leese in consultation with Divisional Commanders, but he felt compelled to obtain Monty's approval before acting on it. In the same way General Horrocks hesitated to commit his Corps with out consulting the army commander.'[97] The Army commander did indeed consent at 1100 hours but 10 Corps did not get moving until after 1200 and the progress thereafter was slow and difficult. Horrocks clearly did 'hesitate' and given the command structure there was little 4th Indian Division could do to spur him on to greater efforts. When the whole 10 Corps move stagnated, Horrocks again visited Montgomery at 1630 hours and during that meeting Montgomery decided that a set-piece attack, something

95 Hart, pp. 98–101.

96 Tuker, *Approach*, p. 3.

97 IWM, Tuker Papers, 71/21/3 Folder 3, Cocksedge to Tuker, 29 July 1960.

with which he was very much more comfortable, should be organised for the following day.[98]

Yet in spite of the anxiousness of the Corps commander to seek his approval for major decisions, Montgomery does not really 'grip' this battle. On the morning of 5 April he held a conference with Leese and Horrocks where he 'had explained in detail how the battle was to be fought – the initial break-in, the break-through, and the pursuit. There was therefore nothing for me to do.'[99] As Cocksedge noted: 'I think Gen. Monty had to all intents and purposes handed over command of the battle to General Leese ... and was I think already planning Sicily.'[100] Indeed in the letter to his direct superior the Army Group commander, General Sir Harold Alexander, outlining the plan for Wadi Akarit he is clearly more concerned with the 'woolly thinking' over the plan for Sicily.[101] As he notes in a letter to General Sir Alan Brooke, the Chief of the Imperial General Staff specifically on Akarit and Sicily: 'It is not an easy matter to fight difficult and important battles and at the same time plan an important operation elsewhere.'[102] Tuker felt the Corps Commanders 'were a bit of a hindrance for, had it not been for them, Montgomery would have personally more in the picture at crucial moments e.g. ... the morning of 6 April 1943'. Indeed Montgomery needed to be more engaged and 'should have been up ... at my HQ directly I'd broken through at Akarit, ready for the last blow'.[103]

Akarit demonstrated that 4th Indian Division was a formation that was somewhat different to its fellow units in 8th Army, as Tuker was from his fellow commanders. The Division embraced manoeuvre and innovation, whereas the bulk of the 8th Army acted in proscribed if generally effective manner. The 8th Army won its battles but rarely exploited them properly. Tuker corresponded with Basil Liddell-Hart after the War and Liddell Hart probably gets to the key issue with Akarit:

> Monty's main fault being excess caution, but it was much increased by the lack of interest in the problem of exploitation that he had always shown ... I have a series

98 TNA, WO 169/8591, Main HQ 10 Corps, War Diary, 6 April 1943.

99 IWM, Montgomery Papers, BLM 33, 7 April 1943.

100 IWM, Tuker Papers, 71/21/3 Folder 3, Cocksedge to Tuker, 29 July 1960.

101 TNA, WO 214/ 18, The Papers of Field Marshal Lord Alexander of Tunis, Montgomery to Alexander, 3 April 1943

102 IWM, Montgomery Papers, BLM 49, 9 April 1943.

103 IWM, Tuker Papers, 71/21/1 Folder 6, *History of 4th Indian Division*, and *Montgomery's Memoirs, 1958.*

> of letters from him ... which show how apt he was, in concentrating on the set piece battle, to overlook the key importance of exploitation.[104]

Or as Tuker put it: 'The 8th Army of 1942–43 ... lived in 1918 where the barrage and its implications ousted manoeuvre.'[105] The Indian Army in its approach to war differed somewhat to the Montgomery dominated British 8th Army. However, despite that 8th Army and its senior commanders were willing to listen to people such as Tuker and profit from this. Indeed at Akarit Tuker won the 8th Army one major battle in Tunisia and, arguably went on to win a second at Medjez el Bab though this time for the neighbouring 1st Army. Oliver Leese, in particular, was willing to take advice. However, Tuker was never ever able to change the rigid upward looking culture of the Army and hence the failure to exploit at Akarit. Furthermore Tuker was always slightly outside the inner circle of Montgomery's commander, something he, no doubt, resented. When the Tunisian campaign ended Claude Auchinleck recommended Tuker for a corps command. However, given his sponsor and the fact, as a friend of his explained 'as you were up against people who had been unable to swallow your criticism of their technique' this came to nothing and he would watch a number of those junior to him promoted past him in Italy.[106] The 8th Army might have been able to take advice but criticism was another matter.

---

104 Ibid., 71/21/6 Folder 5, Liddell-Hart to Tuker, 10 February 1961.

105 IWM, Tuker papers, Box 71/21/1 Folder 1, Hisory of 4th Indian Division, 1958.

106 IWM, Tuker papers, Caroe to Tuker, 16 June 1959.

Chapter 6
'Debunking the Bunker': From Donbaik to Razabil, January 1943–March 1944

Tim Moreman

Introduction

The land war waged by the British Indian Army against the Imperial Japanese Army (IJA) in South East Asia threw up many new tactical problems. During its early phases in Malaya and Burma Japanese troops employed bold, imaginative wide outflanking manoeuvres through supposed impenetrable jungle, for example, to 'hook-in' behind British units tied to the roads by their lavish scales of arms, equipment and motor vehicles and cut them off from their lines of communication. This tactic proved devastatingly effective and trapped troops had little recourse other than fight their way clear on foot. Further problems emerged later during the war in Burma after the IJA was thrown back onto the defensive. This chapter explores how the British tackled the pressing tactical problem posed by overcoming heavily fortified Japanese defensive positions encountered from January 1943 onwards in Burma. It looks in detail specifically at two key engagements: Donbaik and Razabil.[1]

The Road to Donbaik

The British-Indian Army first encountered dug-in Japanese troops during the offensive mounted by 14th Indian Division, commanded by Major-General Wilfred Lloyd, down the jungle-clad Arakan coast in late 1942–early 1943 to secure vitally needed airfields on Akyab Island. On 27 December 47th Indian Infantry Brigade occupied Indin on the Mayu Peninsula and a few days later a Bren Gun Carrier patrol reached its tip without encountering Japanese resistance, whose II/213th battalion wisely withdrew from their forward

[1] For a full discussion of British fighting methods in Burma see: Tim Moreman, *The Jungle, the Japanese and the British Commonwealth Armies at War 1941–45. Fighting Methods, Doctrine and Training for Jungle Warfare*, (London: 2005).

positions at Buthidaung-Maungdaw. The British advance paused given the immense logistical problems facing 14th Indian Division and fears for the safety of its uncovered left flank. Unfortunately this halt also gave the Japanese high command time to begin shifting reinforcements – 55th Division – 600 miles from central Burma to Arakan and Miyzaki Force, part of the 33rd Division already in Arakan, to consolidate their defences, at Akyab and build new carefully reconnoitred positions in the Donbaik-Laungchaung area on the Mayu Peninsula and at Rathedaung on the eastern side of the Mayu River.

The Japanese deployed a single company, commanded by Lt. Watanabe Satao, from the III/213th Regiment at sunset on 4 January at Donbaik, on the eastern side of the Mayu Range, while the remainder of the unit garrisoned Akyab Island. This 250-man strong composite company – consisting of two infantry platoons, a machine gun platoon, a section equipped with a captured mortar and 47mm anti-tank gun and an anti-tank platoon – was hardly formidable on paper.[2] The position chosen by Satao for his defensive stand, however, a mile to the north of Donbaik had considerable natural strength given the coastal strip narrowed to 1,000 yards, with its flanks anchored on the Bay of Bengal and the supposedly impassable densely jungle-covered Mayu Range. The forward edge of this defensive position ran along a wide deep *chaung* (watercourse), filled with water until it reached the jungle, whose crumbling up to 9-foot high banks were both a formidable anti-tank obstacle and difficult to climb on foot, that ran inland from the water's edge to the jungle-clad foothills where it twisted into the shape of a crook. Both sides of the tidal chaung were shielded from view by mangrove trees. A smaller secondary chaung ran off from the main one to the north-east 200 yards from the jungle. The 600 yard wide open paddy fields lying immediately to the front of the position nearer the coast provided a wide field of fire that had to be crossed by attacking troops. The only real physical weakness of the position, however, was that when the tide receded it exposed a wide expanse of hard packed sand negotiable on foot and by vehicles. Further eastwards the whole position was overlooked by two jungle-clad low hillocks – later dubbed North and South Knobs – and then steep, densely wooded hills, cloaked with vegetation dense enough to seriously impede vision and movement on foot, rising gradually in height towards the Mayu Range.

The Japanese set about improving this already strong position and that at Rathedaung with a will, correctly expecting the British to deploy superior artillery, displaying great knowledge, skill and ingenuity in building field defences based on earlier experience fighting in China. The mainstay of the defences was

---

2 Louis Allen, Burma. *The Longest War 1941–45* (London, 1984), p. 98 and John Nunneley and Kazuo Tamayama, *Tales by Japanese Soldiers* (London, 2000), p. 123.

a series of well-sited, skilfully constructed and impressively strong bunkers – essentially pill-boxes made from natural materials – that ran along the southern bank of the chaung and its subsidiary and that were eventually also distributed in depth behind it. Two particularly strong positions – dubbed Sugar 4 (S4) and Sugar 5 (S5) by the British – were located along the secondary chaung. The exact layout and construction differed from location to location being dependent on ground. Each bunker was dug deep into the ground, however, with its walls revetted with timber. Overhead cover consisted of thick logs and soil up to 5 feet thick protection from a direct hit from the field and mountain artillery or a direct hit from all but a 500–1000lb aerial bomb. Indeed, bunkers had such physical strength they could easily withstand fire from supporting Japanese MGs, mortars, rifle grenades and artillery called down by their occupants upon themselves. Each bunker normally contained between 5–25 men armed with rifles, medium and light machine guns and mortars. A narrow aperture or firing slit (normally 3 feet long and 6 inches in height) enabled the garrison to defend themselves from attack, while a strongly constructed small escape hatch or door opening onto a crawl trench or similar provided access into the bunker for resupply and reinforcements. If time allowed underground tunnels or narrow communication trenches were dug interconnecting individual positions so that troops could be shifted around defensive positions as required and to reoccupy positions attackers thought had been cleared. The Japanese bunkers were camouflaged with considerable skill, carefully exploiting the terrain for cover, with any spoil from construction carefully hidden. Live vegetation was left intact or carefully replanted concealing the outline of the bunkers and firing slits such that most were invisible to the eye except at very close range by determined searchers. S5, for example, was built inside a small hollowed-out hillock. The side of a chaung was used as the site of S6 with a series of bunkers hollowed out of the ground. Hessian or other camouflage concealed firing slits and if available these were strengthened with steel or similar shutters.

The real strength of Japanese defensive position lay in the sum of its parts, with bunkers always built in mutually supporting groups normally organised for all-round defence. If enemy troops attacked one bunker they came under fire from at least two others to their flank and rear nearby whose own existence was carefully concealed until they opened fire, normally with correspondingly devastating effect at extremely short range. All Japanese defensive localities were sited in great depth with bunkers covering likely avenues of approach with interlocking and overlapping fields of fire. Further carefully concealed foxholes and trenches added to the strength of the position with snipers liberally distributed throughout a defensive locality. The forward Japanese bunkers positions at Donbaik were covered by machine gun (MG), mortar and artillery positions to the flank and rear, from higher ground overlooking the battlefield, with the result the whole area was covered by overlapping fire.

The Japanese defenders were ready by the time 47th Indian Infantry Brigade, commanded by Brigadier E.H. Blaker, advanced on 7 January, with one column moving along the coastal strip and a battalion on the eastern flank of the Mayu Range. On 6 January Bren Gun carrier patrols met organised opposition north of Donbaik. Early on the morning of 7 January the 1st Royal Inniskilling Fusiliers 'bumped' into a series of positions along the line of the tidal creek, quickly dubbed by British officers the FDL Chaung (Forward Defensive Locality). A hasty attack by a single company failed ignominiously. A battalion strength assault was made on 8 and again on 9 January, with support from a field and mountain battery, but both assaults ground to a halt in the face of intense short range defensive fire with the loss of 100 casualties. Progress proved impossible across the 600 yards of flat ground between the sea and the jungle. The dense jungle badly slowed progress made by a company advancing on the left flank which took 12 hours to cover two miles. It proved impossible, however, to locate enemy MG and mortars hidden in the jungle. The impact of British shellfire, fired by 25-pounders and 3.7" howitzers, proved far more limited than expected since the Japanese quickly learnt to go to ground under intense bombardment, leaving a lone sentry to watch for advancing British infantry and alert the others defenders as they approached.[3]

The British offensive had been fought to a standstill by the Japanese defenders at Donbaik, with similar occurring at Rathedaung where 123rd Indian Infantry Brigade had encountered strong resistance. Lt.-General Noel Irwin, commanding Eastern Army, ordered 14th Indian Division to concentrate its primary effort on capturing Donbaik. Unfortunately the intricate planning and massing of the requisite guns, troops and ammunition took time that the Japanese employed to strengthen their defences.

47th Indian Infantry Brigade, supported by a newly deployed field and mountain artillery regiment (equipped with 25-pounders and 3.7-inch howitzers), a Jat machine gun company and Bren Gun carriers, finally attacked the Japanese defences at Donbaik again on 18/19th January 1943, employing two infantry battalions in a set-piece attack on a narrow frontage. While a third battalion remained in reserve, the other guarded the left flank in the foothills. As one eyewitness serving in the 1st Inniskilling recorded: 'For ninety minutes an artillery barrage was laid down on the "Chaung Area" and from where we were sitting it was a grand sight. I never thought anything could live through it ... We all thought it was just a case of getting to the Jap position and gathering

[3] Ibid., p. 125.

up the pieces.'[4] Nothing could be further from the truth. The initial attack, with the 1st Iniskillings methodically advancing from its trenches along the coast and the 1/7th Rajput Regiment attacking through the foothill further eastwards following a fierce rolling barrage, had mixed results. On 18 January the 1/7th Rajputs occupied the Shepherd's Crook and the area between the North and South Promontories before being forced back to South Knob overnight, but the 1st Inniskillings were immediately held up near the coast by intense machine gun, mortar, grenade discharger and artillery fire after reaching the mouth of the FDL Chaung. A combination of inadequate infantry training, inflexibility once battle was joined and poor cooperation between the assault troops and artillery was partly at fault. As Major L.H. Landon, commanding 8th (Lahore) Mountain Battery firing in support, later wrote:

> Artillery support consisted of a rolling barrage in front of the infantry attack and/or smoke screens – everything was tried. But the Japs were too well dug in for the artillery preparation to have much effect – and the infantry always started late and so kept too far behind the barrage, so giving the Japs plenty of time to man their fire positions and repel the attack.[5]

Further attacks next day, supported by Bren Gun carriers, failed with heavy loss leaving the battlefield littered with quickly rotting corpses. By evening when it was clear further progress was impossible Blaker ordered a withdrawal to a defensive position between the sea and foothills 400 yards north of the FDL Chaung. The sheer tenacity of Japanese troops, fighting literally to the last man and round from within their apparently impervious bunkers, astounded British and Indian troops, whose own morale began a downward spiral, because they had confidently expected them to surrender or withdraw when surrounded or under heavy pressure. As Robert Lyman has written: 'The Japanese position began to develop a legendary status for the British and Indian troops, reinforcing the "superman" myth and convincing them that the bunkers were constructed of some new type of armour plating or concrete.'[6]

The fresh 55th Indian Infantry Brigade, commanded by Brigadier J.M. Hunt, attacked Donbaik on a narrow front with two battalions on 1 February, with 'added punch' provided by the bulk of the divisional artillery and eight Valentine

---

4 Capt. D.P. Farrell, 'An Inniskilling Battalion in Burma', in *The Sprig of Shillelagh. The Journal of the Royal Inniskilling Fusiliers*, 26, 313 (1943), p. 98.

5 L.H. Landon, 'Holiday on Full Pay' (Unpublished TS Memoir, nd), p. 63. OIOC Mss.Eur.C519.

6 Robert Lyman, *The Generals. From Defeat to Victory, Leadership in Asia 1941–45* (London: 2008), p. 156.

tanks, part of C Squadron 146 Regiment RAC, rushed forward from XV Indian Corps in Bengal. It was hoped that these heavily armoured AFVs would solve the problem of the Japanese bunkers despite protests from various quarters about using tanks in small 'penny-packets' inadequate for the task in hand.[7]

This attack did not go to plan with the Japanese, by now reinforced to a complete infantry battalion, yet again offering determined resistance from within their bunkers that the supporting artillery was unable to destroy or suppress. Indeed, the resilience of bunkers to artillery bombardments of ever-increasing strength made British gunners think that concrete and steel had been liberally employed in their construction. The 1st/17th Dogra Regiment (1/17th Dogras), tasked with advancing from North Knob westwards along the FDL Chaung with the Valentines, failed to reach their start lines after coming under MG and mortar fire from previously unlocated positions on the western slopes of North Knob. The lumbering Valentines did not justify the faith placed in them by senior officers and during their initial sortie, made under cover of an artillery barrage without infantry support, three of the slow-moving infantry tanks, operating north of FDL Chaung instead of south as planned, got stuck in a ditch. Japanese anti-tank guns or mechanical failure quickly claimed the others. A heavy price was paid by the unfortunate tank crewmen for the decision to employ too few AFVs for the task in hand, inadequate ground reconnaissance and having had insufficient time to practice tank-infantry cooperation before the attack began. A second planned attack by the 1/17th Dogras, with tank support, from FDL Chaung to Wadi Junction-South Knob simply failed to materialise. Instead, the battalion became embroiled in inconclusive heavy fighting along the FDL Chaung and on North Knob that resulted in heavy casualties, including the commanding officer (CO).

The leading *jawans* of the 2nd/1st Punjab Regiment) fared much better, after securing North and South Knobs during a preliminary operation on 30 January, and successfully outflanked the enemy positions near the chaung. The 2/1st Punjabis advanced through the foothills and by the evening of 1 February successfully occupied Wadi Junction. Losses, however, were heavy. On the morning of 2 February Wooded Village fell to the battalion from the rear. The cut-off Japanese occupying bunkers along the FDL Chaung characteristically refused to give up, however, despite being attacked from the front and rear and repeated Japanese counterattacks were launched on Wooded Village, Shepherd's Crook and South Knob. Although these were unsuccessful on 4/5 February Blaker admitted defeat and ordered the 2/1st Punjabis to withdraw back to South Knob.

---

7 Field Marshal Sir William Slim, *Defeat into Victory* (London, 1956), p. 152.

The British high command did not abandon hope of breaking through at Donbaik and at Rathedaung to the east, despite having now been held up by the Japanese for a month and suffering heavy losses in casualties and prestige, although evidence was accumulating that 14th Indian Division's flank and rear was seriously threatened by elements of 55th Division quickly advancing along jungle tracks down the Kaladan Valley and towards Rathedaung.

The 55th Indian Infantry Brigade renewed the attack on Donbaik with four infantry battalions at 4.30am on 18 February, making yet again a stereotyped direct frontal assault on a narrow front, behind a timed barrage fired by field artillery even though it clearly cost surprise. It reflected the still prevalent belief amongst senior commanders that superior numbers and firepower would ultimately prevail. The 1st Inniskilling, shielded by darkness and covered by a timed artillery barrage, successfully occupied the FDL Chaung from the coast up to M17 and infiltrated into Wooded Village. Unfortunately the 2/1st Punjabis, tasked with clearing the chaung between M16 and S5 and exploiting southwards, were held up by Japanese bunkers at M18, M16, S4 and S5 and suffered 130 casualties during the advance. Although M16 was briefly taken the assaulting company, under heavy fire from both flanks, withdrew. Later that day Japanese troops infiltrated westwards down the FDL Chaung and reoccupied M17. An attack by the 1/7th Rajputs, the reserve battalion, at 1pm on S4 and S5 failed despite a heavy artillery concentration fired in support. By evening all the surviving attacking troops were back at their start lines having yet again achieved little.

The Japanese had not been idle with successful month long defence at Donbaik and Rathedaung buying sufficient time for the Japanese 55th Division's main body to arrive in Arakan. On 7 March Japanese troops advanced out of the Kaladan Valley and began a devastatingly effective counteroffensive, using tried and tested encirclement and infiltration tactics through supposedly 'impassable' jungle, against the tired, demoralised and over-extended 14th Indian Division.

The lacklustre British high command foolishly clung to its long-held plans for capturing Donbaik, now occupied by the Japanese 143rd Infantry Regiment (part of 55th Division), despite growing evidence that 14th Indian Division's left flank was seriously threatened and warnings from Lloyd and Irwin. The Commander-in-Chief, however, overruled his subordinates concerns about its wisdom, with General Sir Archibald Wavell firmly believing that a success was essential before the impending monsoon to restore shaken British morale and ordered that the fresh 6th Brigade and 71st Brigade should overwhelm the Donbaik position by sheer weight of numbers. When the British 6th Brigade arrived at Donbaik on 9th March to make the next assault it found a battlefield resembling the Western Front during the First World War, with the opposing sides occupying trench lines running down to the coast separated by a No-Man's Land littered with abandoned equipment and the quickly decomposing dead from earlier attacks.

The initial plan proposed by the despairing Major-General Lloyd and his subordinates for the sixth and ultimately final attack on Donbaik differed from earlier attempts, in that it involved an advance on a wide front, with the fresh 6th Brigade advancing along on the coastal plain to Donbaik, 71st Indian Infantry Brigade moving along the foothills and 47th Indian Infantry Brigade advancing along the summit of the Mayu Mountains. To secure surprise a silent night attack, deliberately without a preparatory bombardment, was to be employed. Unfortunately Lt.-General Noel Irwin overruled his unfortunate subordinate, whose plan he criticised as lacking imagination and failing to make use of 'deception, subterfuge, close and concentrated cooperation by artillery or air, nor the employment of any special measures to overcome the JAPS in concealed, probably unlocated and certainly in very inaccessible positions'.[8] Instead, Irwin, still wedded to his own ideas, took over and insisted upon making a highly concentrated frontal attack made in depth and with limited objectives, after meticulous planning, employing just 6th Brigade (led by Brigadier RVC Cavendish), with concentrated air and artillery support, to overwhelm by sheer weight of numbers the Japanese defences. When the highly experienced Lt.-General William Slim, GOC XV Indian Corps, visited Donbaik he pleaded with Lloyd to outflank the Japanese defences through the jungle or cut them off from the rear by an amphibious landing rather than mounting another frontal assault. Unfortunately his advice was simply ignored.[9]

The final plan for the frontal attack on Donbaik by 6th Brigade employed six infantry battalions (Cavendish's own four and two attached from other formations), supported by two field regiments, who would advance from the flank from Shepherd's Crook down the FDL Chaung and also southwards from the Knobs to Wadi Junction and the North and South Promontories carried out in timed phases, each with a supporting artillery and aerial bombardment. To clear the way for the main attack an attempt was made by the Royal Engineers on 14 March to destroy S5 using a handcart loaded with explosives pushed towards the bunker using long poles. It proved a failure, however, when the cart fell into a trench outside the main bunker and on a second attempt a 500lb charge did not inflict any noticeable damage on the bunker.[10]

---

8 Irwin to Wavell, 9th March 1943, Irwin Mss, IWM IRW/2/1.

9 Slim, op. cit., pp. 153–4.

10 Julian Thompson, *The Imperial War Museum of the War in Burma 1941–45* (London: 2002), pp. 50–51.

The attack by 1st Royal Welch Fusiliers (RWF), 2nd Durham Light Infantry (DLI) and 1st Lincolns at first light on 18th March successfully penetrated the Japanese defensive position after it was deluged at 5.40am with 124 tons of artillery and mortar shells. Little damage, however, again was inflicted on the enemy bunkers, whose now alerted occupants fought back with dogged determination. An attack by a squadron of Blenheim bombers on the positions running along the FDL Chaung also proved a failure when the aircraft mistakenly dropped their loads on Donbaik Village. The 1st RWF, advancing from positions to the north and east, got atop S4 and S5, but were eventually driven off after failing to locate firing slots through which grenades could be posted to kill the occupants. As one soldier described: 'We arrived just in time to be caught in vicious crossfire of machine guns and grenades emanating from Sugar 5 ... We were also being pounded by mortar fire and other artillery ... Our men were falling like flies but our targets had all vanished underground.'[11] Under heavy mortar and MG fire, deluged by grenades and unable to enter the bunkers they stood atop the remnants of 1st RWF predictably withdrew. Another company was cut off in the FDL Chaung, but eventually made its escape albeit after suffering heavy casualties. The 1st DLI's attack towards 'the Elbow' also met heavy resistance. Elsewhere the Lincoln's attack southwards from the Twin Knobs was held up by Japanese counterattacks after initial progress was made southwards towards the Promontories. Although this attack penetrated some distance the enemy outposts it had by-passed held out and the battalion withdrew. A night attack by the 1st Royal Scots the following day also proved abortive. The British battalions having suffered over 300 casualties had little option but to withdraw leaving the battlefield in the possession of the Japanese.

The final British attack on Donbaik ended in abject failure and bitter recrimination. Despite recent events Irwin remained doggedly convinced that the only way of overcoming Japanese bunkers was by deploying overwhelming infantry strength on a narrow front that would eat up enemy bunkers in 'small mouthfuls'. Writing on 20 March he observed: 'The 6 Brigade attack ... failed obviously because – although the local commanders think otherwise – there were not enough troops following each other up. It was not, in my mind, the frontages that were wrong, but the depths.'[12] Similarly on 22 March a bitterly disappointed Wavell complained about the final attack: 'It seemed to me to show a complete lack of imagination, and was neither one thing or the other ... I should now like to see what can be done in the way of a very gradual point by

[11] '1939–1945, *The Unsung Heroes: A Personal Account by 5186455 Fusilier W.C. Smith 1st Battalion Royal Welch Fusiliers*, unpublished ms, pp. 21–2, cited in Tarak Barkawi, *Soldiers of Empire* (London: forthcoming).

[12] Irwin to Wavell, 20 March 1943. Irwin Mss, IWM IRW 2/1.

point advance, using a little imagination and originality.' As an alternative he went on:

> For instance, it is not possible to bring up a 25-pr gun to point blank range to the nearest of these strong points? Would it not be possible to put one or two low-flying aircraft over the Japanese forward positions and under cover of the noise and distraction make a night advance?

Further suggestions from his fertile brain included damming the chaung and flooding the positions, pounding the bunkers to pieces by concentrated artillery and lastly using a petrol-filled fougasse to incinerate the defenders.[13]

The frustrated, tired and disillusioned troops on the ground at Donbaik, still recovering from the last attack, were not bereft of ideas about destroying Japanese bunkers, with the commander of 6th Brigade calling for medium artillery or some other new method to solve with the problem.[14] Various new means for tackling bunkers, whose exact construction still remained a mystery, were tested on the ground during the remainder of March. The firing slits of Japanese bunkers were sniped at with no discernable result success, for example, by Boys anti-tank rifles. A new expedient was tried by the CO of 99th Field Regiment to destroy S5 with the construction of two roofed gun pits at the edge of the jungle 80 yards from the mound. On 23 March two 3.7-inch howitzers, manhandled into position, opened direct fire, protected by covering fire and a smoke screen, on Japanese positions, but had little impact despite each howitzer firing 100 rounds. Plans to use a 25-pounder firing armour piercing (AP) shells in March in a similar way were abandoned by the withdrawal from Donbaik.[15] A planned 'pin-point' attack on the Japanese bunkers at Donbaik by Vultee Vengeance dive-bombers proved stillborn when the aircraft were unexpectedly withdrawn for servicing due to technical problems.[16]

Although Wavell still hankered after making a further attack, 14th Indian Division had now completely lost the initiative with the Japanese counteroffensive rapidly gaining ground near Rathedaung and uncovering its left flank. Over the night of 24/25 March the Japanese crossed the Mayu River threatening the rear of all British Commonwealth troops in the Mayu Peninsula.

---

[13] Wavell to Irwin, 22 March 1943, Irwin Mss, IWM IRW 2/1.

[14] Report by Commander, 6th Inf Bde Group on the attack carried out on Donbaik Front on the 18/19 March 1943, TNA WO 172/2059.

[15] Gen. Sir Martin Farndale, *History of the Royal Regiment of Artillery. The Far East 1941–46* (London, 2000), p. 130.

[16] Report on Operation of 22 Army Air Support Control in the Arakan Campaign, 3rd November 1942–47, June 1943, 1 October 1945, TNA AIR 23/5119.

On 3/4 April the Japanese crossed the Mayu Mountains and established a block behind 6th Brigade and 47th Indian Infantry Brigade at Indin. Although both eventually escaped, it was at great loss. The Japanese pressed home their offensive and by late April the shattered, demoralised and broken British were back in approximately the same positions they had begun the offensive five months earlier.

Towards a Solution

The Japanese soldier had shown himself to be a skilful defensive fighter, whose remarkable ability to quickly construct elaborate field fortifications resistant to heavy bombardment and whose skill, bravery and stubbornness – glibly dismissed as 'fanaticism' by British observers – in holding them literally to the last man and round had proved decisive in holding Donbaik for 50 days. The battle had set a new tactical problem for the shaken British high command. It should not perhaps have been a surprise, however, since similar problems had been experienced by Australian troops clearing enemy prepared positions in the South-West Pacific Area.

The methods employed to attack the Japanese defences at Donbaik were justifiably heavily criticised at the time. In Wavell's words the: 'Main cause of failure has been inferiority of our tactics both in attack and defence to really skilful and enterprising opponents Japanese have shown themselves to be. I will do my best to have this remedied.'[17] The failure of senior officers to assess and fully appreciate the causes of failure at the time had condemned British troops to repeating the same old mistakes. In particular, the widely prevalent belief that superior numbers of infantry attacking on a narrow front and superior artillery was all that was needed to overcome Japanese defences took a long time to dispel and cost 14th Division dear. Although effective against troops caught in the open, the sad fact was that the 43,000 shells fired by the divisional artillery at Donbaik, in fireplans of ever-increasing sophistication, were too small in calibre to penetrate and destroy Japanese bunkers. The degree of cooperation between infantry and artillery had proved poor, with barrages rapidly outdistancing the assaulting infantry. A lack of training in cooperation and inadequate reconnaissance had also meant that tanks, employed in too small numbers for the task, failed to have any impact.

The best means of defeating Japanese bunker defences – new tactics, fighting methods and equipment – occupied the minds of British officers at senior and

[17] C-in-C India to War Office, 22 March 1943, OIOC L/WS/1/1323.

junior levels in India Command during the breathing space afforded by the monsoon of 1943, as part of wider efforts to improve and standardise jungle warfare tactics, training and badly-shaken morale in India Command. Indeed, the term bunker rapidly became part of the specialised parlance and whose supposed invulnerability to attack quickly became part of the growing damaging mystique associated with jungle fighting. To address this thorny problem a series of demonstrations were held for divisional, brigade and battalion commanders in late April–early May 1944, under the auspices of the Infantry Schools, Saugor, where various methods of attacking 'standard' Japanese bunker defences were studied, with Lt.-General Geoffrey Scoones acting as Chief Instructor, to establish basic principles how such operations should be conducted. A course handout directed: 'It is a question of imagination, determination and training – especially the training of junior leaders and their men.'[18] Four five-day long Senior Officer's courses were held at Sandagir Camp, near Patrikota, with the 2nd South Lancashire Regiment, 60th Field Regiment and a detachment of Queen Victoria's Own Sappers and Miners acting as demonstration troops. Syndicates studied a Japanese defensive position, constructed in the jungle at Nihani, before being given a 'solution' devised by the Directing Staff to the problem. A demonstration in slow time of an attack on this position, phase by phase, was held. The subject was also carefully studied by the quickly increasing number of specialised jungle warfare training establishments – Sevoke, Shimoga and Raiwala Bara – that sprang up in India during the summer of 1943.

The employment of tanks for 'bunker-busting' in the jungle in particular was the subject of acrimonious debate in India Command, with the Valentines' failure at Donbaik reinforcing a view held by senior officers at General Headquarters (GHQ) India that tanks had no future role in South East Asia. Fierce lobbying by Slim and other senior officers, convinced of their important future role in Burma when employed in larger numbers, eventually won the day. On 5 July 1943 Slim instructed Lt.-Colonel 'Atte' Persse to prepare the 25th Dragoons for deployment in Arakan. The use of tanks for buster-busting was carefully studied for three weeks at Lohardaga where 161st Indian Infantry Brigade trained in cooperation with the 25th Dragoons in country resembling the Razabil area in Arakan, although no firm conclusions were reached about tank-infantry cooperation. Similarly Lt.-General Geoffrey Scoones, the General Officer Commanding (GOC) 4th Corps, insisted that tanks had a limited role in the jungle-covered mountains of Assam, with 254th Indian Tank Brigade commanded by his brother later deployed on the Imphal Plain. The critics were

18 Moreman, op. cit., p. 98.

quickly confounded and by November 1943 it was fully accepted medium tanks could be brought forward, maintained and had a definite role in jungle fighting.[19]

The units and formations undergoing instruction in India Command also studied the tactical problem presented by Japanese bunkers, with officers trying to devise suitable battle drills to winkle them out and adapting the use of infantry weapons, tanks and artillery to destroy them. A Training Instruction issued by 36th Division Headquarters, for example, began: 'The attack on JAPANESE Bunker Positions is no mystery. Such an attack confirms to the normal principles of war. It is in the application of which, however, that special variations may be necessary.' It outlined a drill to deal with bunkers, but emphasised each attack should be carefully assessed on its own merits.[20] Similarly the British troops in 2nd Division, for example carefully practised cooperation with tanks and artillery in December 1943 when dealing with Japanese bunker complexes in thick and open jungle.[21]

The comparatively new science of Operational Research also played its part in devising a solution to Japanese bunker defences. A long series of experiments and trials were initially held in November–December 1943 by the newly arrived No. 10 Operational Research (OR) Section, part of the Research Directorate at GHQ India. A bunker position was carefully constructed near Delhi, to study the effect of particular infantry weapons, tanks and artillery pieces – employing different types of ammunition and fuses against bunker positions.[22] Similar trials were held by the Armoured Fighting Vehicle School at Ahmednagar and by the School of Artillery at Deolali that dragged on into 1944 testing the capabilities and effectiveness of various weapons, ammunition and fuses.[23]

The British high command also profited from successful Australian experience in overcoming Japanese bunkers at Buna-Gona-Sananada in New Guinea, with Brigadier J.E. Lloyd and two other experienced 2nd Australian Imperial Force officers lecturing throughout India Command. To gain further knowledge members of No. 10 OR Section toured Australia and New Guinea between June–August 1944, where they visited training establishments and

---

19 Lt.-Gen. E.L. Morris, CGS, India, to CIGS, London, 16 November 1943, OIOC L/WS/1/441.

20 36 Ind Div Training Instruction No. 5 Attack on Japanese Bunker Positions or 'Debunking the Bunker', TNA WO 172/2029.

21 2 Div Training Directive No. 5, 7 December 1943, TNA WO 172/1924.

22 Welch to Godwin Austen, 4 November 1943, TNA WO 203/606 232/6 and Lt.-Gen. E.L. Morris, CGS, India, to CIGS, London, 18 February 1944, OIOC L/WS/1/441.

23 A.F.V. Liaison Letter No. 7, April 1944, TNA WO 203/2472.

studied recent combat experience in the South West Pacific Area with a view to assessing its relevance to Burma. [24]

Those troops serving at the 'sharp end' along the jungle-covered mountains of the Indo-Burmese frontier during the Autumn/Winter of 1943–44 gave serious thought to the problem after encountering Japanese bunker positions on the Tiddim Road after the newly-formed 14th Army, commanded by Lt.-General William Slim, embarked on a policy of active patrolling to improve jungle training, confidence and morale. The best means of overcoming them was carefully studied at courses, conferences and demonstrations of tanks and artillery, for example, held by 4th Corps on the Imphal Plain. As Lt.-General Scoones in Assam wrote to an incoming divisional commander in August 1943: 'Our recent experience here shows that mopping up and dealing with bunkers are problems we haven't got to the bottom of.'[25]

4th Corps experimented against a 'live' enemy, with members of No. 10 OR Section watching carefully from the sidelines, during the winter of 1943–44. An attack on Japanese bunkers at Point 8225, Milestone (MS) 52, near Fort White, for example, by the 1/3rd and 1/4th Gurkha Rifles (part of 63rd Indian Light Brigade), in December 1943 – Operation Pumpkin – drove home that a drill was still badly needed to overcome a mutually supporting bunker position. The supporting artillery barrage proved too far in advance of the assaulting troops, who were also held up by an obstacle outside the defensive positions. Although both battalions penetrated the position and dropped grenades into the firing slits, they eventually withdrew in disorder. This abortive attack underlined the need for improved command and control, a slower pace for a barrage in the jungle, that the infantry needed a weapon of its own to deal with bunkers and lastly the importance of using smoke to reduce casualties. A report on the operation drew the conclusion that: 'The problem of the bunker is not yet solved. Arty fire had little success in this case.'[26]

Further useful lessons about overcoming well-defended Japanese positions were learnt by 17th Indian Light Division in January–February 1944 that later stood it in good stead during the advance in Burma, as further abortive efforts were made to clear the Japanese from positions in the jungle-covered mountains astride the road covering Fort White at MS 22. A report on an attack on Point 8225 near MS 22 by 48th Indian Light Brigade in 6–11 February 1944 produced by No. 10 OR Section, for example, highlighted that it was difficult to locate accurately even 50 per cent of Japanese bunkers prior to launching

[24] Visit to Australia and New Guinea of Members of No. 10 (Indian) Operational Research Section, nd, TNA WO 203/688.

[25] Scoones to Gracey, 13 August 1943, Gracey Mss LHCMA.

[26] Abridged Report – Operation Pumpkin, TNA WO 203/2468.

an attack.[27] A range of different supporting weapons were employed during attacks on the Japanese defences at MS 22 later that month. During attacks made by 48th Indian Light Brigade between 26–28 February, for example, a two-pounder and six-pounder anti-tank gun and a 3.7-inch howitzer firing HE damaged the weapon slits of several bunkers. Several 5.5-inch medium guns, dragged by bulldozers down the Tiddim Road, were successfully employed firing in an indirect role to destroy enemy bunkers. A two-inch mortar was also employed firing high explosive (HE) shells at a low angle at the slits of a bunker. The lesson drawn by a British participant from repeated attacks in late February on the MS 22 position for the assaulting infantry was that enemy positions should be bypassed whenever possible, that artillery fire could not destroy large bunkers, the assault troops needed to follow up an artillery barrage immediately before the defenders recovered, captured positions needed rapid consolidation to prevent the Japanese reoccupying them, damage could be inflicted by two-pounder, six-pounder and 3.7-inch howitzers on weapon slits and lastly that further experimentation was needed to find suitable means of neutralising strong bunkers.[28]

Second Arakan: Infiltration versus Direct Assault

The fierce fighting in Arakan in January–February 1944 as XV Indian Corps, deploying the two most highly-trained formations available in India Command, slowly edged its way southwards towards the Maungdaw-Buthidaung line and ultimately Akyab Island yielded many important new lessons about Japanese defensive methods and attacking heavily fortified positions in the jungle.

The 7th Indian Division began operations to drive in the outposts in the Kalapanzin Valley, covering the heavily fortified Japanese main defensive position on the Maungdaw-Buthidaung line dubbed the so-called 'Golden Fortress of the Mayu Range', at midnight on the night of 30 November/1 December 1943. This naturally strong defensive position was centred on the two tunnels running through the Mayu Range and had two self-contained outlying bastions, consisting of networks of bunkers and dug-outs tunnelled deep into the ground, at Razabil in the west and Letwedet in the east. A policy of infiltration and encirclement was ordered by Major-General Frank Messervy, instead of making deliberate assaults on Japanese positions, during the early stages that exploited the wide gaps between enemy outposts and the cover provided by the intricate

[27] No. 10 Operational Research Section Operation No. 4, 1 March 1944, TNA WO 203/683.

[28] Col. J.B. Chaplin, *Action in Burma 1942–1945* (London, 1984), pp. 44–5.

jungle-covered terrain, in addition to the fact the Japanese had few troops on the ground. To an extent it was also dictated by the fact his formation was without artillery until the end of December. It proved highly successful with reconnaissance patrols locating gaps through the Japanese defences through which infantry battalions infiltrated at night and established defensive positions that cut-off the flow of supplies and reinforcements. Most encircled Japanese garrisons withdrew without further ado.[29] A similar approach was followed by the newly deployed 5th Indian Division, commanded by Major-General Harold Briggs, after it took over responsibility for the western side of the Mayu Range in early November. A note on tactical policy issued to his subordinates by the GOC directed: 'Until such time as the enemy posns are so thick on the ground that large scale infiltration is impossible it must be our object to infiltrate compete units onto such VITAL FEATURES on the flanks and rear of enemy localities as will force the enemy to counter attack us, and thus incur hvy cas, or else withdraw, whilst our fighting patrols ambush his line of withdrawals.'[30]

This approach bore fruit for XV Indian Corps, commanded by Lt.-General Sir Philip Christison, which infiltrated forward during November and December 1943, although it was not clear whether the Japanese actually intended to fall back in any event. By 1 January both formations were in close touch with the main Japanese defences from the Naf River to the Arakan Hill Tracts. Planning and preliminary operations by 7th Indian Division for the main attack on the Letwedet bastion got underway to seize vantage and jumping-off points required for the planned offensive. 5th Indian Division encountered stiffening opposition as it leading units, advancing on Maungdaw and Razabil, encountered a network of fortified positions in the scrub-covered low foothills and paddy fields that their Japanese garrisons were determined to hold.

161st Indian Infantry Brigade frontally attacked Point 124 near Hathipauk, on 30 December – Operation Jericho – lying before Razabil, for example, but the assaulting troops were driven back by intense MG and mortar fire. This attack revealed typical problems encountered in Arakan. For six days the 4/7th Rajputs continued attacking and repeatedly reached the barbed wire trench encircling the position before been driven back by hand grenades lobbed from behind cover. It was a formidable introduction to Japanese defensive methods. As the divisional historian later wrote:

> Each scrub covered hilltop had a ring of trenches dug round the summit, and each was covered by the fire of at least one machine-gun from another hillock. When a

---

[29] 7 Ind Div Comd's Operational Notes No. 5, 15 November 1943, TNA WO 172/1943.

[30] 5 Ind Div Comd's Tactical Policy, 4 January 1944, TNA WO 172/4276.

> particular hill was attacked by our men, the defenders would fire a red Verey light and at once take cover. This was the signal for all other posts giving covering fire to open up with machine-guns on the post being attacked. The enemy soldiers holding the post would lob showers of hand grenades over the parapet, when the assaulting troops were only five or ten yards from the crest.[31]

Although artillery bombardment denuded the hilltop of vegetation, it had little other apparent effect. On 7 January the Japanese abandoned the position, however, after a policy of 'strangulation, starvation, and attrition were adopted'.[32]

The difficulties facing British, Indian and Gurkha troops operating further eastwards in the Kalapanzin Valley in assaulting enemy defensive positions located high on jungle-covered hillocks, combined with earlier experience at Donbaik, reinforced in Messervy's mind the need for an indirect approach, given problems locating enemy defensive localities, difficulties in suppressing them with the available artillery and the infantry's inability to advance close enough behind rolling barrages due to dense jungle. Writing on 8 January Messervy observed: 'It is NOT defeatist to recognise that our usual method of supporting inf does NOT work in the circumstances here. Recognition of this, however, does NOT mean that we are unable to capture a posn and kill JAPS – far from it. There are other ways and means.' In amplification of his earlier orders Messervy directed his brigade and battalion commanders:

> All experience in Arakan has demonstrated the utter futility of a formal infantry attack supported by artillery concentrations or barrage against organized jungle positions ... Normally, one appreciates that superior fire power and superior numbers are dominating assets. Here this is NOT so ... The right answer to capturing JAP posns and killing JAPS in this type of country and in these tactical circumstances is quite simple. It is infiltration and encirclement for which the country is extraordinarily suitable.[33]

As 7th Indian Division battled closer to the main enemy positions it became increasingly apparent, however, that infiltration tactics would not shift Japanese troops from densely held and heavily fortified positions they were determined to hold.

---

31 Antony Brett-James, *Ball of Fire. The Fifth Indian Division in the Second World War* (Aldershot, 1951), pp. 261–2.

32 Ibid., p. 262.

33 7 Ind Div Comd's Operational Notes, 8 January 1944, TNA W0 172/ 4290.

The Battle of Razabil, January 1944

The frontal assault on the Japanese heavily-defended 'fortress of hillocks' at Razabil, the eastern bastion of the main Japanese defensive position, by 5th Indian Division, in accordance with orders from 14th Army to launch a general offensive before the end of the month by infiltrating into or through the enemy's main defensive positions on the Maungdaw-Buthidaung line, was the first real test of British skill in tackling a large and elaborate Japanese defensive position since Donbaik. This self-contained formidable objective was heavily fortified with mutually supporting bunker defensive positions located in a maze of jungle-covered small hillocks and gullies and on a horseshoe-shaped central hill feature – dubbed Tortoise – near the crossroads cloaked with dense scrub and thick tiger grass, whose capture regarded by all as a vital first step to establishing a position astride the Buthidaung-Maungdaw road. From the outset it was anticipated it would be a hard nut to crack. Senior officers had clearly learnt the lesson the hard way from Donbaik that infantry attacks supported by divisional artillery was insufficient to destroy Japanese field defences. As a result XV Corps had been allocated a far larger scale of arms, equipment and ammunition than ever before deployed in Burma, including lavish support from the Strategic Air Force, a troop of 6th Medium Regiment, equipped with 5.5-inch medium guns and a regiment of Lee-Grant medium tanks.

161st Indian Infantry Brigade, led by Brigadier 'Daddy' Warren, began its frontal attack on the Razabil Fortress – Operation Jonathan – on 26 January 1944. The initial aerial bombardment of positions on Tortoise indicated by Vultee Vengeance dive-bombers – employing 16 Liberator heavy bombers and 12 Mitchell medium bombers from the Strategic Air Force and a further 16 dive-bombers from Third Tactical Air Force looked spectacular from the distance. Despite careful target indication by other dive-bombers it proved inaccurate and ineffective in practice with several tanks suffering damage after bombs dropped short and had little impact on the defences. Similarly an intense bombardment by corps medium and divisional field and mountain artillery had little apparent effect on the enemy will to resist, although it cleared vegetation cloaking the hillsides and briefly neutralised enemy positions.

The assaulting 4/7th Rajputs, supported by Lee-Grants of C Squadron, 25th Dragoons (initially withdrawn 1,000 yards for safety reasons because of the preliminary air attack), made good initial progress. Since the low hills were too steep and densely vegetated for the supporting armour to climb onto the final objective, a slow, methodical 20-minute shoot was carried out from the valley floors by the 25th Dragoon's tanks that destroyed all located enemy bunkers. The deeply-dug Japanese defences on Tortoise, however, proved far more elaborate than initially thought. Unfortunately the advancing Rajputs failed to move sufficiently closely behind the barrage and during the brief interlude between the artillery and tanks ceasing fire and the final assault being made the Japanese recovered and manned firing slits in bunkers, foxholes or nearby trenches on the little hillocks east of the road. Although the assaulting infantry eventually got onto the lower slopes of the northern end of the main Razabil Ridge feature, they were held up ten yards from their final objectives by still intact Japanese bunkers that came to life, and driven off by defensive MG fire, grenades and mortar fire brought down on the position from previously undisclosed bunkers on reverse slopes or on neighbouring hill features. Since they were incapable of climbing the steep jungle-covered hillocks the Lee-Grant tanks proved unable to deal with these reverse slopes defences that brought the infantry, lacking weapons of their own to destroy them, to a grinding halt. This first engagement set the pattern for the rest of Operation Jonathan. Over the next three days repeated infantry attacks were made on Tortoise and surrounding hillocks with artillery and tank support, gradually encountering growing albeit ineffective anti-tank fire, from different directions to no avail and at a heavy cost in lives. A supporting attack on the densely jungle-covered Wrencat Hill on 28 January by 123rd Indian Infantry Brigade saw further refinement of British methods, with Lee-Grants tanks on this occasion maintaining fire, after supporting artillery concentrations had lifted, until the last minute of the assault using AP to avoid inflicting casualties on the assaulting 1/17th Dogras. Despite destructive shoots by tanks, medium artillery and close support by mountain artillery and MMGs, Japanese positions on reverse slopes and neighbouring hills forced them back from the positions initially captured on this steep cone-shaped hill feature. On 30 January with casualties mounting and little progress made Operation Jonathan was finally called off.

The ill-fated frontal attack on Razabil ended in bitter disappointment like that at Donbaik a year before, despite initial high hopes that aerial bombardment, heavy artillery and tanks would unlock the enemy defences. The key problems facing attacking troops that emerged at Razabil and Wrencat were how to keep the Japanese defenders' heads down during the first phase of an assault, how to neutralise incoming defensive fire from previously hidden neighbouring positions, and perhaps most significantly, how to cross the last 50 yards of exposed ground after covering fire had ceased to assault enemy bunkers before the occupants had recovered sufficiently to offer resistance. As Slim later wrote in his memoirs: 'It was the old problem of the First World War – how to get the infantryman onto his enemy without a pause in the covering fire that kept the enemy's head down.'[34] Several important lessons had been learnt from this bitter defeat, however, about handling both supporting AFVs and artillery in the attack.

The infantry bore the brunt of the work and casualties during deliberate assaults on Japanese positions in Arakan. The inability of the supporting arms to suppress the Japanese defences meant assault troops fell back on the careful use of ground, fire and movement, the hours of darkness and smokescreens to close with enemy bunkers. It seldom proved enough, however, to capture enemy positions unaided. A range of new weapons in addition to No. 36 Grenades, however, assisted assaulting troops, in winkling Japanese troops out of bunkers and consolidating captured positions on the few occasions they successfully run the gauntlet of defensive fire, including M9A1 rifle grenades and easily constructed pole charges made from lengths of bamboo onto which were taped blocks of Ammonol explosive fitted with a 4–20 second fuse.

The tactics of tank-infantry cooperation during assaults on fortified Japanese positions were far from settled at the beginning of Operation Jonathan, but had displayed considerable promise. The 25th Dragoons had discovered at Razabil that the lengthy time between the artillery and tank fire lifting and the infantry's final assault had allowed the Japanese to man their defences. A key lesson that emerged from the attack on Wrencat, however, was that the accuracy of the Lee-Grant's flat-trajectory 75mm main gun had not been fully appreciated by tank crews and infantry alike and was such that it could maintain fire in extremely close proximity to them without risking undue casualties. The necessity for identifying and then engaging enemy defences on reverse slopes from the flank or rear by AFVs firing from the valley floor was also now fully appreciated by tank crew, although finding suitable fire positions to do so presented difficulties. Following Operation Jonathan, the 25th Dragoons and supporting infantry refined old methods of tank-infantry cooperation specifically for overcoming bunkers, with Major Hugh Ley, the 2/ic of the 25th Dragoons playing a leading part.[35] A technique quickly evolved for tank-infantry cooperation that bridged the gap in covering fire given to assault troops and ultimately saved many lives. The Lee-Grant used its highly accurate 75mm main gun in slow, methodical shoots firing super-quick HE shells to strip vegetation and remove camouflage, solid AP rounds to loosen up packed soil and then delayed HE shells to blast apart bunkers at close range. The Lees would then switch to firing accurate solid AP shot and Browning MG fire to suppress the surviving Japanese defences

[34] Slim, op. cit., p. 250.

[35] Tom Grounds, *Some Letters from Burma. The Story of the 25th Dragoons at War* (London, nd), p. 49.

without endangering the advancing infantry until they had covered the last 25 yards and actually entered the Japanese defensive positions.

The Royal Artillery learnt much about handling artillery in the jungle. The delay imposed by thick jungle on movement to troops on foot, however, meant to an extent the creeping barrage fell out of favour during Second Arakan. Instead, greater reliance was placed on firing accurate, heavy artillery concentrations employing 5.5-inch medium guns, 25-pounders and 3.7-inch howitzers, to soften up positions and on given objectives during attacks, despite the recognised fact that fire from field and mountain artillery had clear limitations, especially in the last phase of the assault when it lifted to prevent 'friendly' casualties. A report by the Director, Royal Artillery (DRA) in India Command summed up:

> Concentrations by the Corps and Div arty have been fired over advancing infantry, This has resulted in extensive, accurate and very heavy fire being put down for a considerable period but is not always satisfactory. The Japanese fire was neutralised, the jungle destroyed or thinned and a certain amount of damage done to defences, though most by lucky shots. The infantry were able to approach the objective under this cover, but had to assault the top of the hill without arty sp and were either driven off or prevented from capturing the objective by fire from the posn or supporting areas.[36]

The vital importance of maintaining fire until the last moment on objectives in increasingly close proximity to the assault troops and suppressing all identified or suspected enemy defences on all neighbouring hill features, from where MGs, mortar and artillery fire could be brought to bear on attacking troops, was a major lesson learnt at Razabil and Wrencat by the gunners

The Royal Artillery made growing use of single six-pounder anti-tank guns during the spring of 1944 in Arakan in a sniping role for accurate 'bunker-busting', with assaulting infantry able to close safely within five to ten yards of the point where solid AP rounds were hitting during attacks. A report by 5th Indian Division noted: 'Single guns have been dealing very successfully with all types of bunkers and gunners are confident they can get a bullseye in 15 rounds.'[37] Although newly-available 5.5" medium guns were reserved primarily for indirect use, carrying out slow, destructive shoots directed by an observation post in the frontline, to soften up and destroy bunker defences at ranges of 1,500–3,000 yards, medium artillery were laboriously manhandled on several occasions into the front line as close as 800 yards from target and used in a direct

---

36 R.A. Notes No. 15, 15 April 1944, OIOC L/WS/1/1330.

37 5 Ind Div Weekly Newsletter, 28 January 1944, TNA WO 172/276.

fire role. The 5.5-inch gun quickly proved highly effective in devastating areas and destroying individual bunkers firing on average under 15 rounds.[38] On one occasion during the Japanese Ha-Go offensive a 5.5-inch medium gun was taken within 800 yards of a Japanese position on the Ngakeydauk Pass and using direct fire destroyed a bunker and the hill top where it had been built with five rounds. A note by the DRA India Command warned: 'The use of Medium artillery in this way should be confined to very special occasions when necessity requires it and the ground makes it possible.'[39]

The limitations of air support had been exposed during the initial attack on Razabil, which had had little apparent impact on either the Japanese defences or morale. The attacking troops had had to stand well back for safety and the time taken to advance through the jungle to reach the objective allowed the alerted defenders to recover. The close air support provided by two Vultee Vengeance squadrons, which made 28 attacks between 1 January–3 February 1944 in support of 7th Indian and 5th Indian Divisions, proved more effective in softening up enemy positions and thickening up covering fire. Even so the effects of dive-bombing generally proved disappointing, with the jungle and terrain limiting blast effect apart from clearing vegetation and it proved virtually impossible to secure a direct hit on carefully camouflaged bunkers that presented such a tiny target from the air. Even very near misses by 1,000lb bombs had little effect. The RAF developed its own methods to keep enemy troops under cover, with Japanese defensive positions bombed several days before using delayed-action, and then unfused bombs were substituted just prior to an attack. Such 'simulated' delayed-action bombs proved successful in keeping enemy troops' heads down while the infantry rushed the position.[40]

The deliberate attacks made by XV Indian Corps on Japanese defensive positions in Arakan followed a standard pattern following Razabil, with success largely dependent on careful reconnaissance, detailed planning and elaborate supporting fire plans involving tanks, artillery and tactical airpower working closely together in a coordinated combined arms attack. As one observer who visited XV Indian Corps early in March noted: 'Fire support technique has obviously been carefully studied and the application of combined support is being carried out smoothly, effectively and efficiently.'[41] The assaulting infantry and supporting armour carried out close reconnaissance of enemy positions prior

---

[38] R.A. Notes No. 17, 15 June 1944, OIOC L/WS/1/330.

[39] R.A. Notes No. 15, 15 April 1944, OIOC L/WS/1/1330.

[40] Brig. M.R. Roberts, *Golden Arrow. The Story of 7th Indian Division in the Second World War* (Aldershot, 1952), p. 52.

[41] Tour to 15 Corps Area by Lt.-Col. S.W.M. Whitehead, GSO 1 (Trg), 11 Army Gp, 5–29 March 1944, TNA WO 203/1090.

to an assault to obtain full information about the location of enemy bunkers on forward and reverse slopes. The plan of attack was carefully coordinated with the artillery, who pounded the enemy defences before and during the assault with concentrations of 5.5-inch medium, 25-pounder, 3.7-inch howitzer fire to clear vegetation, suppress the Japanese defences on and around the objective and demoralise the defenders. Under this cover the infantry advanced to their startlines and supporting tanks to positions from which enemy bunkers could be brought under direct fire from the front, flank and if possible rear. The infantry crossed the start line under covering direct tank fire that continued until the infantry were within 25 yards of the objective and which then changed to AP shot and then coaxial Browning over their heads. As the infantry made the final assault artillery concentrations shifted onto all nearby hill features from where defensive fire might originate. As one officer later wrote: 'The above is a broad picture of how nearly all the tank/infantry actions in the ARAKAN were conducted, though the plan was capable of considerable variation.'[42]

The overriding lesson learnt from XV Indian Corps' initial advance and abortive attack on Razabil was that a slow, costly direct assault on a Japanese fortified position should be avoided whenever possible. During the rest of the campaign the tactics of infiltration were increasingly employed at battalion and brigade level exploiting the cover provided by the dense jungle and the intricate terrain in Arakan to move large bodies of troops undetected by the Japanese. The successful Battle of Second Razabil in March 1944 fought by 5th Indian Division, exploiting Japanese weakness and disorganisation following the failed Ha-Go offensive, was a striking demonstration of the effectiveness of infiltration on larger scale. While 123rd Indian Infantry Brigade simulated a frontal attack from the north, 161st Indian Infantry Brigade successfully penetrated unopposed through the jungle behind the Razabil Fortress facilitating its quick capture. Based partly on Japanese methods and inspired by the successes achieved against the Japanese outpost line and Australians troops in New Guinea, this change in tactical approach was primarily made possible by the vastly improved confidence and jungle training of British Commonwealth troops and the growing availability of air supply. A report on the lessons of Arakan submitted by 14th Army in February 1944 stated:

> The chief lesson that we have learned is that the reduction of a Jap bunkered and dug-outed position is a slow business. The successes that we have achieved have been due almost wholly to the 'Five of Diamonds' method, that is the isolating of the Jap position – or a portion of it – so that supplies and reinforcements cannot

42 R.A. Notes No. 21, 15 October 1944, OIOC L/WS/1/1331.

> reach it. The Jap reaction to this is first violent counter attacks, both from the Jap positions and from outside which give us an opportunity if we are properly dug in to inflict heavy casualties, and, later, when these attacks fail, attempts to get out.[43]

Unfortunately this new approach had serious drawbacks, in that it was time consuming, required large numbers of troops on the ground and in certain circumstances was simply not an option leaving little alternative other than a slow, expensive and frequently unsuccessful deliberate assault.

Conclusion

The self-confident and now fully jungle-trained British-Indian Army had by the early spring of 1944 successfully developed two innovative new approaches – carefully coordinated combined arms attacks and large-scale infiltration – for capturing heavily fortified Japanese defensive positions composed of bunkers at acceptable cost. These new methods were quickly disseminated throughout 14th Army and India Command and stood the test of battle during the crushing defeat of the Japanese Ha-Go offensive in Assam at Kohima and in and around the Imphal Plain, with only minor modifications introduced to suit the terrain and changes in Japanese defensive tactics. The lengthy period from mid 1943 onwards spent studying the best means of overcoming Japanese mutually supporting bunker positions, experimentation with different minor tactics, weapons and equipment and lastly the lessons learnt at the 'sharp end' had paid dividends, with the Japanese bunker having effectively been 'debunked'.

The conduct of a deliberate combined arms attack on prepared Japanese defensive positions remained until the end of the Second World War the single greatest tactical problem facing British Commonwealth units in Burma – difficult, time consuming and expensive in casualties – given Japanese skill at siting, constructing and doggedness in holding defensive positions. It was arguably their greatest military strength in contrast to often ill-thought out, stereotyped and badly implemented attacks. Although avoided whenever possible, on occasion there was little alternative other than mounting a deliberate frontal attack when the Japanese held vitally important positions. Such operations always required careful reconnaissance to pinpoint all defensive bunkers, meticulous planning, the marshalling of overwhelming fire support and close cooperation between the three of arms of service and the RAF working together in a 'colossal crump' that kept casualties at a minimum. It was a lesson driven home during the bitter

[43] Lessons from Operations, February 1944, TNA PRO WO 231/20.

attritional battle at Kohima. As a report submitted by the British 2nd Division noted: 'It is beyond question that the success of the final operations for the clearance of KOHIMA was due to the mutual understanding which had by then been achieved by all arms.'[44]

The infantry – always the predominant arm in jungle fighting – shouldered the burden of the final assault and paid a high price in blood of clearing and holding Japanese defensive positions, employing elaborate battle drills for attacking, consolidating and then mopping up bunker positions. By mid 1944 infantry units had a range of weapons at their disposal to assist in addition to its own small arms and No. 36 hand grenades, including: pole charges, M191A rifle grenades, PIATS and man-pack Lifebuoy flamethrowers employed from Kohima onwards.

The medium tank – working in close cooperation with the infantry – employed either in an assault role alongside assault troops or a support role firing from nearby positions – was regarded by early/mid 1944 as an indispensable 'bunker buster'. As one British officer who joined the 4th/8th Gurkha Rifles (4/8th Gurkhas) at Kohima in mid 1944 recalled: 'If tanks were available, and latterly they generally were, and the Japanese supporting artillery grew scarce, bunker busting became routine and inexpensive ... Once a couple of bunkers from the interlocking chain had been knocked out, the rest fell quickly, for they could be approached from a blind side.'[45]

The supporting Royal Artillery always played an important supporting role by firing increasingly heavy concentrations with medium, field and mountain guns to 'soften up' enemy defensive positions, clear vegetation and expose bunkers to view, undermine enemy morale and most importantly suppress defensive fire from neighbouring positions when attacks were made. An assortment of weapons – six-pounder anti-tank guns firing AP shot and 3.7-inch howitzers firing HE were regularly employed in a direct 'sniping' role against bunkers. In particular, 5.5-inch Medium Guns, firing over open sight 100lb shells fitted with delayed action fuses, were employed in a direct role carrying out slow, methodical destructive shoots that proved devastatingly effective against bunkers. As one report noted: 'Whatever fighting has been going on there has always been a demand for Medium Artillery, and it has played a leading part in killing Japs and gaining us successes.'[46]

The RAF, IAF and latterly the USAAF, exploiting Allied air superiority, greatly assisted ground troops during both the softening up phase and the

44 2nd Div General Lessons from the Attack, nd, TNA WO 203/1980.

45 Patrick Davis, *A Child at Arms* (London, 1970), p. 93.

46 Extracts from paper by Fourteenth Army on the Standard Division, 22 April 1944, TNA WO 203/2265.

final assault on Japanese defensive positions. At Kohima, Hurribombers and Vultee Vengeance dive-bombers provide a fast, flexible source of firepower at the disposal of British commanders during bombing and strafing attacks that cleared vegetation, inflicted casualties on troops in the open, had considerable nuisance value and proved good for Allied morale. Unfortunately the pin-point accuracy needed to hit individual bunkers, however, still eluded Allied pilots.

The British high command ensured these two very different approaches to capturing Japanese defensive positions were carefully studied during training in India Command and throughout 14th Army in 1944–45. The drills and minor tactics to deal with bunker positions, for example, were practised over captured or dummy Japanese positions and refined at Kohima and in and around the Imphal Plain by British Commonwealth troops as 14th Army prepared itself to liberate Burma.[47] Although the basic approach remained unaltered until the end of the war, further refinements were made moreover in 'bunker-busting' techniques, most notably the regular employment of 'Earthquake' air strikes, using strategic and medium bombers, on prepared Japanese defensive positions. Such knowledge and training stood 14th Army in good stead during the 1944–45 campaign as it swept across central Burma.

---

[47] A.C. Bickersteth, Odtaa *Being Extracts from the Diary of an Officer who Served with the 4/10th Gurkha Rifles in Manipur and Burma* (Aberdeen, 1953), p. 95.

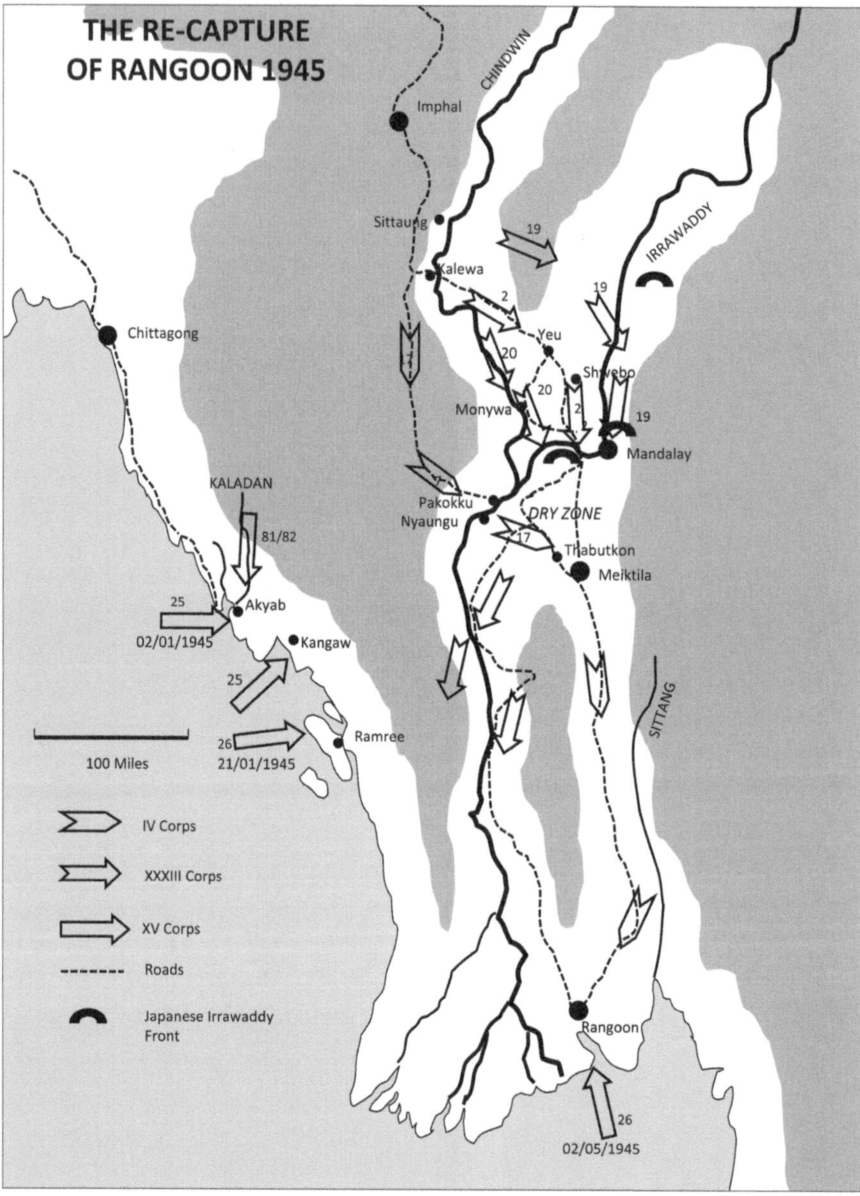

Map 7.1 The Re-capture of Rangoon 1945

Chapter 7

The Re-capture of Rangoon, 1945: The Last and Greatest Victory of the British Indian Army

Graham Dunlop

> This was the old Indian Army going down to the attack, for the last time in history, exactly two hundred and fifty years since the Honourable East India Company had enlisted its first ten sepoys on the Coromandel Coast.
>
> John Masters[1]

On 16 November 1944, the 19th Indian Division, commanded by Major General T.W. 'Pete' Rees, a fiery little Welshman, often to be seen – and heard – leading his men in song as ferociously as he commanded them in battle, crossed the Chindwin at Sittaung and headed eastwards for the Irrawaddy. There they were to meet up with a Chinese army advancing southwards from north Burma. Travelling across country on jungle tracks, making little use of mechanised transport and relying almost exclusively on airborne logistic support, the 19th Division made rapid progress. Thus began the final series of operations that resulted in the destruction of the Japanese Army in central Burma and the re-conquest of the country. Burma was re-captured from the Japanese by an American-led, primarily Chinese, army in the northern part of the country and a British-led, predominantly Indian, army group operating in the central and western part. The latter of these, on which this paper focuses, was the main overall contributor. Its part in the re-conquest of Burma was the last conventional battle fought by the British Indian Army, and was arguably its finest hour. Before examining the justification for that claim, however, it will help to take a brief look at the narrative of the battle.

A little over a month after the start of the 19th Division's advance, over the Christmas period of 1944, the remaining forces of 13 Indian Corps followed on. Major General Douglas Gracey's 20th Indian Division crossed the Chindwin

1 John Masters, *The Road Past Mandalay* (London, Cassell, 2002), p. 311.

a little south of Sittaung. The division followed the general line of the river's east bank, supplied by air, mule and river craft, to capture the important town of Monywa. At about the same time the more heavily mechanised 2nd British Division, commanded by Major General C.G.C. Nicholson, broke out of a bridgehead on the east bank of the Chindwin at Kalewa, further south still, and set off eastwards, clearing the road to Ye-U and Shwebo, opening the 14th Army's main overland supply route, which lay between the two Indian divisions.

In November 1944, when the 19th Division's advance began, Lieutenant General Bill Slim, commanding the 14th Army, was under orders just to capture the Shwebo Plain, in the great bend of the Irrawaddy River north west of Mandalay, and link up with the Chinese coming down from the north. This he was to do in order to secure the ground and air space required for the construction of a new road being built by US Army engineers, under the appropriately named Brigadier General Pick, from north east India into China. That road was intended to re-open the overland link to Chiang Kai Shek's forces, which had been isolated from any ground contact with the outside world since the Japanese capture of Burma in 1942, during which time they had been sustained entirely by air. Throughout the war in South East Asia, as far as the Americans were concerned, the principal objective of any fighting in Burma had been, and remained, to support the Chinese, diverting the enemy away from the American main effort in the Pacific and Philippines. They had no interest whatsoever in helping the British recover their lost Far East Empire, indeed they were hostile to that idea. Since the Americans provided an ever increasing share of the Allied war effort, their intentions became more and more influential in Allied strategic plans. Whatever imperial aspirations might have been harboured by the British, their part of the offensive in Burma was regarded formally by the Combined Chiefs of Staff as just a supporting operation on a subsidiary front in the second priority war. Consequently, Slim's tactical objectives and resources were constrained. When the 14th Army started to cross the Chindwin, the limit of its exploitation was to be the line of the Irrawaddy from Mandalay round to Pakokku, near the junction with the Chindwin. Any further liberation of Burmese territory was a longer term objective, to be achieved by an amphibious assault in the area of Rangoon, most probably no earlier than the autumn of 1945, once the summer monsoon was over.[2] Slim's offensive, however, was destined to achieve results way beyond Allied expectations or intentions. It was known as Operation CAPITAL and Slim had two corps with which to carry it out. IV

---

2 *Report to the Combined Chiefs of Staff by the Supreme Allied Commander South East Asia, 30 June 1947* (hereafter *SEAC Report*), pp. 81–5. Major General S. Woodburn Kirby and others (eds), *History of the Second World War, The War against Japan, Volume IV* (hereafter Woodburn Kirby, *Official History*) (London, HMSO, 1965), pp. 101–11.

Corps, commanded by Lieutenant General Sir Frank Messervy, comprised the 7th, 17th and 19th Indian Divisions, and 255 Indian Tank Brigade. XXXIII Corps, commanded by Lieutenant General Sir Montague Stopford, comprised the 2nd British and 20th Indian Divisions, as well as 254 Indian Tank Brigade. In reserve within the 14th Army were the 5th Indian and 11th East African Divisions along with three independent infantry brigades, two of which were Indian and one East African.[3]

Slim knew that destroying the enemy's army, or at least its ability to fight, was far more important to the success of his mission than seizing ground. In fact it was crucial. Even in the winter dry season he could sustain only four and two thirds divisions in Burma due to the limited capacity of his lines of communication from Imphal, where the 14th Army had stopped the Japanese invasion of India in June 1944. When the wet south west monsoon broke in May 1945, he would have to reduce his force levels still further due to the difficulty of maintaining them along the one tenuous road through the jungle-covered mountains on the Indo/Burmese border and in the extremely hazardous flying conditions likely to be encountered during the rains. Intelligence suggested the forces ranged against him might be up to eight enemy divisions and a tank regiment, albeit three of those divisions were thought to be deployed on the Arakan coast while others were still suffering from the attrition they had experienced in the earlier fighting at Imphal and Kohima.[4] The Japanese Army in Burma was undoubtedly inferior to the 14th Army in armour, artillery and air-power. But Slim could not supply his heavy weapons with all the ammunition necessary to use them to best effect due to the logistic constraints under which he had to fight. The Japanese could still be reinforced and re-equipped, and they had good lines of communication back to their base at Rangoon. In any event, the cunning, courage and tenacity of the Japanese soldier in defence with his back to the wall were not to be under-estimated. In the difficult terrain of central and southern Burma, this enemy would be a very hard nut to crack.

Slim anticipated bringing the Japanese to battle actually on the Shwebo Plain, his tactical objective, where he could make best use of his superiority in materiel and fire-power. He needed to win that battle decisively before the monsoon broke, and he planned initially to use both 4 and 33 Corps alongside each other. Until late in the day, intelligence suggested that the Shwebo Plain was also where the Japanese intended to fight. However, in late November and early

---

3 Woodburn Kirby, *Official History*, pp. 472–86.

4 *SEAC Report*, p. 99 and map 22, opposite p. 96. The National Archive (hereafter TNA), WO 172/6863, 14th Army and 3rd Tactical Air Force Joint Appreciation and Outline Plan, Operation CHAMPION (the preceding name for Operation CAPITAL), undated.

December 1944, even as the 14th Army were starting to cross the Chindwin, the picture began to change, and it became increasingly clear that the enemy were pulling back across the Irrawaddy to defend its south eastern bank either side of Mandalay, using the river as an obstacle.[5] And a formidable one it was, running at up to half a mile wide with currents of up to four knots and shifting sand bars to hinder the passage of assault craft and ferries. Slim could not just seize the ground vacated by the Japanese and leave their forces intact on the far side of the Irrawaddy, for he could not guarantee to contain them there after he had reduced his own forces in readiness for the summer monsoon. But he had neither the resources nor the time before the anticipated arrival of the monsoon in May to destroy the enemy by a simple head-on assault across the Irrawaddy followed by a battle of attrition on the far bank. He had to use more sophisticated means of achieving his aim within the time available and settled instead on a bold outflanking manoeuvre to isolate the Japanese front, precipitating its rapid collapse by threatening its rear and cutting its lines of communication. Then he could destroy the enemy in detail after they had been forced to abandon their main prepared defensive line on the Irrawaddy. That, however, meant dividing his already barely adequate forces.

In Slim's revised plan, 33 Corps would take under command the 19th Indian Division, actually part of 4 Corps but already across the Irrawaddy north of Mandalay, and engage the Japanese head-on across the river either side of Mandalay. Meanwhile, 4 Corps, now comprising just the 7th and 17th Indian Divisions, along with 255 Indian Tank Brigade, was to change its role completely. Instead of fighting alongside 33 Corps on the Shwebo Plain, it was to move covertly down the west side of the Chindwin to cross the Irrawaddy near Pakokku, some 50 miles behind the Japanese left flank. Then the 17th Division and 255 Tank Brigade, led by Major General D.T. 'Punch' Cowan, were to race across the arid 'dry zone' of central Burma to seize the town of Meiktila, which lies on the road and rail routes between Mandalay and Rangoon, before the Japanese could react and strengthen the defences of the town. Slim reasoned that the Japanese would be compelled to weaken their front in order to try and recapture Meiktila to re-open their lines of communication, and that would give 33 Corps the chance to break up the enemy's defences on the Irrawaddy line. But the 17th Division and 255 Tank Brigade would have to hold onto Meiktila until 33 Corps could relieve them, and that could mean withstanding a lengthy siege. The revised plan became known as Operation EXTENDED CAPITAL, and it was a high risk venture, both tactically and logistically.

---

5 *SEAC Report*, pp. 100–101.

With insufficient troops to secure a line of communication to Meiktila as well as holding the town against the anticipated Japanese counter attacks, the 17th Division would have to be maintained entirely by air. At the same time, much of the rest of the 14th Army would be dependant upon air supply as well, due to the limited capacity of the one road between India and Burma. There were just sufficient transport aircraft to cope but potential crisis would lurk in the shadows throughout the operation for many of those aircraft were American and likely to be diverted to other tasks without notice – as, indeed, they were.[6] In any case, the maximum economic radius of action of the Dakota aircraft, the principal supply aircraft, was just 250 miles. Beyond that distance, the payload the aircraft could carry was reduced dramatically and exponentially to allow for the additional fuel required. Meiktila lies just over 250 miles from Imphal and Chittagong, the two nearest supply base airfields capable of supporting the 14th Army in central Burma. Therefore a parallel amphibious and overland operation would have to be mounted on the Arakan coast to seize the Japanese-held airfield at Akyab, which lies well within the 250-mile radius of Meiktila and which had a small port, through which the air supply operation could itself be sustained.[7] This supporting offensive was to be mounted by Lieutenant General Sir Philip Christison's 15 Corps, comprising the 25th and 26th Indian Divisions, the 81st West African Division, the 50th Indian Tank Brigade and the British 3rd Commando Brigade. As well as capturing the airfield at Akyab, it was thought that an offensive on the Arakan coast should also tie down substantial numbers of enemy troops, who would consequently be unable to oppose the 14th Army, as well as protecting the port of Chittagong, which was a major point of entry to the 14th Army's lines of communication. Until the start of Operation CAPITAL, 15 Corps had been part of the 14th Army but, in order to allow Slim to concentrate on operations in central Burma, it had been removed from his command and placed directly under Allied Land Forces South East Asia (ALFSEA), commanded by General Sir Oliver Leese. While this reorganisation simplified Slim's immediate task by limiting the geographical area on which he had to focus his attention, it added an additional level of command with concomitant potential complexities in the essential coordination of progress and priorities on the two fronts.

Despite hard fighting and the huge logistic risks involved, the operation went ahead as planned. The 19th Indian Division made good progress despite crossing appalling country with only narrow, difficult tracks, and closed up on the Irrawaddy, some 40 miles north of Mandalay, on 11 January 1945.

6 Ibid., p. 104.

7 Ibid., p. 107.

Encountering little opposition on the near bank, they 'bounced' a crossing using what local boats they could find as well as improvised rafts in order to maintain the momentum of their advance. The Division's Bren Gun carriers were fitted with flotation tanks fashioned from empty oil drums and floated across under their own power, using their tracks as propellers. In this configuration they were used also as armoured ambulance ferries to bring casualties back across the river with some degree of protection. Once established on the far side of the river the 19th Division fought off a series of ferocious counter attacks on their bridgehead before continuing the advance on Mandalay down the east bank of the river.

The 20th Indian Division, followed by the 2nd British, crossed the Irrawaddy to the west of Mandalay during the latter part of February, overcoming fierce opposition on the far bank. The two divisions had to cross consecutively due to a severe shortage of assault craft and ferries, and sufficient numbers were found only by salvaging barges sunk by the Japanese during their withdrawal across the river. Having no diving equipment, the Indian Engineers improvised underwater breathing apparatus from gas masks, rubber hosepipes and workshop compressors. This was another prime example of the innovation that characterised the way the 14th Army had to fight at the end of its tenuous lines of communication, almost at the bottom of Allied war priorities, and was so effective it was taken into formal use by the Royal Engineers as an authorised expedient device for diving operations in the field.[8]

Once 33 Corps was established ashore on the south east bank of the river, the 2nd Division swung to the east, behind Mandalay, to cut the city's local lines of communication, while the 20th Division covered the right flank by pressing the Japanese southwards towards Meiktila. The Japanese defended Mandalay with the anticipated fanatical determination, finally holding out in the ancient Fort Dufferin against an attack that Slim described as resembling a siege in the time of the Indian Mutiny, with 33 Corps' medium artillery firing over open sights to blow a breach in the walls.[9] The city eventually fell to the 19th Indian Division on the night of 19/20 March 1945.

Meanwhile, 4 Corps made its way covertly 400 miles from Imphal down the west bank of the Chindwin to its confluence with the Irrawaddy near Pakokku, where the corps was due to cross. To maintain the secrecy of the operation, it was completed under radio silence and supported by a complex deception plan, while

8 *The Second World War 1939–1945, Army Supplies and Transport Volume II* (War Office, 1954), p. 86. *The Second World War 1939–1945, Army Military Engineering (Field)* (War Office, 1952), p. 109. *Royal Engineers Training Memorandum 17*, August 1945, pp. 133–4.

9 Field Marshal Sir William Slim, *Defeat into Victory* (hereafter, Slim, *Defeat Into Victory*) (London, Cassell, 1956), p. 469.

scouting enemy aircraft were kept at arm's length by the Allied air force. The route was so bad that it could not sustain logistic traffic once the main body of 4 Corps had passed, so the corps was maintained almost completely by air, having to clear landing strips out of the bush as it went. The 7th Indian Division forced its way across the Irrawaddy between Pakokku and Nyaungu on 13 February 1945 in what was the longest assault river crossing of the entire Second World War.[10] Again, the assault was made with the barest minimum of proper craft and many of those that did arrive were badly worn or damaged from the long, rough road journey. The crossing very nearly came to grief when some of the first waves were swept away on the current. Nevertheless, the 7th Division eventually established a secure bridgehead and, on 21 February, 255 Tank Brigade and two brigades of the 17th Division, mounted in trucks, broke out for their dash to Meiktila. About 10 miles short of their objective, they seized the Japanese-held airfield at Thabutkon and the third brigade of the 17th Division, for whom there been insufficient vehicles, were flown in whilst the airfield was still under fire. By 7 March, Cowan's combined force had captured Meiktila from its 12,000 Japanese defenders and then had to hold the town, besieged, against continuous counter-attacks, until the Japanese finally withdrew in the face of 33 Corps' advance on 28 March. During this time, much of the fiercest fighting took place over the very airfield through which they were being sustained, and aircraft frequently landed and took off through the cross fire.

On the Arakan coast, Akyab was captured – actually without a fight – on 2 January 1945 by the 25th Indian Division and the British 3rd Commando Brigade. The Japanese garrison had already withdrawn, laying waste to much of the town and the facilities needed to run air supply operations in support of the 14th Army. Meanwhile, the 81st West African Division, soon to be replaced by the 82nd, advanced southwards down the nearby Kaladan Valley, driving the Japanese there before them. Fresh from the seizure of Akyab, elements of the 25th Indian Division and 3rd Commando Brigade were put ashore again at Kangaw, near Akyab, to cut the Japanese escape route in front of the Africans. Despite very hard fighting, the block was not entirely successful as substantial enemy forces managed to by-pass it, exfiltrating through the jungle. However, there followed a protracted amphibious battle in the mangrove swamps along the Arakan coast, harrying significant numbers of Japanese and attempting to prevent their movement east, over the hills, to reinforce the defence of central Burma against the 14th Army's advance. Whilst all this was going on, a good deal of engineer and logistic work was required to repair the port at Akyab and

[10] Woodburn Kirby, *Official History*, pp. 264–6.

to extend and stock the airfield, but by mid-March 60 Dakotas were flying out of Akyab, operating in support of the 17th Division fighting at Meiktila.

Even as these battles were just starting, in early January, it became clear that the remnants of the enemy would have to be pursued southwards and destroyed, and that Rangoon would have to be captured and opened before the monsoon broke in May. Otherwise the 14th Army would have to withdraw much of its forces back across the Irrawaddy – and possibly even across the Chindwin – as it would be impossible to sustain them at such distance from India by air and overland means during the monsoon. That in turn would allow the enemy an opportunity to re-group, reinforce and return to the offensive, which would signal the failure of Slim's mission. Thus the limit of exploitation and, indeed, the very purpose of the operation were suddenly much extended. What had started out as a limited offensive to secure the new road to China became effectively the re-capture of Burma. However, despite the second decisive victory soon to be achieved over the Japanese on the Irrawaddy, it was not to be an easy pursuit. By the time the Irrawaddy front finally collapsed at the end of March, there were only some 30 days left before the monsoon was due, and it is 300 miles by road from Meiktila to Rangoon. The 14th Army's logistic capacity was sufficient only to sustain one corps all the way to Rangoon. The other corps would have to be limited to providing flank security. The speed required of the advance demanded that the priority for engineering effort would have to be directed to ensuring the mobility of the divisions at the front of the corps on the main axis rather than maintaining the lines of communication. Once again, therefore, the operation would rely heavily on air supply, and the mechanised forces leading the advance would require a high rate of daily maintenance – estimated at some 1,200 tons per day. That figure was calculated to be the very limit of what the aircraft available could deliver over the distances involved. Akyab alone would not be able to sustain the rate of flying required and, in any case, the last 80 miles or so of the route to Rangoon were beyond the critical 250 mile radius from that field.[11] For this reason the operations on the Arakan coast had to be extended to seize a second airfield at Ramree, 70 miles south of Akyab, from where the whole route from Meiktila to Rangoon lay within 250 miles. The timely arrival of the long-promised amphibious ships and landing craft of Naval Force 'W' made this possible along with further operations, mounted and maintained by sea, to prevent the Japanese defenders of Ramree escaping through the mangrove swamps where overland movement was virtually impossible. On 21 January 1945, the 26th Indian Division landed on Ramree Island, this time against heavy opposition, supported by the guns of the Eastern Fleet, including those of

---

[11] *SEAC Report*, Map opposite p. 112.

the battleship HMS Queen Elizabeth, which had first spoken in anger 30 years previously during another amphibious operation – at Gallipoli.

The capture of Ramree and continuing operations on the Arakan coast required some ferocious fighting by 15 Corps, but the second airfield was operating by mid-April, just in time to sustain the latter part of the 14th Army's final advance to Rangoon. 4 Corps led the way down the Sittang Valley, with the 5th and 17th Indian Divisions, both now mechanised, leapfrogging each other. The 19th Indian Division, now returned to 4 Corps but still mainly on its feet, mopped up Japanese stragglers by-passed by the other two divisions and secured the east flank of the corps against counter attack from the Shan States. 33 Corps advanced parallel to 4 Corps down the Irrawaddy Valley to the west, securing 4 Corps' right flank against any interference from Japanese troops managing to escape from the Arakan coast. Aerial supply was directed almost exclusively on 4 Corps, while 33 Corps and the 14th Army rear area were sustained mainly by river transport, for which the ALFSEA engineers built and ran a fleet of barges made out of local timber on the Chindwin and powered by tugs brought in pieces by rail and road from India. Among the cargoes carried by this makeshift barge fleet were heavy railway locomotives with which to run the railways of central and southern Burma once they had been re-captured.

In the event, the monsoon broke slightly earlier than expected, while the leading elements of 4 Corps were still some 30 miles from Rangoon, and the 14th Army's advance ground almost to a halt in mud and swollen rivers just short of its final objective. Slim had foreseen the possibility of his failure to reach Rangoon before the rains, however, and had asked General Leese to prepare a small scale amphibious operation to seize the port in that event. The 26th Indian Division, fresh from fighting on the Arakan coast, along with the 50th Indian Parachute Brigade, landed by sea and air at the mouth of the Rangoon River on 2 May 1945 only just before the deteriorating conditions rendered airborne and amphibious operations impossible. On that day, one Wing Commander Saunders, flying his Mosquito bomber on a reconnaissance mission over Rangoon observed the words 'Japs gone – extract digit' painted crudely on the roof of Rangoon jail. Landing at the nearby Mingaladon airfield and wrecking his aircraft in a bomb crater whilst doing so, Saunders discovered that the enemy had, indeed, evacuated the city. So he made his way to the docks, where, purloining a sampan, he set off down the river to inform the Navy. Troops of the 26th Division were quickly re-embarked, Rangoon was re-occupied virtually without a fight and, the following day, patrols of the 26th Division met those of the 17th Division about 10 miles north of the city. Further hard fighting was still required to mop up Japanese survivors trying to re-group in the east of the country or escape into Thailand, but effectively Burma had been re-captured, an event not anticipated to take place until the end of 1945 or even early 1946 when the 14th Army's advance began at the very end of 1944.

That, in very condensed form, is a narrative of what happened, and now it remains to examine the claim that this was the last and greatest victory of the British Indian Army. Certainly it was not their last operation. After the war ended, Indian troops went on to fight insurgents in French Indo-China and the Netherlands East Indies, and were centrally involved in internal security operations in India during the tragic period leading up to independence and partition. But this was the last major conventional battle fought by the British Indian Army – and it was, overwhelmingly, an Indian affair. Overall, the British contribution to the Burma campaign comprised three infantry divisions, two of which were not included in the 14th Army, operating instead in support of the Chinese in the north of the country; and a commando brigade, along with numerous combat and logistic support units. Three African divisions as well as an independent African brigade took part. Five Chinese divisions and an American Special Force brigade conducted separate operations in north Burma, outside the 14th Army's front but with the same ultimate objective: linking India and China. In what we might call the British Commonwealth sector, however, the one which eventually effected the re-capture of Rangoon, no less than ten Indian infantry divisions, three Indian tank brigades, an Indian parachute brigade and two independent Indian infantry brigades, one of them almost of divisional size, fought at some stage between 1942 and 1945. Some of these troops, notably the 17th Indian Division, were at the forefront of fighting almost continuously throughout the campaign. This amounted to the greatest concentration of Indian forces to be committed to any single campaign in the history of the British Indian Army. Out of this overall commitment to the campaign in Burma, Operation EXTENDED CAPITAL and the supporting operations conducted on the Arakan coast involved one British, two African and seven Indian divisions, along with one British, one African and five Indian independent brigades of various types. That is certainly the strongest concentration of Indian forces committed to any battle, or indeed any operational theatre, in either of the two World Wars of the Twentieth Century. In contrast, as the numbers of Indian personnel peaked, a crisis of British manpower was developing by late 1944. Shortly after the fall of Mandalay, the 2nd British Division and the 36th British Division, the latter of which had been fighting alongside the Chinese in the north, had to be withdrawn to India as they were proving too expensive to maintain and there were insufficient British reinforcements in the pipeline to replace losses due to enemy action, sickness or the routine repatriation of men with long service in India. For these reasons, the 14th Army's final advance from Meiktila to Rangoon and the supporting operations on the Arakan coast were almost exclusively Indian on the ground, save for the diminishing number of British units in Indian formations, chiefly (but not exclusively) artillery, signals and logistic units. Perhaps the relative proportions of Indians and British in the 14th Army and 15 Corps account for that Army's reputation as 'forgotten' in Britain. But most overlooked were the Indian naval and air forces that supported these operations. These included 27 warships and 49 minor combatant vessels of the Royal Indian Navy, along with innumerable landing and logistic support craft, as well as seven squadrons of the Royal Indian Air Force, all manned by Indians. Those people – men and women – were drawn into armed forces which expanded from 189,000 in 1939 to some 2,500,000 by 1945 – every single one of them a volunteer.[12] India produced the largest all-volunteer armed forces of any belligerent nation during the Second World War, and can lay unassailable claim to majority share-holding in the re-capture of Burma that contributed so much to victory in the East.

If it is accepted that this operation was, historically, the 'greatest' in terms of the numbers of Indian troops committed, assessing its claim to being 'the greatest' in qualitative terms is inherently more challenging. All manner of qualitative comparisons could be drawn from a wide variety of circumstances and operations over the years of the Raj. There is a compelling case, however, for stating that the re-capture of Burma was among the finest joint service, all-arms manoeuvre battles fought by the western Allies at army group level throughout the Second World War, and the lion's share of the credit must go to the Indians of all three services who contributed so much to making it happen. Slim, commanding 14th Army, the largest component force of this manoeuvre, was confronted by a desperate, cunning and tenacious enemy, holding a strong position behind a most formidable natural obstacle, and had very limited time in which to achieve his mission. He did, however, have the space and means to manoeuvre and used them to best advantage, accepting in the process enormous tactical and logistical risks. 4 Corps' 400-mile march from Imphal down the west bank of the Chindwin and the subsequent dash of the 17th Division and 255 Tank Brigade to Meiktila caught the Japanese almost completely by surprise, leaving them unable to react in sufficient strength to defend the town effectively. Holding Meiktila against sustained counter attacks for three weeks, maintained by air at the very limit of aircraft range and capability was a carefully calculated risk. Although a tried and tested technique proved in the winter fighting in the Arakan of 1943–44, it relied upon huge resilience and courage at every level from the high command to the individual soldier. Success hung in the balance throughout the operation but in the end it led directly to the

---

12 Philip Mason, *A Matter of Honour* (London, Purnell, 1974) p. 495.

quick collapse of the enemy's Irrawaddy front, giving the 14th Army time to reach Rangoon before the monsoon. It was the very epitome of the outflanking manoeuvre at which the Japanese had excelled when they were on the offensive, and which had defeated the British so comprehensively in Malaya and Burma in 1942. The term was not used then but it was absolutely what would now be described as 'manoeuvre warfare', in which a protagonist seeks to win his battle by concentrating force against his enemy's weak points, shattering his cohesion and will to resist, rather than directly confronting his strength head on. This was not a new concept, even in 1945, and the technique is as old as organised warfare. But British and Indian forces were not good at it in South East Asia until they developed the will and means required to fight off the roads and in the jungle. In the end they proved to be better at it than the Japanese, and with a truly combined arms force that generated far greater combat power than the Japanese could effectively counter. The tactic was used repeatedly at lower levels of command, as well as being emphasised in the battle drills and tactical doctrine developed by the Army in India during the war.

Following the breakout from the Irrawaddy front, the pursuit to Rangoon, again a hugely risky undertaking logistically, was conducted with urgency and skilful concentration of force, which prevented the enemy from offering any really effective organised resistance. Meanwhile, at the army group level of command, the 14th Army's manoeuvres were made possible only by 15 Corps' parallel operations on the Arakan coast, coordinated by ALFSEA, and the capture of Rangoon itself. These turned out to be the longest continuous series of amphibious battles conducted by any British Commonwealth forces in the course of the war, and were characterised by astonishing courage, determination and improvisation on the part of those involved from all three Indian services.

This form of fighting was made possible by a method of command and control which today would fall under the definition of 'Mission Command' or 'Directive Control'. Those expressions would have been unknown to Slim, although he practised the method extensively – partly because he had to and partly because it fitted into existing Indian Army practice developed during operations on the North West Frontier.[13] It is the art of giving subordinates a clear understanding of the commander's intentions and what they are to do in order to enable the commander to achieve those intentions, allocating resources and setting any parameters on freedom of action; then, crucially, letting the subordinates get on with it without constant interference from above. In short, it means telling subordinates what to achieve, not how to achieve it, trusting that they know

[13] Patrick Rose, 'British Army Command Culture 1939–1945: A Comparison of Eighth and Fourteenth Armies', PhD Thesis, King's College London, 2009, ch. 2.

how to conduct their affairs within the bounds of a commonly understood tactical doctrine. Good use of mission command is essential if subordinates are to be allowed the scope to use their initiative without repeatedly referring back for new instructions when events do not develop as expected. That use of initiative, in turn, is vital to the quick, responsive decision making needed to win a fast-moving battle such as Operation EXTENDED CAPITAL, particularly on a remote and far-flung battlefield with poor communications. It was a style of command which did not appear to come naturally to the British Army early in the war during large scale operations. To be fair, it is a good deal more difficult to use mission command in the withdrawals that characterised Allied operations early in the war than it is in the advance or attack, and it is more difficult to apply when resources are scarce than it is when they are plentiful. But resources and initiative could only be delegated properly in a fluid battle if commanders at every level were confident in the manner in which their subordinates would tackle the problems that would face them, and that confidence could only come from a commonly understood way of fighting – or tactical doctrine, imbued through training and practice. To coin a phrase, tactical doctrine is for the guidance of wise people and the blind obedience of fools. Following the disasters of 1942 and early 1943, the Army in India quickly recognised this requirement and worked hard to develop sound doctrine for large scale conventional fighting and trained in its application in combat.[14]

Slim believed wholeheartedly in the ideas of a common doctrine and mission command. He understood that as an army commander on such a widespread battlefield, with poor communications, he could not be everywhere to supervise the details of the battle. He had to give his subordinates scope for local initiative within clear parameters if he was to outfight the Japanese, who actually turned out to be notoriously bad at delegating authority, and it worked well.[15] Consequently, the Operation Instruction which launched the re-capture of Burma runs to just four sides of foolscap paper and stands as a supreme example of good mission command, trusting in the way his subordinates would fight.[16] It generated the sort of freedom of action that allowed 'Pete' Rees's 19th Division to bounce its crossing of the Irrawaddy on local and makeshift craft, without stopping to seek permission, and before Japanese reaction could turn the quick attack into a long-drawn-out deliberate assault.

---

14 For example, see 20th Indian Division Battle Instruction 1 of 44, 25 September 1944, in the Liddell Hart Centre for Military Archives, Gracey Papers, 2/24.

15 Slim, *Defeat Into Victory*, pp. 541–2.

16 Fourteenth Army Operation Instruction No. 82, 19 December 1944, TNA WO 172/4164.

Slim also realised the importance of having a thoroughly integrated ground/air organisation and, to that end, formed a completely unified joint HQ to command the 14th Army and 221 Group RAF, which provided the tactical air support.[17] The concept of joint operations had been almost entirely lacking amongst British Commonwealth forces earlier in the war, contributing much to the defeats of 1942. At the theatre level, that problem was largely addressed, though not entirely solved, by the formation of the Allied South East Asia Command in October 1943. The concept was finally adopted lower down at the tactical level after Brigadier 'Tubby' Lethbridge, subsequently Slim's Brigadier General Staff, had seen how well the Americans unified their single service commands in the Pacific.[18] Like Slim, Christison, commanding 15 Corps, on receiving his orders for the further operations on the Arakan coast, promptly formed a tri-service HQ, with Rear Admiral Martin, the Commander of Force 'W' as his Naval Commander, and Air Vice Marshal the Earl of Brandon, commanding 224 Group RAF, as the Air Commander.[19] He took this joint HQ to sea and worked afloat throughout most of the operation. At that time, this was all very up-to-date, if not futuristic, thinking in the armies of the British Commonwealth, and the 14th Army and 15 Corps were at the forefront of it.

For all the skilled tactical thinking and sophisticated methods of command and control employed at the higher level, none of this would have been possible without thoroughly competent troops of the highest quality, who could be trusted to do what was expected of them without constant close supervision. By the beginning of 1945, Indian soldiers met this definition admirably, but that had not been the case earlier in the war in South East Asia. At the start of the German war, a large proportion of the small, highly professional peacetime Indian Army was deployed to the Middle East to form the core of the 4th and 5th Indian Divisions, which carved out for themselves a fine reputation in that theatre. However, the concurrent rapid expansion of the Indian Army resulted in a marked lowering of quality among newly recruited soldiers as war with Japan approached. It was not the fault of the soldiers. Prior to 1939, India had been instructed by the British Government not to concern itself with any threat from Japan or the Far East. That would be dealt with by the Royal Navy operating out of the 'fortress' of Singapore and India was to look only towards Afghanistan and the Middle East. The Army in India was established and trained to do just that. As so often happens in peacetime, however, Britain had tried to 'punch above her weight', with a predictable and inevitable panic when the truth dawned that

17 Slim, *Defeat into Victory*, p. 411.

18 220 Mission Report, 25 March 1944, TNA WO 202/881.

19 *SEAC Report*, p. 108.

she could not meet her defence commitments as war approached. India did now have to face east into the jungle at the rush and she was not resourced to do so. Men were recruited faster than the weapons, equipment and accommodation could be built or bought to house, train and prepare them for war. They were drawn increasingly from areas and communities not already imbued with a martial tradition and required a longer period of induction and training than their professional forbears to absorb a military ethos. Due to the urgent need to deploy forces to Malaya and Burma in 1941, they would not get that time. The standard of British officers appointed to the Indian Army decreased as fast as the numbers needed increased. Again, it was not their fault. In peacetime, young officers aspiring to serve in the Indian Army were selected on the basis of their cultural and military suitability for working with Indian soldiers. The pressures of war demanded that filling spaces too often took precedence over selection for suitability but there were also accusations voiced in India that the British were dumping their worst officers on the Indian Army, saving the best for the British Army at home.[20]

For all these reasons, the standard of training and preparation of many Indian soldiers deploying to Malaya and Burma in 1941 was insufficient for the task they faced, and that was reflected in their generally poor performance in those countries during the campaigns of 1942 and early 1943. Ill-trained and ill-equipped, afraid of the jungle and tied to the roads, often poorly commanded, Indian and British troops were easily out-fought by an enemy experienced and hardened by years of fighting in China. Following the early defeats, quite substantial numbers of Indians captured in Malaya and Burma turned and joined the pro-Japanese Indian National Army (INA), largely because they lacked the *esprit de corps* that would have been bred from proper induction, training and leadership. They felt abandoned by the British and perceived service in the INA as offering an existence preferable to that in captivity. Some were affected also by the Indian nationalist movement. It has to be borne in mind, though, that much larger numbers of Indian prisoners of war stayed loyal and endured captivity despite the political pressures and the shortcomings in the way they had been prepared for war. Many individuals and units also fought well despite their inadequate preparation. Nevertheless, Wavell, then the Commander in Chief in India, recognising the causes of failure in Malaya and Burma during 1941 and 1942, felt compelled to issue a strongly-worded rallying call that needs no clarification:

---

20 Report of the Infantry Committee, 11 October 1943, TNA WO 106/4708. Letter from Director Military Training, Faults in Cadet Training, 43/Training/3255(MT14), 4 December 1943, OIOC L/WS/1/761.

> We have experienced in the five months of war against Japan a series of humiliating defeats which may tend to destroy the morale and confidence of the Army in India, unless we realise what is wrong and take steps to put it right. As a result of these defeats our fighting reputation stands low in the East at the present – a reproach which every member of the Army in India must concentrate on removing as soon as possible. It can be done by training, but only by real hard intensive training such as we have not yet undertaken. The exploits of the 4th Indian Division, which has established for itself a reputation under all conditions second to none in the Middle East, have set a standard to be aimed at by Indian troops .... Our motto should be LIVE HARD, FIGHT HARD, and when necessary DIE HARD.[21]

Sadly though, the worst was yet to come. Following a catastrophic performance in the first Arakan campaign over the winter of 1942/43, the fighting reputation of both British and Indian soldiers in South East Asia fell yet further to an all-time low.

Following the abortive first Arakan campaign, however, the nadir had been reached and recovery began. Very largely due to the efforts of Slim, General Giffard, the Commander of 11th Army Group, Field Marshal Auchinleck, the Commander in Chief in India from 1943 onwards, and many of their subordinate commanders, the quality of training and leadership in the Indian Army in South East Asia improved out of all recognition in the latter three years of the war. It is not the purpose of this chapter to examine that training in detail. That has already been done admirably and in depth by Daniel Marston and Tim Moreman.[22] It is sufficient here to record that, at last, adequate time, energy, realism and challenge were devoted to the training of individuals and units before they were committed to battle. The importance of posting high quality men to the infantry was recognised. Recruits and replacements were properly inducted into the culture and traditions of the formations and units in which they were to serve. British officers were properly trained in how to command and live alongside Indian soldiers, and ever increasing numbers of Indians were commissioned and promoted to higher ranks. Consequently, at the crucial battles of the second Arakan campaign, Kohima and Imphal during the spring and summer of 1944, when the tide of the whole Burma campaign swung in favour of the Allies, Indian soldiers demonstrated beyond doubt that they were every bit as brave, resourceful and enduring as their enemy. Most importantly,

---

21 *A Note on Training for Commanding Officers by the Commander in Chief, India*, May 1942, OIOC L/MIL/17/5/2223.

22 Daniel Marston, *Phoenix from the Ashes* (Westport CT, Praeger, 2003). Tim Moreman, *The Jungle, the Japanese and the British Commonwealth Armies at War 1941–1945* (London, Cass, 2005).

they were also generally more skilful in the field. Having been tied to the roads and easily out-manoeuvred by the Japanese in the campaigns of 1942/43, by 1944, Indian troops were thoroughly at ease in close country and could operate far removed from roads, relying on animal transport and air supply to give them the edge over the enemy, who soon lost his reputation – largely based on myth – for invincibility in the jungle facing this superior force.[23]

Indian soldiers were, by then, also remarkably adaptable. The skilful and sophisticated use of mechanised, air and amphibious transport that made the manoeuvres of 1945 possible were put into practice by soldiers who, until a short time before, had been experienced only in operations on foot in the jungle with very little transport of any sort – and most of that having four legs and a notoriously stubborn character. Tanks had, until the time of the crossing of the Chindwin, been used essentially as mobile pill boxes and there had been only one serious tank vs tank action – at Imphal. Mechanising the 17th Division for its dash to Meiktila required every spare vehicle in the 14th Army to be rounded up, and even then there were sufficient for only two brigades to be mechanised. The third brigade was organised and trained at very short notice for air mobility and was flown in, under fire, to join the division at Thabutkon airfield near Meiktila while it was still in the process of being captured. On the Arakan coast, while the 26th Division and the British commandos had the benefit of amphibious warfare training, the 25th Division and the 50th Tank Brigade had none, and had to learn on the job – very quickly and in the face of the enemy. Many of the smaller landing craft, which operated in desperately difficult conditions, far removed from base facilities for weeks on end, were manned by Indian soldiers given a crash course in seamanship (not literally!). The culture of improvisation, deeply ingrained in the 14th Army and 15 Corps by the environment in which they had lived and fought for most of the war, along with persistent shortages of equipment and supplies came to the fore in making these changes 'on the hoof' possible. Indians of all three services proved themselves to be more than up to the challenge. In Slim's own words:

> My Indian Divisions after 1943 were among the best in the world. They would go anywhere, do anything, go on doing it, and do it on very little.[24]

And they did all that despite the political tensions of the Indian nationalist movement, winning 20 of the 27 Victoria Crosses awarded in Burma.

---

23 War Office Notes from Theatres of War, No. 19, Burma 1943/44, May 1945.

24 Slim, *Defeat Into Victory*, p. 539.

For all these reasons the re-capture of Rangoon by the 14th Army and 15 Corps can assuredly take its place right up alongside operations such as the capture of Sicily and the breakout from the Normandy beachhead as an example of sophisticated large scale manoeuvre warfare. Like Operation EXTENDED CAPITAL, Sicily and Normandy both involved the technique of pinning down the enemy's strength by attritional frontal pressure (in both cases done by Montgomery) while a bold, outflanking attack against weaker opposition (in both cases done by Patton) got round behind him. They were both conducted with less space available against a more powerful enemy than that facing Slim. Ultimately, though, especially in Normandy, they succeeded through the application of overwhelming combat power and every conceivable up-to-date device for overcoming the obstacles in their path. Slim enjoyed considerable superiority of artillery, armour and air-power, but it was not overwhelming due to his logistic difficulties. Numerically, the opposing forces in Burma were pretty evenly matched, and the Japanese may well have had a slight advantage. Not only were they on the defensive behind the best natural obstacle in Burma with good lines of communication but, at that stage, they would still fight to the last man and the last round, and die rather than surrender. Only at the very end of the campaign, after Rangoon had fallen, were Japanese taken prisoner in significant numbers. Possibly the greatest differences between Burma and the European theatres were in logistics and equipment scales. Sicily and Normandy were, in their time, the points of main effort of the western Allies and, though in both cases, supplies had to come across the beaches, copious quantities of the most up-to-date materiel were available and the lines of communication ashore were short and secure. Montgomery himself described the logistic conditions in the European theatres in the latter part of the war as 'lavish'.[25] Slim, by contrast, was fighting at the end of a long, tenuous line of communication, the limited capacity of which severely constrained the force levels he could commit to battle, and his troops fought much of it on half rations to make room in the supply chain for ammunition and fuel. His campaign was near the bottom of allied war priorities, with concomitant provision of supplies and equipment for his army. It had to live largely on its wits through ingenuity and improvisation, of which several of the more colourful examples have been outlined here. These were huge tactical and logistic challenges, and the formations that faced them so successfully were overwhelmingly Indian. Overcoming them, and the hardships they entailed, surely allows the Indian Army to claim the re-capture

---

[25] Field Marshal the Viscount Montgomery of Alamein, *El Alamein to the River Sangro* (London, Hutchinson, undated), p. 65.

of Rangoon, its last great conventional battle, as its finest – and right up among the finest of its type fought by the western Allies in that great war.

Chapter 8
The 20th Indian Division in French Indo-China

Daniel Marston

Introduction

This chapter focuses on a difficult and controversial aspect of the Second World War and the immediate aftermath: occupation responsibilities throughout the Imperial Japanese Empire. When His Majesty's Government (HMG) in London agreed to expanding the area of responsibility for South East Asia Command (SEAC) with regard to occupation duties in July 1945 at Potsdam, Germany, this put SEAC in the position of relying upon the largely volunteer Indian Army to carry out the mission. The conscript British Army could not meet this need, as it was having great difficulties keeping numbers high enough amid demobilisation pressures at the end of the war in the east. In the immediate aftermath of the Second World War, the Indian Army found itself carrying out occupation duties not just in British colonies such as Burma and Malaya, but also in the colonies of French Indo-China and the Dutch East Indies (later Indonesia).

The Indian Army's involvement in French Indo-China (FIC) and the Dutch East Indies (DEI) was to prove one of its most controversial assignments.[1] In both

---

[1] This chapter will focus on the Indian Army's difficult campaign in French Indo-China (FIC); its ability to deal with a complex mission; and the impact of its involvement, and of the political situation in India, on Army morale. There has been considerable research into this period in the last 20 years, mostly within the context of the post-Second World War political environment; there has not been much specific emphasis on the Indian Army's role as distinct from the larger strategic context of British decolonisation and the impending wars in French Indo-China that would engulf the French (and later the Americans) in two costly wars, as well as the Indonesian war of independence. For further details on the larger issues surrounding this chapter, see the following: John Springhall, 'Kicking out the Vietminh: How Britain Allowed France to Reoccupy South Indo-China, 1945–6', in *Journal of Contemporary History*, Vol. 40 (1), 115–30, January 2005; Ronald Spector, 'After Hiroshima: Allied Military Occupations and the Fate of Japan's Empire, 1945–7', *Journal of Military History*, Vol. 69, No. 4, October 2005, 1121–36; Peter Neville, *Britain in Vietnam: Prelude to Disaster, 1945–6*, London: Routledge, 2007; Peter Dennis, *Troubled Days of*

places, Indian Army divisions found themselves, as one officer would later state, in the position of 'piggy in the middle'[2]. The divisional and corps commanders had to navigate a minefield of political issues, involving emancipation of Allied prisoners of war and civilians, disarming more than 300,000 Imperial Japanese soldiers, and eventually embroiled in fighting counterinsurgency campaigns against nationalist guerrillas who perceived them as instruments of the returning French and Dutch colonial administrations in colonies that did not belong to the British. For some battalions, the campaigns during this period involved fighting almost as bitter as anything they had encountered against the Japanese in Burma.[3]

The occupation was further hampered by a well-defined strategy; mission statements appeared to change over the course of the occupation, and indicate considerable gaps in understanding between SEAC, HMG, and India Command on what the Indian Army's remit and goals should be. Attempting to define, and articulate, why the Indian Army should be involved in occupation duties

---

Peace: Mountbatten and South East Asia Command, 1945–6, Manchester: Manchester University Press, 1987; T.O. Smith, *Britain and the Origins of the Vietnam War: UK Policy in Indo-China, 1943–50*, Basingstoke: Palgrave, 2007; Louis Allen, *The End of the War in Asia*, London: Hart-Davis MacGibbon, 1976; Peter Dunn, *The First Indo-China War*, London: C. Hurst & Co, 1985; F.S.V. Donnison, *British Military Administration in the Far East, 1943–6*, London: HMSO, 1956; Woodburn Kirby, *The War Against Japan*, Vol. 5, London: HMSO, 1969; Earl Mountbatten of Burma, *Report to the Combined Chiefs of Staff by the Supreme Commander, South East Asia, 1943–1946*, London: HMSO, 1951; *Post Surrender Tasks; Section E of the Report to the Combined Chiefs of Staff by the Supreme Allied Commander South-East Asia, 1943–1946*, London: HMSO, 1969; and *Transfer of Power (TOP)*, Vols 5, 6, and 7; as well as the papers of General Sir Douglas Gracey, Liddell Hart Centre for Military Archives (LHCMA), King's College London. For more details on the Dutch East Indies, see John Springhall, 'Disaster in Surabaya: The Death of Brigadier Mallaby during the British Occupation of Java, 1945–6', *Journal of Imperial and Commonwealth History*, 24, 3 September 1996, 422–43; Richard McMillan, *The British Occupation of Indonesia, 1945–1946*, London: Routledge, 2005; papers of General Christison, Imperial War Museum, London; and the papers of Lt. Colonel A.J.F. Doulton, National Army Museum, London.

[2] Interview with Major G.C. Coppen, 1/11/1999.

[3] A sad commentary regarding this point was the death of Lt. Col. Sarbjit Singh Kalha of the 2/1st Punjab Regiment at Soerabaja in Java, DEI. He had risen to command the battalion during the Burma Campaign and was highly respected. As noted in the 5th Indian Divisional history, he was 'calm and unruffled in battle, fearless, and with delightful manners, he had won the DSO and Bar. His remarkable ability included that of commanding both British and Indian officers, and there was no one in his battalion or in the Division who did not hold him in the highest regard. He was one of those senior Indian Army officers whom India could least to afford to lose.' Antony Brett-James, *Ball of Fire: The Fifth Indian Division in the Second World War*, Aldershot: Gale & Polden, 1951, p. 463.

in non-British colonies and as a result find itself fighting a counterinsurgency campaign against nationalists that had nothing to do with India or the British Empire, presented a number of problems for both the Viceroy, Lord Wavell, and Commander in Chief, India (CinCI), General Sir Claude Auchinleck. Along with the postwar trials of Indian Army personnel who had joined the Indian National Army as Japanese prisoners of war, the Indian National Congress Party made significant political use of the Indian Army's involvement in FIC and DEI, part of an ongoing societal debate on India's independence and the role of the Army in that context.

While the Indian Army's involvement was being discussed and debated in New Delhi, the Indian Army itself quietly got on with carrying their difficult duties with competence and dispatch. They were commended on all sides for their professionalism, providing a vivid example of how Jawaharlal Nehru[4] failed to comprehend the essential motivation of most Indian soldiers, VCOs, and officers, regardless of the circumstances or the problems therein: to perform to the best of their abilities. To supply but one example from this period, consider the performance of the 23rd Indian Division in the Dutch East Indies by assessing awards listings for gallantry and leadership: the Distinguished Service Order, Military Cross and Military Medal. Nine DSOs were given to commanders during the Burma Campaign, three in the DEI. Seventy MCs were given out in Burma; 23 were given out in the DEI. Last but not least, 100 Military Medals were awarded in Burma, and another 38 in the DEI. Then consider that the 23rd served just over one year in the DEI, compared to just under three years in Burma against the Japanese.[5]

One need only refer to the various war diaries and divisional and regimental histories to see that, for the men, VCOs, and officers, these campaigns were a strange continuation of the Second World War – and one which some authors felt that this should not have occurred.[6] Some units added battle honours to

---

4 Nehru attempted to use both the INA trials and the operations in FIC and DEI as political levers against the Viceroy and the C-in-CI. His objections reached the United States, and the *New York Times* reported on a speech he gave late in 1945, in which he stated that Indian troops were 'doing Britain's dirty work against our friends [Viet Minh and Indonesian nationalists]', *New York Times*, 1 January 1945 and cited in Neville, p. 124. The irony about the complexity of relationships among Nationalist populations at the end of the war is exemplified by Ho Chi Minh, then operating in the northern section of Vietnam who, despite his Nationalist credentials, was instrumental in the capture and handing over of the deputy commander of the Indian National Army, Major General A.J. Chatterjee, to the British military.

5 A.J.F. Doulton, *The Fighting Cock: Being the History of the 23rd Indian Division, 1942–1947*, Aldershot: Gale & Polden, 1951, p. 311.

6 See Richard McMillan's work.

their unit's credentials during this period; more than one indicated that they accomplished this without any obvious support from the British Army. The pre-war model of one British battalion in each Indian Brigade, to toughen it up, was a thing of the past by 1945 and 1946, and the Indian Army took responsibility for being both the spine and the body within all of the divisions: bearing the brunt of higher level decision making, expanding the area of responsibility for SEAC; and carrying out occupation duties in non-British colonies.

Strategic Context

As stated above, Lord Louis Mountbatten, commander of SEAC, arrived in Potsdam, Germany, on 24 July 1945, to meet with the Combined Chiefs of Staff. There he was informed that SEAC would be taking over responsibility for more of South East Asia – chiefly Borneo, Java, and Indo-China, all of which had previously been under the control of South West Pacific Area, or General Douglas MacArthur's command. At first, Mountbatten did not feel that this would be too large a task for SEAC to take on. SEAC had already been planning Operation ZIPPER, the amphibious attack and campaign for Malaya and Singapore.

It was during the meetings in Potsdam that Mountbatten was advised of the impending atomic bomb drop on Japan. He was sworn to secrecy, but told to prepare for the possibility of an early Japanese capitulation. Mountbatten duly informed SEAC HQ in Kandy, Ceylon, without revealing information about the atomic bomb, to prepare for potentially imminent capitulation, and to begin planning to manage the enlarged area of responsibility that SEAC had inherited. SEAC HQ responded to this information with concern, fearing that Operation ZIPPER would not go forward if an early capitulation occurred. Military and political leaders in SEAC and London considered the invasion and re-occupation of Malaya and Singapore of particular psychological importance, necessary to wipe clean the humiliation of the 1942 Malayan and Singapore capitulations.[7]

Mountbatten immediately set out to prepare SEAC, chiefly formations from the 12th and 14th Armies, to make ready to seize strategic areas from the Japanese in Burma and then prioritise specific areas expected to be handed over to SEAC control. On 13 August SEAC established priority areas as follows: Malaya, Saigon, Bangkok, Batavia (DEI), Surabaya (DEI) and Hong Kong.

[7] See Dening to Foreign Office, 31 July 1945, *Documents on British Policy Overseas*, Series 1, Vol. 1 (1945) (London: HMSO, 1984), Calendar I to no. 599, also quoted in Dennis, pp. 11–12.

With this plan in place, SEAC was able to move quickly and naval forces were able to begin carrying out Operation ZIPPER in short order.[8]

The increased level of responsibility caused consternation for some senior British officers, including General Sir William Slim, commander of Allied Land Forces South East Asia (ALFSEA). As he wrote: 'The area of South East Asia Land Forces had suddenly expanded to include Malaya, Singapore, Siam [Thailand], Dutch East Indies, Hong Kong, Borneo and the Andaman Islands. ... [I]n two of them, Indo-China and the Dutch East Indies, nationalist movements armed from Japanese forces had already seized power in the vacuum left by the sudden surrender.'[9]

Another major issue for Generals Slim and Auchinleck, back at India Command, was that Operation PYTHON, the repatriation scheme for British personnel, was also in full force. Many conscripted British officers, NCOs, and soldiers were being released from service due to pressure on the British government to end conscription with the war's end. With the expanded area of operations for SEAC and the need to re-occupy many areas, SEAC needed formations that were going to fill the space for the required occupation duties. The political reality of Operation PYTHON meant that this duty fell to the professional Indian Army,[10] and this was unlikely to be welcomed by nationalist politicians in India.[11] General Auchinleck stressed to Mountbatten[12] that it was not a forgone conclusion that all the Indian Army troops that were needed could come from India Command. SEAC had asked for the 7th Indian Division to deploy to Siam, the 20th Indian Division to deploy to Indo-China, and the 23rd and 26th Indian divisions to deploy to Malaya and then the DEI, with the 5th Indian Division following on.[13] Auchinleck specifically cited the need for troops

---

8 Saigon was placed high on the list due to the fact the Japanese HQ for their Southern Army was housed there. Dunn, p. 119.

9 Slim, *Defeat into Victory*, pp. 529–30.

10 As Professor Ronald Spector noted: 'Mountbatten suffered from the most critical shortage of troops as well as the worst timing. ... [A] large proportion of Mountbatten's non-British forces were divisions of the Indian Army. ... [A] good number of the Indians were career soldiers and many of the rest were in no hurry to be discharged.' Ronald Spector, 'After Hiroshima: Allied Military occupations and the Fate of Japan's Empire, 1945–1947', *Journal of Military History*, 69 (October 2005), pp. 1128–9.

11 See below for more discussion.

12 It is interesting to note that, in Mountbatten's private diary, he never alludes to any tension regarding the use of Indian Army troops or to Auchinleck's and Slim's concerns, despite mentioning both men numerous times. See *Personal Diary of Admiral The Lord Louis Mountbatten: Supreme Allied Commander, South-East Asia, 1943–1946*, edited by Philip Ziegler, London: Collins, 1988.

13 Slim, pp. 530–31 and Dunn, p. 124.

for internal security duties in India, which would be necessary later in the year and into 1946 as the INA trials moved forward. It was clear that the political situation in India was extremely delicate; Mountbatten understood this and was quick to respond to Auchinleck that he saw the need to be cautious. Even so, neither they nor HMG were prepared for what would be required of the Indian Army in the DEI and FIC, or the political fallout that would ensue.[14]

Even as planning went ahead, formations were earmarked and assigned, and shipping began to move, inter-allied relations deteriorated. The American General MacArthur announced that he wished for all commanders to stop movement and for no landings to take place in the Japanese Empire until the formal surrender in Tokyo Bay had taken place. At this point, this ceremony was planned for 28 August. MacArthur's reasoning was that Japan had not yet signed any surrender treaty, and that unilateral action by theatre commanders could prejudice the surrender process, and ultimately lead to the Japanese commander of forces in South East Asia, Field Marshal Terauchi, refusing to obey surrender orders from SEAC.[15] It was well known that communications between Tokyo and field commanders were erratic at best during this time,[16] and while some of MacArthur's points may have been valid,[17] Mountbatten and SEAC were outraged. They complained bitterly to the Joint Chiefs, pointing out that some of their forces were already six days out from Rangoon and preparing to land in Malaya. The British Chiefs of Staff agreed with Mountbatten, but HMG in London disregarded these concerns and told Mountbatten and SEAC to halt the invasion of Malaya and follow MacArthur's instructions. To add insult to injury, not all allied forces did the same. The Russians ignored MacArthur and continued to destroy the Japanese Army in Manchuria; even worse, the American General Albert Wedemeyer,[18] serving with the Chinese Nationalist forces, did the same.[19] This delay contributed significantly to the subsequent issues that arose in the occupations of both the DEI and FIC; British/Indian forces lost time and traction in dealing with both Japanese and nationalist groups, the latter

---

[14] Dennis, p. 7.

[15] Dunn, p. 123.

[16] Dennis, p. 13.

[17] It was feared that many Japanese soldiers would still fight on until they heard that the Emperor had actually surrendered. It was estimated that there were close to five million Japanese soldiers in the Empire, and the impression was that they had not been defeated.

[18] General Wedemeyer had been the Chief of Staff to Mountbatten in SEAC, but in October 1944, he replaced General Joseph Stillwell, to assume command of all US forces in China and to serve as Chiang Kai-shek's Chief of Staff.

[19] See Gairdner to Mountbatten, 21 August, 1945, TNA WO 172/1778, and Dunn, p. 123.

of whom had successfully filled the political vacuum that had been created with the Japanese surrender.[20]

The British/Indian Army mission for both the DEI and FIC continued to evolve over the next several months. Issues remain unresolved to this day regarding the intent of senior commanders and what actually occurred. Overall, the commanders had three specific aims in entering into each area: rescue Allied Prisoners of War (POWs), disarm the Japanese military, and maintain law and order to ensure internal security.[21] The ability of commanders to carry out these orders was compromised by the delay imposed by General MacArthur, and the ensuing internal political maelstrom. The plight of the POWs was an excellent example of this; as Slim noted: 'Our men and those of our Allies were daily dying in their foul camps; thousands were at the limit of weakness and exhaustion.'[22]

SEAC's campaigns in the DEI and FIC began simultaneously; however, while the DEI campaign lasted through most of 1946, the FIC campaign was over for all intents and purposes by the end of February 1946. This chapter will focus on the FIC campaign, named Operation Masterdom.[23]

French Indo-China

The British were placed in charge of only part of French Indo-China; specifically, they were assigned to control the area south of the 16th parallel,[24] while the Chinese Nationalists controlled the area to the north. The British area of responsibility included not only southern Vietnam, but also Cambodia and parts of Laos. The Chinese troops, having disregarded General MacArthur's orders, arrived in the area first, in early September. Their efforts were focused on pillage, rape, and loot in the northern areas of Indo-China.[25] The British mission was organised into two groups, the Control Commission[26] and the Allied Land

[20] Dennis, pp. 14–15.

[21] See 28 August 1945, ALFSEA Operational Directive No. 12, 'Masterdom', TNA WO 203/5444, and Springhall, p. 119.

[22] Slim, pp. 530–31.

[23] See Operational Directive, No. 12, 28 August, 1945, TNA WO 203/5444, and Springhall, p. 119.

[24] In the end, the 20th Indian Division expended most of its time and effort in and around Saigon.

[25] See Springhall, p. 119 and Dunn, p. 139.

[26] This organisation was made up of resources from SEAC and reported directly back to SEAC HQ in Kandy, Ceylon. General Gracey had nine tasks to fulfil for SEAC: assume control of HQ Japanese Southern Army; supervise the surrender; transmit SEAC orders to the Japanese; obtain information regarding Japanese dispositions and supplies; control

Forces French Indo-China (ALFFIC[27]), and headed by the seasoned and well-respected 20th Indian Division commander, Major General Douglas Gracey.[28]

As commander of Allied Land Forces South East Asia (ALFSEA), General Slim issued Operational Directive No. 8 to his senior commanders to effect the military occupation of Malaya, Burma, the Dutch East Indies and French Indo-China. Commanders were instructed to disarm and concentrate all Japanese forces; protect, succor, and ultimately evacuate Allied POWs and civilian internees; establish and maintain law and order; introduce food and other civil affairs supplies; and set up appropriate civil administration.[29] Gracey received further detailed orders; in addition to the points raised in Operational Directive No. 8, he was instructed to pay special attention to law and order and, more importantly, 'liberate Allied territory is so far as your resources permit', which implied possible future operations against the Vietminh.[30] This last directive[31] has been interpreted by later historians as Gracey potentially going beyond his remit.[32]

By the time the British were able to send troops into Indo-China, planning had become quite difficult. The British had minimal intelligence about the state of the Japanese Army in the area, as well as the state of the administration and relations with the Vietnamese nationalists, the Viet Minh.[33] The French had administered the area under five different colonies: Cochin-China, Tongking, Annam, Cambodia, and Laos. Until March 1945, the Vichy French had worked alongside the Imperial Japanese Army, at which point they had been ousted by Japanese occupation forces. Before the British arrived, Ho Chi Minh had

---

Japanese communications; study the Recovery of Allied Prisoners of War and Internees problems and render all possible aid; report on Indo-China's lines of communication, airfields and the port of Saigon; open river and sea approaches to Saigon; using Japanese resources, reduce size of Japanese HQs as soon as possible; and maintain liaison with the French local government, keeping Mountbatten informed. File 4/2, 30 August 1945, Gracey Papers, LHCMA.

27 This was a larger organisation than the commission; it included French military forces and directly reported back to General Sir William Slim and ALFSEA.

28 Springhall, p. 119.

29 ALFSEA Operational Directive No. 8, 23 August 1945, file 4/2, Gracey Papers, LHCMA.

30 Operational Directive No. 12, 28 August 1945, file 4/2, Gracey Papers, LHCMA.

31 Slim sent a message to Gracey that the French were to be in charge of civil administration; however, in designated key areas, he would be responsible for full authority over both the military and civilian but working through the French administration.

32 See debate in Dunn, pp. 140–47.

33 Dunn, p. 134 and Gracey papers. More information started to trickle out to the British, but it was not of a high quality.

declared independence from the French authorities for the new nation of Vietnam, with the tacit support of the Japanese. The resistance movement was named the League for the Independence of Vietnam or Viet Minh. The Viet Minh provisional executive committee in the south set out to fill the political vacuum there, acting at the behest of Ho Chi Minh.[34] The Viet Minh slowly started to take over governmental control in Saigon and the surrounding areas. On the same day as the Japanese surrender occurred, there were mass demonstrations in Saigon in support of the Viet Minh and declaration of independence. Violence erupted between French civilians, Viet Minh, and other political factions wishing to take advantage of the power vacuum. There were rumours of many people being killed, and escalating violence.[35]

The British needed to get troops to Saigon quickly, but were hampered by acute transport shortages, both by air and by sea. This was the start of an ongoing problem for the British and, later, the French forces. The first elements of the 20th Indian Division, 80th Indian Brigade,[36] arrived at Saigon's Tan Son hut airport on 6 September and began immediately to assess the situation.[37] More troops arrived on 11 September and Gracey arrived from Rangoon with his staff on 13 September.[38] Gracey immediately recognised the need for more troops with the city and surrounding areas apparently in chaos. Ironically, Japanese troops were being used to provide security at the airfield. They would play both defensive and offensive roles under British command in the following days, weeks, and months, and not just in FIC but also in the DEI.[39] And this would lead to controversy, especially with the Americans.

While one of the chief missions for Gracey and the Indian troops was disarming the Japanese,[40] they recognised that they would need to keep quite

---

34 Kirby, Vol. V, p. 290.

35 Springhall, pp. 117–18.

36 It would not be in fully in country until the 26th, due to the many transport issues.

37 There is some discrepancy on the date: some authors such as Springhall state the first troops arrived in the 8th. The first detachment was a COY minus from the 1/19th Hyderabad Regiment.

38 Upon arriving, Gracey and his staff walked past the small Viet Minh delegation and met with the Japanese contingent. This action specifically stated that the Allies did not recognise the Viet Minh as a legitimate government.

39 Interestingly, many Indian Army veterans recalled, from their command of Japanese POWs, the professionalism and discipline that the Japanese displayed. Some even indicated their preference for commanding Japanese over their own Indian jawans. Interviews with Indian Army officers, 1999–2007.

40 The process of disarming and rounding up soldiers and weapons was complicated. The British and Indian soldiers would do it first and then hand over the weapon stores to the French authorities and military, as the Japanese refused to deal with them.

a few in place as defensive and static forces. Indian troops were slowly starting to arrive, and the rising violence between the French and the Vietnamese communities was causing problems. As the days progressed, tensions between the British/Indians and the Viet Minh increased apace. The Viet Minh were inciting Japanese soldiers not to surrender, but to desert with their weapons and join the Viet Minh.[41] They also set out to spread anti-British propaganda amongst the Indian soldiers in the division (which fell on deaf ears).

Gracey and his staff viewed the Viet Minh as a direct threat to law and order. On 19 September, SEAC issued contradictory directives, simultaneously ordering Gracey and the 20th Division to seize Saigon Radio and censor other broadcasts of the Viet Minh, and issuing a general statement about not interfering in local affairs.[42] Gracey and his staff decided on more far-reaching moves to contend with rising violence. Brigadier Maunsell, Chief of Staff on the Control Commission, met with the Viet Minh provisional government on the 19th, and issued a proclamation closing all newspapers, banning provisional government seizure of buildings or other property, lists of all Vietnamese police and armed units, banning all public meetings, demonstrations, and processions, and carrying weapons, and enforcing a night curfew. This amounted to declaring martial law, which Gracey then had to enforce, relying on the equivalent of two battalions of troops.[43] Gracey advised SEAC of his proclamation, asserting that: 'I would stress that though it may appear that I have interfered in the politics of the country, I have done so only in the interest of the maintenance of law and order and after close collaboration with some senior French representatives.'[44] Mountbatten backed Gracey at the time, although later in life he questioned Gracey's decisions at this point in the campaign.[45]

Gracey's proclamation was read out and in theory took effect on 21 September. In reality, however, without sufficient troops the British were limited in their ability to enforce its tenets, particularly the curfew. On the 22nd, former

---

41 It was estimated that over 2,000 Japanese soldiers did desert before and after the arrival of the British and Indian troops. Springhall, p. 119.

42 It was stressed by Mountbatten in a communiqué: HMG's goals in sending British troops into FIC, were fourfold – to control Field Marshal Terauchi's headquarters, which commanded the Japanese Armies in the Southern Regions; to disarm the Japanese; to release and repatriate Allied POWs and internees; and to maintain law and order until the arrival of French Forces. He stressed that HM Government had no intention of using British forces in FIC to crush resistance movements. Dunn, 167.

43 Gracey to Mountbatten, TNA WO 172/1784.

44 Gracey to Mountbatten, 21 September 1945, TNA WO 203/5562; Dennis, p. 39 and Springhall, p. 120.

45 See Mountbatten, *Post Surrender Tasks*, Section E as well as Dunn, p. 173 and Dennis, p. 41.

French POWs were released and rearmed to support the effort.[46] While at first this idea seemed like a good solution to the manpower problems in Saigon, it was to have wider repercussions within 24 hours. British and Indian troops had been moving through the city, trying to round up and disarm the Viet Minh police and armed groups. Units of the 80th Indian Brigade also moved against the Viet Minh-controlled administrative buildings, handing over the buildings to the small amount of French forces after they had taken possession. The French were able to seize control of the administrative elements of Saigon without too much bloodshed, pushing out the Viet Minh provisional government and raising the tricolor above Hotel de Ville.[47] A *coup d'etat* had occurred, however, and more blood was to be spilled.[48]

The released French POWs had been guarded by the Viet Minh and had suffered at their hands. Sadly for Gracey and the British/Indian forces, within 24 hours of the coup, French discipline started to loosen and French troops began to kill Viet Minh and so-called Viet Minh in retaliation. The French civilian population also became involved with the ensuing mob violence. This had repercussions for the British and Indian troops, and Gracey attempted to make the French commanders aware of the issues and to get their men back in control. These men still fell under the command of Gracey and he and his men would be accountable for the situation's deterioration.[49]

The Viet Minh now truly saw the British as part of the attempt to re-impose French colonial government in Indo-China.[50] Some authors cite this episode as the beginning of the first Indo-China war. The Viet Minh launched a general strike on 24 September, paralysing sections of the city with lack of water or

46 The French 9th DIC (Colonial Infantry Division) was still not in Vietnam, but was to be released soon, to relieve the 20th Indian Division.

47 See Saigon Control Commission, Political Report, 13 September to 9 October, 1945, Gracey Papers, LHCMA for a more detailed account, as well as Dunn, pp. 183–9.

48 Throughout this period, a series of debates was ongoing in both SEAC and in London, where the British mission began and ended. Mission creep had been occurring since mid-August and there was at times a lack of clear strategy and end goal. General Gracey felt that he had to carry out the coup to allow for law and order to be restored, and that the French forces and administration were best placed to carry this out, since the Viet Minh were not a recognised organisation. See Dennis, Springhall, and especially Dunn for a much more detailed account of the higher-level issues regarding strategy and joint British and French planning and thinking on Indo-China.

49 See Dunn, pp. 195–7 and Dennis, pp. 43–8.

50 As noted 'On September 23, armed and protected by the British forces, the French colonialists launched their attack and occupied Saigon. Our people replied by force of arms, and from that moment, our heroic resistance began.' Truong Chinh, *Primer for Revolt*, New York: Praeger, 1963, p. 17 and Dunn, pp. 202–3.

electricity. Violence also began to increase; on 25 September, more than 300 French and Eurasian families were butchered in a northern section of Saigon by Viet Minh and other paramilitary gangs. Violence escalated as the Viet Minh set up road blocks and British and Indian troops engaged them during their expanded patrols.[51] The sounds of gunfire, mortars, and other weapons were heard each night, as British/Indians, French, and Viet Minh forces skirmished through the city. Many Burma veterans noted the difficulty of fighting guerrillas in an urban environment.[52]

Mountbatten praised Gracey for his actions in communicating with the Chiefs of Staff,[53] but on the 24th he cabled Gracey and asserted that British and Indian troops should be used only in designated 'key areas'; the French and Japanese needed to handle sections outside of Saigon.[54] Mountbatten appeared to be growing concerned that Gracey had exceeded his orders, and began to question his ability to command. General Slim, by contrast, supported Gracey, and pushed Mountbatten to release all of the 20th Indian Division to provide support.[55] The course of action now contemplated was for British/Indian forces to take complete control of Saigon; this would require a whole division, to restore law and order and re-partriate POWs as well. General Gracey was also expected to start working to find a political solution to the problems between the Viet Minh and the French, so as to allow the withdrawal of British and Indian forces.[56] It was also at this juncture that a politically fraught decision was made: to expand the use of Japanese troops. Not only would they be protecting airfields; they were also allocated to more offensive roles alongside and sometimes under the command of British officers[57] to support Gracey's efforts to impose law and order in and around Saigon, until the rest of the 20th Indian Division and the follow-on French military forces arrived.[58] The Japanese refused to work

[51] The first American casualty in the history of US intervention in Vietnam occurred during this period. LTC Thomas Dewey of the OSS was killed in a Viet Minh ambush. The role and position of the US OSS during this period is quite controversial; see Dunn and Dennis for a more detailed discussion of their stance in relation to the British and French activities.

[52] See War Diaries from the 20th Indian Division for more information; see also Dunn, pp. 200–201.

[53] Dennis, p. 50.

[54] See Dunn, pp. 200–210 and Dennis, pp. 50–54.

[55] Springhall, p. 124, as well as Dunn, pp. 229–30.

[56] Dennis, pp. 59–61.

[57] Interviews with Indian Army veterans, 1999–2007 and 1/1st Gurkha Rifles, War Diary, October, 1945, TNA WO 172/7769, as well as Dunn, p. 204.

[58] The Japanese forces followed a multifaceted approach to the campaign. Some units clearly did not want to support the British and French, and actively aided the Viet Minh with

for the French, and requested that all orders and actions were directed through the British command structure. In the end, however, the main French build-up of forces took longer than expected.[59]

It was at this juncture that both General Auchinleck and the Viceroy, Wavell, began to note the political fallout that operations in FIC and the DEI were causing in India. Cognisant of the pressure on the Indian Army, due to the INA trials that were about to begin in New Delhi, Wavell stated to the Secretary of State for India, Lord Pethwick-Lawrence, on 1 October 1945:

> The situation in French Indo-China and the Netherlands East Indies will give us some trouble. Indian troops are involved in both places, and we shall be attacked for allowing HMG to use them to suppress national movements. It was of course most necessary to disarm the Japanese, and to maintain law and order while this was being done. But I hope that HMG will be able to disengage the troops, both British and Indian, as soon as possible and leave the business to the French and the Dutch.[60]

General Slim was aware of and in agreement with both Wavell and Auchinleck. He advised the Chief of the Imperial General Staff, Alanbrooke, that 'directions we have been receiving from various sources seem to me to have been somewhat involved and at times contradictory'. In the same letter, he also recounted a conversation with the British Secretary of State for War, Lawson. He noted that, while Lawson intended that the British not become involved in nationalist struggles, French forces still operated under Slim's command, and that 'as long as we retain this command ... we cannot divorce ourselves from the responsibility for their actions'.[61]

Meanwhile, back in Saigon, the fighting continued. On 1 October, the same day that Wavell was asking for an end to the Army's commitment, the British Chiefs of Staff reversed an earlier decision, and expanded Gracey and the

---

weapons and lack of support to the British and Indian troops. Other units actively worked with British and Indian troops, and fought and died alongside them in battle with the Viet Minh. See Dunn for a more in-depth discussion.

59 The 9th DIC was not formally in place until the end of November 1945, although other forces started to arrive in October and early November. General Philippe Leclerc, commander of the French Forces, arrived on 5 October. See SACSEA Joint Planning Staff, 'Turnover of Command', 19 November 1945, TNA WO 203/5608 and Dennis, pp. 59–61.

60 *TOP*, VI, 127, Wavell to Lord Pethick-Lawrence, 1 October, 1945, p. 306. Wavell would reiterate this point in a follow-on letter to Lord Pethick-Lawrence on 9 October 1945. See *TOP*, VI, 135, p. 323.

61 Slim to Brooke, 6 October 1945, annex to COS 9450 607 (0), CAB, 80/97 and cited in Dennis, p. 165.

British and Indian troops' remit to work outside the Saigon area in support of the French. It was also on 1 October that talks were held between the British and the Viet Minh. Gracey's stated position was to curb violence and restore order in Indo-China. The Viet Minh expected the British to act as arbitrators, but Gracey was under strict orders not to do so, since such a role was political and outside his remit. A ceasefire was agreed, to take effect on the evening of the 2nd. Meetings between the French and Viet Minh were scheduled for the 3rd. Despite these efforts, sporadic fighting continued.[62] The truce ended definitively on 10 October, when the Viet Minh attacked a British/Indian engineer reconnaissance party. Gracey had warned the Viet Minh that they would reap the consequences of violence against his troops; he ordered his 20th Indian Division and the newly arrived 32nd Indian Brigade, to clear the areas to the north of the city.[63] Mountbatten had agreed as well and asserted: 'I ordered strong action should be taken by the British/Indian forces to secure further key-points and so to widen and consolidate the perimeter of these areas. At the same time I insisted that further attempts to negotiate must continue.'[64]

At this time political pressure was increasing on Auchinleck and Wavell in India, focusing on the escalating violence in both FIC and the DEI. General Auchinleck telegraphed the British Chiefs of Staff on 7 October, asserting that Indian troops must be withdrawn to alleviate political pressure.[65] Lord Pethick-Lawrence responded to both Wavell and Auchinleck; he confirmed that it was HMG's intent to withdraw as soon as possible, but that, in the meantime, 'our endeavor to keep out of political trouble in these areas as much as we can be entirely withdrawn until French and Dutch troops arrive. ... [W]e cannot totally disregard the interests of our French and Dutch Allies. ... [I]n any case it is clearly our duty so long as we are the only people on the spot with effective forces to prevent so far as we can conditions deteriorating into civil chaos with great loss of life.'[66]

---

62 Gracey to Mountbatten, 1 October, TNA WO 172/1786, and Dennis, pp. 66–7. See also Dunn's chapter 'Truce' for a very detailed discussion of the truce talks and the higher level political issues that occurred.

63 Gracey was quick to point out that it was not going to be wanton killing; there would be no provocation use of force, and troops would cause minimal disturbance to law-abiding citizens. However, this did not mean he would not use all of his weapons against the violent elements of the Viet Minh. Dunn, pp. 259–60.

64 Mountbatten, *Post Surrender Tasks*, Section E, p. 282 and Dunn, p. 257.

65 Auchinleck to the Chiefs of Staff, 7 October 1945, OIOC L/WS/1/716.

66 *Transfer of Power (TOP)*, Vol. VI, 140, Lord Pethick-Lawrence to Wavell, 12 October 1945, p. 337.

Throughout October and November, the remaining units and formations of the 20th Indian Division arrived and set out to establish control in and around Saigon and to provide support for the French. The French also began to arrive in early October; their commander, General P. Leclerc, arrived on the 5th, along with the 5th Colonial Infantry.[67] Fighting continued during this period between the British/Indians and the Viet Minh, and between the Viet Minh and the French.[68] Japanese troops were also utilised. The British also brought in more Royal Air Force support, in the form of Spitfire fighter squadrons. These were to be used sparingly and under strict controls, but to be called upon if necessary.[69]

By 17 October, the last units and formations of the 20th Indian Division had arrived and were ready to move against the Viet Minh. It was decided to send the 100th Indian Infantry Brigade, commanded by Brigadier C.H.B. Rodham, and supporting arms to the north and north-east of Saigon into the Thu Duc/Thu Dau Mot/Bien Hao areas. Intelligence reports stated that the Viet Minh strength lay in these areas, and there was a clear need to break the Viet Minh ring of control surrounding Saigon. Brigadier Rodham informed the Japanese command in the region that the 100th Brigade was coming to occupy the area and assume responsibility for the maintenance of law and order over the course of 23–25 October.[70] The Japanese were asked to continue disarming the Viet Minh, searching for weapons, and clearing areas around the main towns. The Japanese troops now fell under the command of Brigadier Rodham and his brigade. The various units of the 100th Indian Brigade – the 1/1st Gurkha Rifles, 4/10th Gurkha Rifles, 14/13th Frontier Force Rifles[71] and the 16th Light Cavalry[72] --carried out a well-planned and executed operation to clear the areas to the north of Saigon. The Japanese carried out the static duties of defence,

67 Kirby, Vol. V, pp. 302–3.

68 For some battalions, serious fighting ensued. See the Newsletters of 9/14th Punjab and the 2/8th Punjab regiments in the Gracey Papers, files 5/5 and 5/12, for more details of the actions as well as Dunn, pp. 257–9. As one battalion stated: 'As far as the BN was concerned the shooting season for the Annamites [word used for the Viet Minh by British and Indian troops] had opened.' Also see battalion history of the 9/14th Punjab, which stated: 'it was an unsatisfactory sort of fighting. The enemy wore no uniform and usually did not carry arms visibly.' Anon. *Ninth Battalion Fourteenth Punjab Regiment* (Cardiff: Western Mail and Echo Limited, 1948), p. 97.

69 See Dunn, pp. 236–7 and Dennis, p. 64.

70 100th Indian Infantry Brigade, War Diary, November, 1945, TNA WO 172/7135.

71 This battalion was considered one of the best in the Burma Campaign; at this point in the Indo-China campaign, it still had many of the veterans from Burma. See Marston, *Phoenix from the Ashes* for much more detail on the battlefield performance of this battalion.

72 This was a pre-war Indianised regiment and performed well during the war. It was commanded at this point by an Indian officer, Lt. Colonel Chaudhuri.

while the Brigade operated mobile columns to destroy any opposition and deal with any road blocks.[73]

The units of the 100th Brigade defaulted to their wartime experience, and created combined arms mobile units. An example of this, an operation known as GATEFORCE, was established by the 14/13th Frontier Force Rifles, who were based to the northeast of Saigon at Bien Hao. Major L.D. Gates took his company, plus a squadron of armoured cars from the 16th Cavalry, a section of mortars from the 14/13th Frontier Force Rifles, a detachment of Royal Engineers and an attachment of Japanese troops, and pushed east towards Xuan Loc. They were ordered to create a patrol base in Xuan Loc on 29 October and patrol for three days, to try to destroy and capture 2,000 Viet Minh and members of the HQ staff that had been reported to have fled to the area. Gates was ordered to use maximum force to clear the area and track down and destroy the Viet Minh.[74] One of the most controversial aspects of this operation was the instruction to destroy any village that resisted their efforts.[75] Over the course of several days, GATEFORCE engaged elements of the Viet Minh and succeeded in destroying various roadblocks and fortified positions. After two days of fighting, it was estimated that close to 200 Viet Minh had been killed in the Xuan Loc region; thus, in theory, breaking the back of the overt Viet Minh military presence.[76] It was reported that GATEFORCE was also able to rescue some 20 French civilian hostages.[77]

[73] Dunn, pp. 270–77 and 100th Indian Infantry Brigade, War Diary, November 1945, TNA WO 172/7135.

[74] 14/13th Frontier Force Rifles War Diary, November 1945, TNA WO 172/7743.

[75] Dunn, p. 280. This was not the first time that buildings were burned in retaliation by the British and Indian troops. Members of the Bombay Sappers and Miners Company had destroyed huts after the killing of one of their men. See Dunn, p. 277. The issue with this is that although the Indian Army was an army that understood 'minimum force', many within the 20th Indian Division were mistakenly viewing this campaign through the prism of conventional operations, due to the level of violence and the military organisation and activities of the Viet Minh. It must also be remembered that the burning of villages followed the doctrinal practice of 'punitive expeditions' in the North-West Frontier Province over the previous 80 years. The British attempted to drop leaflets to inform the population, as they had done in the NWFP. See letter from Gracey to Mountbatten, 9 November 1945, TNA, WO 203/4271, and Dennis, pp. 174–5 for some of General Gracey's explanations for the destruction of houses and, potentially, villages.

[76] 14/13th Frontier Force Rifles, War Diary, November 1945, TNA WO 172/7743, and 100 Indian Infantry Brigade, War Diary, November 1945, TNA WO 172/7135.

[77] Dunn, p. 282. By the end of November, 18 British and Indian soldiers had been killed and 51 wounded, 19 Japanese killed and 13 missing. It was estimated that close to 400 Viet Minh had been killed and more than 400 had been captured by the 20th Indian Division; estimates from the French and Japanese were lacking. Dunn, p. 285.

The month of November brought about a partial shift in the campaign. As the 20th Indian Division was able to consolidate its gains, it decided to re-focus on its primary operational task, disarming the Japanese Army. More and more French troops were arriving in FIC and were able to start taking over key security tasks from the British/Indian troops, as well as from the Japanese outside of Saigon. The various units and formations of the 20th Indian Division continued to send out mobile combined arms patrols to show the flag and disrupt any Viet Minh attempts to seize key areas within the 'Saigon' area of operations, at the same time as disarming the Japanese soldiers.[78]

At the same time, General Auchinleck, still pressing for the withdrawal of the Indian forces in the region, sought to make clear to the British Chiefs of Staff that the Indian Army was not an open-ended resource which they could use throughout Asia: 'If we continue to use Indian troops in Java [and FIC], as HMG apparently propose to do, for the purpose of reinstating Dutch rule in the Netherlands East Indies [French rule in FIC], we can have no defence whatever against the accusations that these troops are mercenary troops who are acting at the bidding of the British Government against the wishes of the Indian people.'[79] He followed up a similar letter to the War Office on 15 November 1945.[80]

By the end of November, units of the 100th Indian Brigade had been used in mobile columns to engage pockets of the Viet Minh and had disarmed thousands of Japanese. The 14/13th FFRifles had disarmed over 1,000 Japanese on one day in November.[81] At the same time, some Japanese frontline units were still being employed in battle, doing a professional job and being commended for it.[82] The complexity of the war and the 'strangeness' was staggering to many Burma

---

78 See 100th Indian Infantry Brigade War Diary for the month of November 1945, as it lists 'Jap Surrender Instr No 1' as well as other key tasks and operations for the brigade, November 1945, TNA WO 172/7135.

79 Auchinleck to Wavell, 13 November 1945, no. 1112, Auchinleck Papers, University of Manchester. He followed this with another letter on 20 November to G.E.B. Abell, Private Secretary to the Viceroy, no. 1116, stating that the Government of India should be consulted before Indian troops were used in other areas. General Auchinleck and Wavell were under immense pressure due to the INA trials that were taking place and were aware of the potential additional pressure that would be applied to the Indian Army.

80 Auchinleck to the War Office, 15 November 1945, OIOC L/WS/1/1488.

81 See both the battalion and brigade war diaries, TNA WO 172/7135 and WO 172/7743 for more detail.

82 Dunn, p. 311.

campaign veterans.[83] The 9/12th Frontier Force Regiment[84] was earmarked to set up a large Japanese internment area, in Cap St. Jaques (Vung Tau) to repatriate Japanese POWs.[85] On 28 November, the 32nd Indian Infantry Brigade handed over their area of responsibility north of Saigon. By the end of November, the drawdown was to begin as Mountbatten arrived to formally accept the surrender of the Japanese General Terauchi and his forces on the 30th. While in Saigon, Mountbatten met with General Gracey and the French Army commander, Leclerc, to discuss the withdrawal of the 20th Indian Division, due to the needs of SEAC in other Areas of Operations (AOs) and the political pressure being applied by the Indian National Congress against the Government of India, just as the Indian National Army trials were being carried out. The 32nd Brigade was earmarked to leave by the end of the year, and the 80th Brigade to leave with the divisional HQ and General Gracey, by the end of January 1946, as French forces geared up to take over.[86]

While the planning for withdrawal was in full swing, operations continued and took on a different flavor during December. The 32nd Brigade carried out an operation to clear Han Phu Island of the Viet Minh, which it did with minimal casualties. By the 19th, it had relinquished command of the area to the French.[87] As 80th Indian Brigade was earmarked next, it slowly started to hand

---

[83] Interview with Indian Army officers, 1999–2007. It is also noted in W.E.H. Condon's *Frontier Force Regiment* Aldershot: Gale & Polden, 1962: 'As the concentration of surrendered Japanese troops increased, the men of the battalion [9/12th Frontier Force Regiment] had naturally to come into closer contact with their late enemies, and had the opportunity to observe them closely. It is recorded that their discipline was first class, and they co-operated and carried out orders 100 percent. Never was there a cause for complaint, and the men grew to respect them and showed a tendency to fraternize', pp. 512–13. The 9/14th Punjab Regiment's battalion history, while respecting the Japanese soldiers' discipline, still could not see them other than an enemy. As the battalion stated: 'Many of them [surrendering Japanese soldiers], handing over their swords which were family heirlooms, were in tears but after what we had seen of them [in Burma] our hearts were closed to any pity for the Jap.' Anon, p. 99.

[84] The battalion arrived in FIC in early October 1945. The battalion was initially commanded by an ICO, Lt. Col. Hayaud Din, who had commanded the battalion during the heavy fighting in Burma in 1945. The battalion had served throughout the Burma campaigns of 1943–45 with the 80th Indian Infantry Brigade. Upon the ending of the Burma campaign, the battalion became the recce battalion for the division. During the first weeks of deployment to FIC, it served in the Cholon area of Saigon and participated in many clearing patrols of the area. In mid-October it was ordered to proceed to Cap St Jacques to set up a series of internment camps for the Japanese POWs. See War Diary, January to December 1945, TNA WO 172/7738 as well as file 4/26, Gracey Papers, LHCMA.

[85] 9/12 Frontier Force Regiment, War Diary, December, 1945, TNA, WO 172/7738.

[86] See Dunn, pp. 314–16 for more details.

[87] 32nd Indian Infantry Brigade, December, 1945, TNA WO 172/7098.

over various areas of responsibility to the French, at the same time as disarming the Japanese.[88] It became so quiet in their sector that the battalion was able to revert to peacetime training.[89] This was not true for the 100th Indian Brigade and its units, which continued to be engaged in various skirmishes with the Viet Minh at the same time they were disarming the Japanese and seizing arms stocks, during December 1945 and January 1946.[90]

While the British were beginning to withdraw and hand over to the French, French arrogance and lack of discipline, which had already caused problems in September, began to get out of hand again. General Gracey sent a letter to General Leclerc, stating forcefully his anger with the French units and their arrogant and racist behaviour towards the Japanese forces and his own Indian troops. He wrote in part:

> It might be of value for them [French troops] to realize that, had not the Japanese in most cases carried out my orders faithfully, there would have been a disaster of the first magnitude in Southern French Indo-China with a massacre of thousands of French people, and the destruction of a vast amount of French property. ... [In terms of disrespect of the Indian troops] the camaraderie which exists between officers of the Indian Army and their Gurkha and Indian soldiers must be explained to them. Our men, of whatever colour, are our friends and not considered 'black' men. They expect and deserve to be treated in every way as first-class soldiers and their treatment should be, and is, exactly the same as that of white troops.[91]

As noted previously, as the 32nd and 80th brigades began to hand over control to the French and organise withdrawal, in preparation for service in British Borneo and other AOs of SEAC, the fighting in the north and north-east of Saigon, in the 100th Brigade's AO, continued throughout December and early January. The Brigade was stretched, due to the lack of supporting forces to the south and west. The 14/13th Frontier Forces Rifles carried out countless patrols

88 80th Indian Infantry Brigade, December, 1945, TNA WO 172/7128.

89 9/12th Frontier Force Regiment, December, 1945, TNA WO 172/7738 and see also Condon, *Frontier Force Regiment*, pp. 509–13.

90 100th Indian Infantry Brigade, December 1945, TNA WO 172/7135.

91 See file 4/16, 12 December 1945, Gracey Papers, LHCMA. Also quoted in Dunn, pp. 325–6 and Dennis, 177. Gracey wrote more regarding the Indian Army, 'There is no more fruitful source of friction between Indian Army officers and their men on one side, and French troops on the other, than when our Indian and Gurkha troops are regarded and treated as 'black' by French officers and men. I mention this point particularly as cases have occurred in which it is obvious that our Indian Army traditions have not been understood.'

in and around Bien Hao, reverting to the term, 'Sher Forces', used to refer to their patrolling activities in the Burma campaign. This exemplifies how many within the battalion saw this as a continuation of the Burma war, even against a different enemy.[92] While the battalion sent out 'Sher Forces' to engage the Viet Minh, they slowly started to see a Viet Minh build-up of forces and became aware that the Viet Minh controlled the night once again. Many patrols were able to surprise the Viet Minh, partially due to the 'jungle warfare' experience they had earned in Burma. A marked similarity between the campaigns in Burma and in FIC was evident in the Viet Minh attack on the patrol base at Bien Hao. Overnight on 2/3 January 1946, a Viet Minh battalion attacked the main patrol base for the 14/13th Frontier Force Rifles at Bien Hoa, with attached troops from the Jats. The Viet Minh launched five well-coordinated, simultaneous attacks supported by heavy fire. The Indian troops were able to beat off the attacks, with heavy fire from machine guns and supporting mortars. The attack lasted for four hours and resulted in an estimated 100 Viet Minh killed, with no losses for the troops at Bien Hao, including the Japanese, who were still defending.[93] While the Viet Minh lost the battle, many noted their bravery afterwards.[94]

Units of the 100th Indian Brigade continued to send out patrols to keep up the pressure, before the brigade handed over responsibility to French forces.[95] The Viet Minh in return kept the pressure on the brigade and the various patrol bases, including Bien Hao. The 'mobile' ability provided by the 16th Light Cavalry's armoured cars ended with the 16th's departure on 12 January.[96] The 80th Indian Brigade had stood down the day before, and the 20th Division HQ and General Gracey were scheduled to leave FIC at the end of the month for Malaya. The date set for the transfer of all forces, including some Indian battalions in FIC to French command, was 28 January, the day that Gracey was scheduled to leave.[97] More than 54,000 Japanese soldiers had been disarmed and concentrated at Cap St Jacques; 40 soldiers from the 20th Indian Division had died and more than 100 had been wounded between October and late January. It is estimated that more than 2000 Viet Minh were killed during the same period.[98] Initially the

[92] Interviews with officers from the 14/13th Frontier Force Rifles. See Marston's *Phoenix from the Ashes*, for more details on the 14/13th Frontier Force Rifles and the 'Sher Forces'. Also December 1945, TNA WO 172/7743.

[93] 14/13th Frontier Force Rifles War Dairy, February 1946, TNA WO 172/10272.

[94] Dunn, p. 334.

[95] December 1945, TNA WO 172/7135.

[96] See TNA WO 172/7353 and WO 172/10060 for more details of the 16th Light Calvary.

[97] 20th Indian Division HQ War Diary, February 1946, TNA WO 203/5995.

[98] Dunn, p. 341.

100th Indian Brigade was assigned to support the French but this was stopped in response to political pressures in India and objections from Auchinleck and the Viceroy. The brigade left on two days, on 8 and 9 February.[99] Over the course of January and February close to 12,000 troops from the 20th Indian Division withdrew from FIC.

The 9/12th Frontier Force Regiment[100] and 2/8th Punjab remained in FIC, the latter to guard the mission in Saigon and the former to guard Cap St Jacques and continue the repatriation of Japanese POWs. Both battalions served until the end of March under the authority of Allied Commander's Inter-Service Liaison Mission to French Indo-China, under the command of a British Brigadier, F.K.S. Maunsell. Only small miscellaneous sub-units remained, including Coy 2/8th Punjab, until May 1946.[101]

Conclusion

The 20th Indian Division's time in FIC highlighted many complexities of war and strategy. Contrary to the common assertion that the Second World War was not a complex war, the post-war occupation duties for the Indian Army in the Far East provide an excellent encapsulation of the complexity of the Second World War. HMG's government was never quite clear about the role the British and the Indian armies should play in support of their European allies in the restoration of their former colonies. Furthermore, one cannot help but wonder whether HMG would have been as quick to allow the expansion of SEAC AO, if British soldiers, NCOs, and officers had been the ones to do the fighting. The political pressure brought to bear by Operation PYTHON indicates that the answer is clearly no. The other irony is that the new Labour Government, in haste to end the British presence in India, nevertheless saw the Indian Army as an imperial reserve with unlimited abilities to project British power and support for allies, with the added benefit of few casualties to trouble the British electorate.

The so-called evolving strategy within SEAC also highlights some of the issues that had arisen during the war between India Command and SEAC. While both the 14th and 12th armies fell under the command of SEAC, their

99 December 1945, TNA WO 172/7135.

100 Condon notes an interesting aspect of the withdrawal of the 9/12th Frontier Force Regiment, in his book: 'on 29th of March the battalion embarked at Cap St Jacques. ... Many Japanese senior officers and men lined the route to say goodbye to the Battalion, and it was a curious, if not pathetic, scene to find the very men who had fought against us so bitterly, now so manifestly sorry to bid the Battalion farewell', p. 513.

101 Dunn, pp. 355–6.

formations were predominantly Indian. It was one thing to have forces working in former British colonies, such as Burma and Malaya – which Indian Army units did. Their roles in FIC and the DEI, on the other hand, created a major political issue in India, at the same time as the INA trials were getting underway. To General Auchinleck, the long-term stability of the Indian Army was the most important factor for India during the coming years leading to independence, and he felt very strongly that involvement in these operations caused far too much unnecessary pressure.

Due to the lack of clear strategy, and contradictory advice from both SEAC and London, General Gracey was left to develop planning and strategy on his own, as the man on the ground. While he made mistakes, particularly in the early days with the Viet Minh, he had specifically been told not to engage the Viet Minh, but to work with French authorities, even if there was minimal French presence. Gracey and his staff set out to carry out their mission, at first with minimal support, and along strict military lines, they did a professional job. The officers, VCOs, NCOs, and soldiers of the 20th Indian Division carried out this difficult mission with the same level of professionalism and ability as they had shown in Burma from 1943 to the end of the war. Many veterans had remained with the division, and applied their experiences and knowledge to the campaign in Vietnam. In the minds of many of the officers, VCOs, NCOs and jawans, they were professional soldiers and recent victorious veterans of Burma, and their job was to carry out the orders of their commander, Major General Gracey. However, lack of strategy and of political awareness at the highest levels, both in SEAC and London, left the division the 'piggy in the middle' in a difficult political and combat situation.

In the end, the Indian Nationalists' rhetoric, though troublesome, had minimal impact on the Indian forces. This was partially due to the duration of the campaign, but more because they were a frontline veteran formation that tended to view their present through the prism of the profession of arms against an enemy. This was further reinforced by the role and support provided by the Japanese forces. The British/Indian troops, at first bemused by their role, came to respect and develop a feeling of camaraderie with their former enemy. Those who had been fighting and killing one another a few months previously discovered common ground as fellow professional soldiers, serving and dying alongside one another. In such paradox is embodied the fog and complexity of war.

Chapter 9

Re-forging the Damascus Blade: Partition of the Indian Armoured Corps, 1947

Ashok Nath

The partition of India in August 1947 saw the unified Indian Army dismembered and separated into the armies of India and Pakistan. The task of dividing the army's regiments was accomplished in less than three months largely due to the efforts of senior British and Indian officers and was made possible with the spirit of camaraderie and goodwill existing amongst all ranks. This chapter examines how this seemingly 'impossible task' was achieved in one of its most respected fighting arms – the Indian cavalry or more appropriately its descendent the Indian Armoured Corps.

A Difficult Task

'The biggest crime and the biggest headache' is how Mountbatten's Chief of Staff, Lord Ismay described the partition of the Indian Army.[1] Field Marshal Claude Auchinleck, Commander-in-Chief (C-in-C) India, hoped that, in spite of the birth of the independent dominions of India and Pakistan, the army might remain intact under a joint command. He expressed the view that it would take from five to ten years satisfactorily to divide the Indian Army. John Connell in his biography of Auchinleck has explained the reasons: 'Auchinleck and the surviving cadre of British officers wanted to preserve that Army, not as an instrument of some devious policy of British imperialism, not as a museum piece, not even as an end in itself, but to hand it on, strong and unimpaired to their successors.'[2] He was supported in his view by the Viceroy Lord Louis Mountbatten and the vast majority of British and Indian officers of the Indian Army. The plan proposed by the Cabinet Mission had also envisaged a unified

[1] Alan Campbell-Johnson, *Mission with Mountbatten* (London: Robert Hale, 1952), p. 137.

[2] John Connell, *Auchinleck: A Biography of Field Marshal Sir Claude Auchinleck* (London: Cassell, 1959), p. 839.

army. A notable exception was Lieutenant General Sir Francis Tuker the commander of Eastern Command. He was convinced partition of India was inevitable and already in 1946 had proposed a scheme for the division of the Armed Forces into Muslim and Hindu units before communal feeling became too fierce.[3] Nehru and the Congress were opposed to the idea of the partition of India and of its army; however, when partition became inevitable he is reported to have opposed a unified Indian Army for the two dominions. Therefore both Mr Jinnah and his pro-partition Muslim League along with Mr Nehru and Congress wanted two separate armies sooner than later.

A subcommittee headed by Major General Stephen Fenemore Irwin as chairman was hastily established to implement the task of dismembering the Indian Army. This was called the Armed Forces Reconstitution Committee. The term 'Reconstitution' was applied instead of ' Division' so as to avoid an adverse psychological effect on the Indian officers and men who had for so long regarded themselves as a closely integrated and unified body. By mid July 1947, the division and allocation of regiments were announced. In broad terms, the army was split on a ratio of two (India) to one (Pakistan). The task of dividing the Armed Forces unprecedented in the military history of the world was accomplished largely due to the efforts of senior British and Indian officers. Describing the huge task facing his headquarters Auchinleck in his letter to the Editor of the *Fighting Forces* wrote: 'In the Army the task was more complicated still, as many units, of mixed class, Hindu and Muslim composition, had to be torn apart and rebuilt into new units of one class or religion only.'[4]

In 1947, the class structure of the Indian Armoured Corps with the exception of one regiment[5] was based on the so called 'Martial Races' from the North. Martial Races was a designation coined by officials in British India and increasingly in vogue after the Second Afghan War of 1878–80. It represented a collective expression of beliefs prevalent amongst in the British Indian Army officer corps which had gained wide currency under Field Marshal Lord Roberts

[3] C.H. Philips and M.D. Wainwright (eds), *Keeping the Peace in India 1946–47; the Role of Lt Gen Francis Tuker in Eastern Command. The Partition of India: Policies and Perspectives 1935–47* (London: G. Allen & Unwin, 1970), pp. 127–47 (Tuker's scheme for classing Army into Hindu and Muslim units prior to the partition of the country would have created the conditions for a civil war instead of checking communal frenzy).

[4] Auchinleck Papers (John Rylands University Library Manchester), File LXXXVII, MUL 1311.

[5] This was the 16th Light Cavalry, by March 1947, most of its so called Martial Classes, i.e., Jats, Rajputs and Kaim Khanis were posted out and South Indians replaced them.

(Kipling's *Bob's Bahadur*), a popular Victorian military hero and considered the main architect of victory over the Afghans.[6]

The Indian Armoured Corps Prior to Partition

Just prior to Partition in 1947, the Indian Armoured Corps comprised 18 regiments, as well as the Indian Long Range Desert Squadron, the Governor General's Body Guard and the various Indian Armoured Corps training establishments.

These were the following:

Governor General's Body Guard (split equally between India and Pakistan).
Skinner's Horse (1st Duke of York's Own Cavalry).*
2nd Royal Lancers (Gardner's Horse).*
3rd Cavalry.*
Hodson's Horse (4th Duke of Cambridge's Own Lancers).*
Probyn's Horse (5th King Edward's Own Lancers).
6th Duke of Connaught's Own Lancers.
7th Light Cavalry.*
8th Light Cavalry.*
The Royal Deccan Horse (9th Horse).*
The Guides Cavalry (10th Queen Victoria's Own Frontier Force).
Prince Albert Victor's Own Cavalry (11th Frontier Force).
13th Duke of Connaught's Own Lancers.
The Scinde Horse (14th Prince of Wales's Own Cavalry).*
16th Light Cavalry.*
The Poona Horse (17th Queen Victoria's Own Cavalry).*
18th King Edward VII's Own Cavalry.*
19th King George V's Own Lancers.
The Central India Horse (21st King George V's Own Horse).*
Indian Long Range Desert Squadron.
The Indian Armoured Corps training establishments and records located in Ahmadnagar, Lucknow, Ferozepur and Babina

6 A. Nath, 'Martial Race Theory in the South Asian Context', Rydeberg, Thisner, Åselius (eds), *Militärhistorisk Tidskrift* (Stockholm, 2007), pp. 3–4.

Twelve regiments (marked with *) remained with the Indian Army and six were to go to Pakistan. The Governor General's Body Guard which required exceptional treatment was to be divided equally between the two. The Indian Long Range Desert Squadron comprising four 'Class' patrols: J (Jats); M (Muslims), R (Rajputs), S (Sikhs) was disbanded, the men reverting to their parental units.

Allotment of Regiments

A committee under Major General Irwin appropriately called the Irwin Committee was given the delicate task of allotting the regiments. In addition to its British chairman, it included representatives from both India and the future Pakistan. It proceeded to make its difficult and hurried decisions based upon a simple principle. The ethno-religious preponderance within each regiment should determine its allocation to either India or Pakistan, in accordance with the communal majorities of each country.[7] Pakistan's share was six regiments, *viz.*, Probyn's Horse (5th King Edward's Own Lancers), 6th Duke of Connaught's Own Lancers, Prince Albert Victor's Own Cavalry (11th Frontier Force), 13th Duke of Connaught's Own Lancers and The Scinde Horse (14th Prince of Wales's Own Cavalry)[8] changed later to The Guides Cavalry (10th Queen Victoria's Own Frontier Force) and the 19th King George V's Own Lancers. It is immediately evident from the percentages below that ethno-religious criteria for allocating regiments could not be universally followed. Considerations such as immovable regimental property were important. Another factor that hindered the implementation of the Committee's decisions in allocation of regiments in a fair manner has been underlined by Major General G.S. Sandhu.

It was becoming clear at the time that the sympathies of a large number of British officers lay in Pakistan. The fact that Pakistan accepted a much larger number of British officers for retention in their country after partition and then promised them employment for a much longer period contributed to the bias. Nevertheless, in the allotment of regiments to Pakistan a distinct partiality can be discerned.[9]

---

[7] Ashok Nath, *Izzat: Historical Records and Iconography of Indian Cavalry Regiments 1750–2007* (New Delhi: USII, 2009), p. vii.

[8] Maj-Gen. Jehanzeb, 'From Bitter Lakes to Bitter Thoughts', in *Sabre and Lance (Journal of the Pakistan Armoured Corps)*, 1997, p. 54.

[9] Maj-Gen. G.S. Sandhu, *The Indian Armour, History of Indian Armoured Corps 1941–71* (Delhi: Vision Books, 1987), p. 246.

Regiments with considerable assets such as Probyn's Horse, 13th Duke of Connaught's Own Lancers (the oldest cavalry unit of the old Bombay Army) and The Guides Cavalry are examples of this bias. A particular case in point was the allotment of The Guides Cavalry to Pakistan and The Scinde Horse to India. The Guides, possibly the most written about cavalry regiment of the old Indian Army and sometimes styled 'God's Own Guides' in good-humoured malice by envious brothers in arms, was one of two surviving Piffer[10] cavalry regiments with a non Muslim majority. The other Piffer unit, Prince Albert Victor's Own Cavalry (11th Frontier Force) had a Muslim majority. The Corps of Guides' historical association with Mardan and the Frontier, added to the pressure from its British officers who would enjoy a longer tenure if the regiment went to Pakistan, resulted in intense lobbying against the decision.[11]

A feasible way to implement division of the manpower assets required a practical approach. Sixty squadrons formed the Indian Armoured Corps regiments; twenty three squadrons were Muslims and 37 Hindu/Sikh and South Indian Classes. Many of them had to be separated from their parent units and re-allocated to new units. The squadron themselves as far as possible were to be left intact, transferred or retained as the case might be. Although, the division which looked possible on paper was not quite that simple as subsequent events unfolded. A Muslim soldier domiciled in Pakistan and a non-Muslim domiciled in the rest of India had no option but to serve his respective dominion or be discharged. Also, it was erroneously presumed that all class Muslim squadrons would automatically opt for Pakistan. Furthermore, Muslim communities with traditional homes outside the areas which were likely to constitute 'Pakistan' several of whom had initially opted to remain in India, changed their opt later for Pakistan, after witnessing the horrific scenes following the outbreak of communal violence, e.g. the Kaim Khani squadron of the Poona Horse, the Ranghar squadrons of Skinner's and Scinde Horse are some such typical examples (See Table 9.1).

10 Piffer is a term used for units of the former Punjab Irregular Force (PIF) comprising cavalry, artillery and infantry, their mission was to maintain order on the Punjab Frontier. Considered a tight knit brotherhood of soldiers, bound by a distinguished military history and a long tradition of soldiering. Most of them were allotted to Pakistan at the time of Partition of India in 1947.

11 Nath, *Izzat*, p. 516; see also *Sabre and Lance*, p. 54.

Table 9.1 The Class Squadron Composition Prior to Partition

Class or ethnic composition	Squadrons
Hindustani Muslim and Ranghar	6
Punjabi Muslim	9
Pathan (Muslim)	4
Kaim Khani (Muslim)	4
Rajput (Hindu)	6
Jat (Hindu)	11
Dogra (Hindu)	5
Sikh	12
South Indian Classes	3

Source: A. Nath, Izzat: Historical Records and Iconography of Indian Cavalry Regiments 1750–2007 (New Delhi: USII, 2009), p. 515.

Regiments Remaining with the Indian Army, with Percentage of Men Transferred to Pakistan

The Governor General's Body Guard (part of). 50 per cent (Punjabi Muslims) to Pakistan.

Skinner's Horse (1st D.Y.O. Cavalry). 33 per cent to Pakistan.

2nd Royal Lancers (G.H.). 23 per cent to Pakistan (circa 10 per cent Hindustani Muslims stayed in India and were later transferred to 18th Cavalry).

3rd Cavalry. 33 per cent to Pakistan.

Hodson's Horse (4th D.C.O. Lancers). 33 per cent to Pakistan.

7th Light Cavalry. 33 per cent to Pakistan.

8th K.G.V's O. Light Cavalry. 33 per cent to Pakistan.

The Royal Deccan Horse (9th Horse). 33 per cent to Pakistan.

The Scinde Horse (14th P.W.O. Cavalry). 67 per cent to Pakistan.

16th Light Cavalry. Not affected (converted to South Indian classes in 1946).

The Poona Horse (17th Q.V.O Cavalry). 33 per cent to Pakistan.

18th K.E VII's O. Cavalry. 33 per cent to Pakistan.

The Central India Horse (21st K.G.V's O. Horse). 33 per cent to Pakistan.

Regiments Allotted to Pakistan, with Percentage of Men Transferred to India

Governor General's Body Guard (part of). 50 per cent (Sikhs) to India.
Probyn's Horse (5th K.E.O. Lancers). 67 per cent to India.
6th D.C.O. Lancers (Watson's Horse). 67 per cent to India.
The Guides Cavalry (10th Q.V.O. Frontier Force). 67 per cent to India.
Prince Albert Victor's Own Cavalry (11th Frontier Force). 33 per cent to India.
13th D.C.O. Lancers. 33 per cent to India.
19th K.G.O. Lancers. 67 per cent to India.

The Class Structure of Indian Cavalry Regiments

Indian cavalry regiments unlike the infantry were not named after any particular class or region. 'Class', a term in vogue since the 1880s in the Indian Army, described a type of Indian recognised for recruiting purposes being distinct from others. Its usage was fluid and inexact. Criteria could be race or language, religion, caste, domicile, or tribe; at times, it could be two or more of these attributes. It did not necessarily mean an ethnic type.[12] Three cavalry regiments, the Royal Deccan Horse, Scinde Horse and Central India Horse retained geographical or regional titles. This was continued solely as part of regimental tradition. Therefore, in reality a typical cavalry unit comprised at least three different classes, the majority being recruited from so called established martial races.[13] These were segregated respectively as the case may be, into three 'sabre' or fighting squadrons numbered Alpha, Bravo, Charlie, a fourth squadron the HQ squadron was a mixture of all classes drawn from the three squadrons and its task was mainly administrative. Each Squadron maintained its distinctive social identity; this was evident not only by the separate *langars* (communal kitchens) but also by the type of pagri worn on ceremonial dress by each squadron. For example Probyn's Horse had a squadron each of Punjabi Muslims, Sikhs and Dogras. Officially on paper they were designated as A, B, and C squadrons, but in reality they were identified and took great pride in being called after their respective class, e.g. Sikh squadron, Dogra squadron, Punjabi Muslim squadron etc.

---

12 Nath, *Izzat*, p. vii.

13 See Nath, 'Martial Race Theory in the South Asian Context', pp. 31–41.

The Indian Cavalry had always considered itself socially superior to other arms or services, drawing mainly from the traditions of the old surviving irregular cavalry regiments which had been based on the silladar system.[14] Several such units had remained loyal to the British cause during 1857 and had thereby been regularised in the post 1861 reorganisation that followed. The silladar system of the Indian cavalry had also appealed to the East India Company as is evident in Lord William Bentick's comment in 1835, when he was Governor General and C-in-C India:

> I need not repeat what has often been stated, that the Rohillas and all the highest caste and bravest of men of India, who will not enter our ranks from dislike to our rigid discipline ... have no repugnance to serve in the Irregular Cavalry. The Irregular Cavalry is of peculiar importance in India. It is the favourite arm of the native. It attaches him to our service by the strongest ties of interest and affection. It prevents their being engaged against us, and if the system were sufficiently extended it would at a trifling expense afford us all the advantages, moral and military, which the Russians have derived from the Cossack, who from being the bitterest of enemies of Russia, in the time of Peter the Great, have become the most faithful subjects ...[15]

Lord Kitchener implemented the first big change in the organisation of Indian cavalry by abolishing the old Presidency titles, re-numbering regiments from one to thirty-nine, and making all liable to serve in peace anywhere in India. Nevertheless, each regiment remained a separate entity. The silladar system, never really intended to meet the needs of modern warfare, broke down completely during the Great War. The Esher Committee expressed itself in favour of the abolition of this system, and the conversion of 36 of the 39 regiments to a non-silladar basis was commenced in 1920.

Before their conversion, it had been decided that only 21 regiments were to be retained in the post-war Indian Army. This involved the loss of 18 regiments but, rather than disband them, it was resolved to follow the British Army practice of that time and to amalgamate them in pairs. The 39 regiments were re-formed as 18 linked pairs with three retained as separate entities. The amalgamation or re-structuring of one or more regiments did not necessarily threaten the existence

---

14 In the silladar system, each man supplied and maintained his own horse, clothing, equipment, arms (other than his rifle) and barracks. Though individually men in silladar regiments were paid more, a silladar regiment actually cost the State less than a non-silladar one. One major disadvantage, however, was that the provision of equipment was a regimental responsibility in non-silladar units and therefore no two units had identical patterns.

15 Nath, *Izzat*, quoted on p. 4.

Table 9.2 Indian Cavalry Reorganisation of 1921–1923 and the Formation of Seven Cavalry Groups based on a Fixed Class Composition[123]

Group Nos	Group Centre Location	Designation on Amalgamation	New Designation by 1922–23	Class composition
I	Poona	1st/3rd Skinner's Horse 2nd/4th Cavalry 5th/8th Cavalry	1st D.Y.O. Skinner's Horse 2nd Lancers (G.H.) 3rd Cavalry	One squadron each of: • Hindustani Muslims & Rangars • Rajputs • Jats
II	Lahore	9th/10th Hodson's Horse 11th/12th Cavalry 13th/16th Cavalry	4th D.C.O. Hodons's Horse 5th K.E.O. Probyn's Horse 6th D.C.O. Lancers	One squadron each of: • Punjabi Muslims • Sikhs • Dogras
III	Secundrabad[16]	28th Light Cavalry 26th/30th K.G.O. Light Cavalry 20th/29th Deccan Horse	7th Light Cavalry 8th K.G.O. Light Cavalry 9th Royal Deccan Horse	One squadron each of: • Jats • Sikhs • Deccani Muslims[17]
IV	Rawalpindi	Q.V.O. Corps of Guides Cavalry (FF) 21st/23rd Cavalry 22nd/25th Cavalry	10th Q.V.O. Corps of Guides Cavalry (FF) 11th P.A.V.O Cavalry (FF) 12th Cavalry (FF)	One squadron each of: • Dogras • Sikhs • Punjabi Muslims
V	Jubbulpore (Jabalpur)	31st/32nd Lancers 35th/36th Cavalry 7th/37th Lancers	13th D.C.O. Bombay Lancers[18] 14th P.W.O. Scinde Horse 15th Lancers	One squadron each of: • Pathans • Sikhs • Muslim Rajputs
VI	Jhansi	27th Light Cavalry 33rd/34th Cavalry 6th/7th Cavalry	16th Light Cavalry 17th Q.V.O. Poona Horse 18th K.E.O. Cavalry	One squadron each of: • Jats • Kaimkhanis • Rajputs
VII	Delhi	18th/19th Lancers 14th/15th Lancers 38th/39th Cavalry	19th K.G.O. Lancers 20th Lancers 21st K.G.O. Central India Horse	One squadron each of: • Sikhs • Jats • Punjabi Muslims

Source: A. Nath, Izzat: Historical Records and Iconography of Indian Cavalry Regiments 1750–2007 (New Delhi: USII, 2009), p. 407.

16 Bangalore proposed earlier, but later changed to Secundrabad.

17 Changed to Punjabi Muslims from 1932/34.

18 13th D.C.O. Lancers; the last to amalgamate, did so in September 1923.

of the regimental system as was demonstrated in the reorganisation of 1922 and again in 1937, it was based on a class structure and so it largely remained when the Armoured Corps was suddenly faced with the prospect of Partition in 1947.

Reorganisation 1937

Another reorganisation took place in 1937. The earlier system of seven cavalry stations considered impractical and unpopular since it tied down seven regiments when mobilisation was called for was done away with. In the new system there were three groups of six regiments each. Three regiments were converted permanently into training regiments, one for each of the groups located at a permanent group centre. The new groupings also involved some further adjustments in the ethnic composition. For example the Pathans from 15th Lancers were transferred to the Guides replacing their Punjabi Muslims and the surplus Pathans were taken over by 13th D.C.O. Lancers and the Scinde Horse. A Jat squadron from 20th Lancers went to 6th D.C.O. Lancers, and Dogras were eliminated from 6th D.C.O. Lancers.

What is clearly evident here is that a distinctive pattern emerges – all units comprise a set of different classes, organised into separate squadrons. The squadrons can be interchanged between regiments as long as the organising principle is adhered to.

No one class regiment or single religious identity existed in the post 1922 cavalry, unlike that of the Infantry (Gurkhas, Garhwalis, Dogras, Sikhs etc).

Expansion and Changes 1939–1947

The metamorphosis of Indian cavalry into Indian armour became official on 1 May 1941. Mechanisation proceeded until every Indian cavalry regiment was converted and became a part of the new Indian Armoured Corps. All new raisings were ordered to include 'Indian Armoured Corps', or 'I.A.C.' for short after the regimental title. On paper, armour strength in India was sanctioned from 20 regiments (18 Indian and two British) to 32 regiments (28 Indian and four British). In reality this did not happen mainly due to shortage of equipment and the low priority given for the mechanisation of the Indian cavalry. The pre-1939 class structure mainly remained unaffected, except that the recruitment base broadened to take in non traditional classes[19] (circa 11 per cent) for the

19 Ibid., p. 786, see also caste returns of the Indian Armoured Corps for 1945.

Table 9.3 ORBAT of the Indian Cavalry was now 18 Active and Three Training Regiments[12]

Group No.	Group Centre Loc	Training Regiment	Regiments Affiliated	Ethnic composition
I	Jhansi[20]	15th Lancers	Skinners Horse (1st D.Y.O. Cav) 2nd Royal Lancers (G.H.) 3rd Cavalry 16th Light Cavalry The Poona Horse (17th Q.V.O. Cav) 18th K.E.O. Cavalry	• Rajputs • Jats • Rangars and Hindustani Muslims • Jats • Rajputs • Kaimkhanis
II	Ferozepur	Sam Browne's Cavalry (12th Frontier Force)	Hodson's Horse (4th D.C.O. Lancers) Probyn's Horse (5th K.E.O. Lancers) Guides Cavalry (10th Q.V.O. FF) P.A.V.O. Cavalry (11th FF)[22] 13th D.C.O. Lancers The Scinde Horse (14th P.W.O. Cavalry)	• Dogras • Sikhs • Punjabi Muslims (Pathans[21]) • Pathans • Ranghars • Sikhs
III	Lucknow	20th Lancers	6th D.C.O.Lancers 7th Light Cavalry 8th K.G.V.'s O. Light Cavalry The Royal Deccan Lancers (9th Horse) 19th K.G.O. Lancers The Central India Horse (21st K.G.V.'s O. Horse)	• Jats • Sikhs • Punjabi Muslims • Dogras[23] • Jats • Punjabi Muslims

Source: A. Nath, Izzat: Historical Records and Iconography of Indian Cavalry Regiments 1750–2007 (New Delhi: USII, 2009), p. 408.

20 This was shifted to Ferozepur.

21 A.V.O. Cavalry's 'B' Squadron comprising Dogras was transferred intact to the Central India Horse in 1940, and to replace them a new 'B' Squadron comprising Ranghars and Hindustani Muslim was raised.

22 Pathans from 15th Lancers replaced the Punjabi Muslims in the Guides and Jats from 20th Lancers replaced the Dogras in the 6th D.C.O. Lancers.

23 Dogras only after 1940. Earlier Sikhs.

duration of the war, but reverting to its more traditional pre-1939 structure by 1946 (an exception was the 16th Light Cavalry which was being restructured into a South Indian class unit).

The two primary elements that created an effective Indian cavalry regiment was firstly the overall regimental identity, its guardian were the officers, British primarily but increasingly Indian. The second were the squadrons based on their respective class identities, integral to but not necessarily indispensable to the regiment as squadrons could be inter-changed and adopt new regimental identities being secure in their own sub-unit class identities which remained intact. The soldier of the Indian cavalry therefore primarily fought for his squadron which represented the honour of his own community, after that for his regiment. That was basically the character of the Indian Cavalry regiment at its core, and given its construction it was to be expected. Take the case of the mutiny of the Sikh squadron of the Central India Horse which refused to embark on the troopship at Bombay to fight in what they called an 'Imperialist war'. The Sikh squadron from 19th King George V's Own Lancers volunteered to a man to replace them in order to uphold Sikh honour – although this was not accepted and the authorities decided to play it safe by transferring a complete Dogra squadron from the Prince Albert Victor's Own Cavalry to replace the disgraced Sikhs of the Central India Horse.

As regards the British officers and later Indian officers commissioned from Sandhurst and Dehra Dun, the regimental identity was paramount and all successful regiments were usually a closely knit family bonded together. To what extent this bonding existed between British and Indian officers is open to question? Most historians tend to show an amiable relationship with a few minor hiccups. The relationship certainly varied depending on the regiments. Especially between regular pre-war commissioned British officers (by no means all) who resented the inclusion of Indian officers into their regiments. It was only when a large number of young Englishmen fresh from schools and colleges in England and unburdened by colonial inhibitions, came out as Emergency Commissioned officers to fill the gaps in junior ranks. It was they with whom the Indian officers, particularly the younger ones, began to establish easy relaxed friendships.[24]

The only units of the Indian cavalry who admitted Indian officers and had been earlier Indianised were the 16th and 7th Light Cavalry, followed by the 3rd Cavalry. These were the least attractive regiments for the British officers to serve in, the first two had been non-silladar units of the old Madras Army

[24] Maj-Gen. D.K. Palit, 'Indianisation of the Army Officer Cadre 1920–47', *Indo-British Review: A Journal of History (Madras)*, Vol. 16, No. 1, March 1989, pp. 55–8.

and therefore not as rich in assets, the 3rd Cavalry without royal patronage was known as 'Nobody's Own'. Therefore the vast majority of Cavalry regiments and certainly the most famous amongst them had barred entry to Indian officers. This was a sort of institutionalised segregation, only rectified after 1940 when all units of the Indian Army (except the Gurkha Brigade) threw open their doors. This was necessitated as a wartime contingency more than anything else. The earlier policy naturally had its repercussions as most of the famous cavalry regiments lacked pre-war regular Indian officers and were often left without their original officer cadre.

Camaraderie under Fire

A good deal of camaraderie existed amongst members of regiments irrespective of class or religion. But the question was whether it would last? British officers did not appear to think so. Those who had earlier volunteered to serve on, in increasingly large numbers now wanted their services terminated. In his report of 28 September 1947 Auchinleck wrote:

> When the decision to partition India was announced, British Officers of the Indian Armed Forces were asked to volunteer to serve on during Reconstitution .... Those who volunteered did so in the general desire to help in a fair and efficient division of the armed forces ... these volunteers are now asking to be released from the contracts in rapidly increasing numbers. One of the chief reasons for this is because they hold that they volunteered to help in the Reconstitution and not help the new governments to keep law and order in their own territories. The conditions of massacre and bestiality of the worst kind in which many of these British officers have been working continuously for so many weeks have sickened them. They have lost faith in their cloth and in their men, of whom they were so proud a short two months back.[25]

Two examples will suffice to illustrate that the *esprit de corps* in the old Indian Cavalry went far beyond the pull of religious bigotry. The first is the case of the 3rd Cavalry which after long years of brutal captivity in Japanese prisoner of war camps, had been reformed as an airborne armoured regiment and was the first and only armoured regiment to experience parachute dropping of both men and armoured vehicles. The regiment had just completed this exercise near

---

[25] Auchinleck Papers, Report on the Situation in India and Pakistan, 28 September 1947, File LXXXI, MUL 1262.

Rawalpindi when news of Partition became known. The resurrected 3rd Cavalry had been raised from volunteers from other armoured regiments, and the intention, revolutionary at that time, had been to make the 3rd Cavalry a mixed class regiment down to troop level, with common messing for its Hindustani Muslims, Ranghars, Rajputs and Jats (although Muslims and Hindus had served together down to the mixed troop level in cavalry regiments prior to 1861), common messing itself was a revolutionary step. After bidding a sad farewell to its Muslim comrades, who had opted for the Pakistan Army, the non-Muslim majority prepared for the move out of Rawalpindi and the hazardous journey south across the new frontier into India. Meanwhile, orders came from the Pakistani authorities that non-Muslim troops leaving for India should be disarmed. Lieutenant Colonel K.M. Idris, the officiating commandant and Risaldar Major Aulia Khan, both Muslims and optees for Pakistan, realised the dangerous implications of this order. They put their foot down, exclaiming that 'they shall depart as soldiers' and, in defiance of authority, allowed the men to retain their arms. If this order had been carried out, the men most probably would have been massacred on their train journey. The second concerns the Sikh squadron of the 19th King George V's Own Lancers. The regiment stationed at Peshawar was allotted to the Pakistan army when Partition took place. The Sikhs were to join Skinner's Horse in India. Their personal security caused considerable anxiety to the regiment, as the local Pathan population's hatred towards them was severe, originating as it did from the days of Sikh rule a century earlier. The operation to get the squadron away safely was carried out with the help of Muslim troops of the 19th Lancers, and such was the secrecy with which this was achieved that not even the police knew of it.

What was left was the incorporation of those squadrons whose parent units had either been allotted as the case may be either to India or Pakistan. An example will suffice to show how tradition of one regiment was symbolically interchanged with another in a simple yet moving ceremony that took place between the Pathan squadron of the Scinde Horse and the Sikh squadron of the Guides Cavalry. Early in August 1947, the Pathan squadron was transferred *en bloc to* the Guides Cavalry, whose Sikh squadron took its place in the Scinde Horse. The Regiment formed a line opposite the Quarter Guard and saluted their old comrades as they left their lines for the last time. On arrival in their new regiment, which was also stationed at Ahmadnagar, they formed up opposite the Sikhs who were to relieve them. Each man of both squadrons removed his Regimental cap or pagri badge, as the case might be, and handed it over to his opposite number. Thus symbolically did the Pathans of the Scinde Horse and

Sikhs of the Guides pass the custody of the traditions of their Squadron to their new guardians.[26]

Conclusion

The fact that both India and Pakistan inherited disciplined armed forces goes to prove the process of reconstitution, in spite of the difficult conditions, went through smoothly and was a success. It was made possible because of the leadership provided by British and Indian officers, along with a high degree of discipline, goodwill and camaraderie existing within the regiments. The regiments themselves did not collapse because switching class squadrons amongst them was not an unusual practice. The class squadron structure introduced from the 1880s, had seen several such interchanges notably in the cavalry reorganisations of 1922 and in 1937. Partition did alter the religious class structure of Indian cavalry regiments; it however, did not affect their efficiency or discipline. The regimental mess, its customs, traditions and *espirit de corps* were passed on to their successors. The 'Damascus blade' which symbolically represented an army in which all creeds and races of Indian served together with the British in mutual respect and concord marched away into history, but its memories and traditions remain intact in the armies of India and Pakistan.

[26] Lt. Col. K.R. Brooke, *The Scinde Horse (14th Prince of Wales's Own Cavalry) 1922–1947* (Privately published: The Scinde Horse Association, 1957), p. 80.

Chapter 10

A Dismal Story? Britain, the Gurkhas and the Partition of India, 1945–1948[1]

David Omissi

There is a familiar narrative about the end of the Indian Army of the British Raj. It runs something like this. In August 1947 the Indian Army, like India itself, was partitioned between the two successor states of India and Pakistan. The Muslim units of the Army went mainly to Pakistan, while the Hindu and Sikh units went mainly to India. The Nepalese Gurkhas, on the other hand, remained part of the British Army, with the exception of a few regiments, which were 'transferred' to the Indian Army at the time of independence.[2]

1 An earlier version of this paper was presented to the University of Hull History Research Seminar in December 2010. I am grateful to the organisers and participants for the opportunity to discuss work in progress, and for their very useful comments. There is an extensive literature on the Gurkhas, much of it written by British officers of Gurkha regiments. For an overview see the bibliography in L. Caplan, *Warrior Gentlemen: 'Gurkhas' in the Western Imagination* (Oxford, 1995). Excellent works on the Gurkhas in this period include T. Gould, *Imperial Warriors: Britain and the Gurkhas* (1999) and R. Gregorian, *The British Army, the Gurkhas and Cold War Strategy in the Far East, 1947–1954* (Basingstoke, 2002). The most important published primary source remains N. Mansergh et al. (eds), *The Transfer of Power, 1942–47* (12 vols, 1970–83), which has been one of the main sources for the present chapter. The Auchinleck papers (henceforth AUC) are held at the John Rylands University Library of Manchester. For a very useful guide to these papers see M.M. Wright, 'The Military Papers, 1940–48, of Field Marshal Sir Claude Auchinleck', *Bulletin of the John Rylands University Library of Manchester*, 70/2 (1988). For some of the legal implications of the transfer of Gurkha regiments to the Crown in 1948 see D.E. Omissi (with Public Interest Lawyers), Witness Statement, 'The Queen (On the Application of Pahalman Gurung and Others) and Ministry of Defence', Court of Appeal (2003). This Statement, which deeply informs this chapter, is based mainly on War Staff (henceforth L/WS) files in the India Office Records held in the British Library. For further references to these documents see the relevant chapters of the books by Gould and Gregorian cited above.

2 This slip of the pen occurs in otherwise excellent books: see for example J. Parker, *The Gurkhas: The Inside Story of the World's Most Feared Soldiers* (1999), Appendix II, 'The Regiments and Battle Honours'.

Broadly speaking this is indeed what happened, with one striking exception – the Gurkhas. No Gurkha regiments were 'transferred' to the Indian Army in 1947, for the simple reason that they already were part of the Indian Army. Instead, four of the Indian Army's ten Gurkha regiments were transferred *from* the Indian Army to the British Army, which had hitherto possessed no Gurkha regiments of its own. The 'British' Gurkha regiments had always previously belonged to the Indian Army, or, before 1858, to its predecessor, the army of the East India Company. The partition of the Indian Army in 1947 was therefore not a two-way, but a three-way process – between Pakistan, India and Britain.

This simple fact prompts several questions. Why did the British Army suddenly acquire (or even wish to acquire) four regiments of Gurkhas? How did the negotiations to acquire the Gurkhas develop, what were the main obstacles to the transfer, and how successful was the outcome? How did the Gurkha rank and file (and their British officers) react to the prospect of being transferred to the British Army? What was the attitude of the Maharaja of Nepal to the proposed transfer, and why did he consent to it? What was the relationship between the partition of the Gurkha Brigade and wider political and military events in South and South-East Asia? In January 1946 Viceroy Wavell told Lord Pethick-Lawrence (Secretary of State for India, 1945–47) that the future of the Gurkhas was a 'most delicate matter in which strict secrecy should be observed by all concerned'.[3] Why did the division of the Gurkha 'brigade' become such a touchy subject?[4] Sir Francis Tuker, Commander-in-Chief of Eastern Command from 1946, and himself a former officer of the 2nd Gurkha Rifles, was an outspoken critic of the partition of the Gurkha Brigade. 'The story', he wrote in his memoirs, was a 'dismal one'.[5] Was it?

Gurkha Recruitment to 1945

The army of the East India Company had begun recruiting Gurkha deserters and prisoners during the 1814–16 Anglo-Gurkha War.[6] Recruitment of Gurkhas continued after the war, even though the treaty ending the war made no

[3] Wavell to Pethick-Lawrence, Secretary of State for India (henceforth SSI), 1 January 1946, *Transfer of Power*, Vol. VI, doc. 325.

[4] Gould, *Imperial Warriors*, p. 286.

[5] F. Tuker, *While Memory Serves* (1950), p. 639.

[6] P. Mason, *A Matter of Honour: An Account of the Indian Army, its Officers and Men* (1974), p. 380.

formal provision for the entry of Gurkhas into British service.[7] Further Gurkha regiments were raised; they won a reputation for loyalty, and they earned the profound affection of their British officers. One Gurkha unit, the Sirmoor battalion (later the 2nd Gurkha Rifles) distinguished itself during the Sikh Wars and in the Indian Mutiny. As a reward, it was retitled a Rifle regiment, laid up its colours, and was presented instead by Queen Victoria with a 'truncheon' – a six-foot staff of bronze and silver, topped with a crown supported by three Gurkhas.[8] This truncheon was to feature prominently during one of the most difficult moments of the transfer in 1947.

By the later nineteenth century, recruiting to the Indian Army was increasingly driven by the theory of the so-called 'martial races', an idea particularly associated with Lord Roberts (Commander-in-Chief in India, 1885–93). According to the martial races theory – a mixture of indigenous notions of caste, Social Darwinism, and British India's collective memory of the Indian 'mutiny' – only certain 'races' in India could be considered both warlike and loyal.[9] Roberts (and others) considered the Gurkhas to be a martial race *par excellence*, and the number of Gurkha battalions in the Indian Army accordingly increased from five in 1862 to 15 in 1892.[10] By the early 1900s the Indian Army included ten regiments of Gurkha Rifles, each composed of two battalions, and organised (and dressed) rather like British Rifle regiments.[11] By this time, the Gurkhas were increasingly regarded as a *corps d'elite* within the Indian Army.[12] They had become, according to one leading historian, the Indian Army's equivalent of the Brigade of Guards – 'the gold standard of Indian soldiering'[13] – and Gurkha officers took a 'distinctly superior attitude' towards the rest of the Indian Army.[14]

[7] 'The Future of the Gurkhas', Draft Memorandum by SSI for Defence Committee, L/WS/1/1022.

[8] Mason, *Matter of Honour*, pp. 280–81.

[9] For excellent discussions of the theory see H. Streets, *Martial Races: the Military, Race and Masculinity in British Imperial Culture, 1857–1914* (Manchester, 2004) and D.M. Peers, 'The Martial Races and the Indian Army in the Victorian Era' in D.P. Marston and C.S. Sundaram (eds), *A Military History of India and South Asia: from the East India Company to the Nuclear Era* (Westport, CT., 2007).

[10] D.E. Omissi, *The Sepoy and the Raj: the Indian Army, 1860–1940* (Basingstoke, 1994), p. 11.

[11] T.A. Heathcote, *The Indian Army: The Garrison of British Imperial India, 1822–1922* (1974), p. 77.

[12] Gould, *Imperial Warriors*, p. 285.

[13] R. Callahan, 'The Great Sepoy Mutiny' in Marston and Sundaram (eds), *A Military History of India*, p. 33.

[14] L. Caplan, 'Bravest of the Brave: Representations of "the Gurkha" in British Military Writings', *Modern Asian Studies*, 25/3 (1991): 575.

During the Great War, Gurkhas served in France, Belgium, Mesopotamia, Persia, Egypt, Gallipoli, and Palestine.[15] Figures for the Indian Army should always be treated with caution, but official statistics suggest that there were 55,589 wartime Gurkha enlistments.[16] From 1919, as a reward, Nepal received an annual payment of 10 lakhs (or 1 million) rupees; and in 1923, through a Treaty 'of Perpetual Peace and Friendship' with Nepal, Britain formally recognised Nepalese independence.[17]

In the interwar period, the Gurkha Brigade reverted to ten regular regiments of two battalions each, making up roughly one-sixth of the total infantry in the Indian Army. Crucially, unlike other types of Indian Army units, Gurkhas were exempt from the process of Indianisation – the gradual introduction of Indian officers holding the King's commission – which was proceeding very slowly during the 1920s and 1930s.[18] By 1939 the Indian Army's officer corps included 1,912 British and 344 Indian officers.[19] None of the latter was serving with a Gurkha regiment, all of which retained their full complement of British officers.

During the Second World War, Gurkhas served with distinction in several theatres, including North Africa, Italy and (especially) Burma. The entire brigade expanded from 20 to 51 battalions. Gurkhas served in 44 infantry and parachute battalions (including 24 war-raised battalions), five training battalions and two garrison battalions.[20] That said, the wartime Indian Army in general had expanded more rapidly than its Gurkha component, and by 1 June 1943 Gurkhas made up only seven per cent of the entire Indian Army.[21]

During the war the Gurkhas maintained their military reputation, winning 10 Victoria Crosses – one in Tunisia, two in Italy and seven in Burma.[22] Like most British officers, General Sir Claude Auchinleck (Commander-in-Chief

---

15 .For a recent overview see D.E. Omissi, 'The Indian Army in the First World War, 1914–1918', in Marston and Sundaram (eds), *A Military History of India*.

16 D.E. Omissi (ed.), *Indian Voices of the Great War: Soldiers' Letters, 1914–1918* (Basingstoke, 1999), p. 367.

17 Tuker, *While Memory Serves*, p. 626.

18 On Indianization see Omissi, *The Sepoy and the Raj*, ch. 5.

19 Establishment of the Indian Army Officer Cadre, L/WS/1/924, Annexure 'A'. All Indian officers then served only in the 12 units that had been selected for Indianisation. From 1940 until independence they could serve in any Indian Army unit other than Gurkhas. These figures do not include Viceroy's Commissioned Officers (henceforth VCOs).

20 'The Future of the Gurkhas', Memo by Pethick-Lawrence (SSI), 7 March 1947, *Transfer of Power*, Vol. IX, doc. 503; Gregorian, *The British Army, the Gurkhas and Cold War Strategy*, p. 246, fn. 42. See also C. Bellamy, *The Gurkhas: Special Force* (2011), p. 370, fn. 1.

21 Government of India (henceforth GI) War Department to Maj.-Gen. Molesworth, India Office, 15 September 1943, L/WS/1/136.

22 For a complete list of Gurkha VC winners see Parker, *The Gurkhas*, pp. 266–8.

in India from June 1943) had a very high opinion of the Gurkhas, whom he considered 'among the best soldiers in the world if properly officered and trained'.[23] According to Wavell, the Gurkhas had proved 'invaluable' in the war.[24] Even the men who had been taken prisoner impressed him. In September 1945, Wavell inspected at Dehra Dun two battalions of the 2nd and 9th Gurkha Rifles, just back from prisoner-of-war camps in Malaya.[25] The men, he wrote, were 'very smart for inspection in spite of being ... very sick and debilitated'. Both battalions were 'exceedingly bitter about the INA from whose hands they had had worse treatment than from the Japs'.[26]

The Maharaja of Nepal hoped that Nepal would get a just reward for its services in the war.[27] Wavell had developed a good relationship with the Maharaja. He visited Nepal in January 1945 and spent five days' camp in Nepal Terai with him. Wavell noted in his diary that the 'atmosphere was very friendly'. The break was 'good fun and a very pleasant change in an attractive part of the country'. The party 'shot twelve tigers and six rhino'.[28]

The Post-War Future of the Gurkhas

The future employment of the Gurkhas had been under consideration since at least 1943.[29] With the prospect of demobilisation after the war, Britain was likely to face a shortage of military manpower, especially for overseas garrisons, where service could be unpopular with British troops.[30] Wavell thought that 'British manpower for fighting purposes' was going to be 'extremely limited'.[31] The post-war British Army might have to be supplemented by a 'Foreign Legion', and Gurkha infantry (who were also cheaper than British troops) could be used to garrison such places as Iraq, Malaya, Singapore, Hong Kong and Borneo.

23 Auchinleck to Brooke, 30 September 1945, AUC/1102.

24 Wavell to Pethick-Lawrence, 5 August 1945, *Transfer of Power*, Vol. VI, doc. 4.

25 Wavell to Pethick-Lawrence, 1 October 1945, ibid., doc. 127.

26 P. Moon (ed.), *Wavell: The Viceroy's Journal* (Oxford, 1973), entry for 28 September 1945. The INA (Indian National Army) had been formed from the 20,000 Indian prisoners of war who went over to the Japanese. The remaining 40,000 Indian prisoners stood firm in their allegiance despite being exposed to propaganda, and in some cases to torture and starvation.

27 Amery (SSI) to Wavell, 23 November 1944, *Transfer of Power*, Vol. V, doc. 110.

28 Moon (ed.), *Wavell*, entry for 19 January 1945.

29 'Future Employment of Gurkha Battalions', Minute by Thompson, 2 October 1943, L/WS/1/1021.

30 Gould, *Imperial Warriors*, p. 289.

31 Wavell to Pethick-Lawrence, 1 January 1946, *Transfer of Power*, Vol. VI, doc. 325.

Tuker wanted all 20 pre-war Gurkha battalions to go to the British Army, but he probably overstated his case when he claimed that the 'whole outlook' of the 'Gurkha Brigade ... was British'.[32]

In early March 1945, when the War Cabinet's India Committee discussed the Gurkhas, Sir James Grigg (Secretary of State for War, 1942–45) thought that a 'ticklish situation might arise' over Gurkha troops since their recruitment was governed by an agreement between the Maharajah of Nepal and HMG.[33] General Sir Mosley Mayne (the principal Staff Officer to the India Office) thought that there was general agreement that 'Gurkhas should be employed in considerable numbers' in the British Army of the future. Authoritative opinion differed widely, however, 'as to the scope of their possible employment under conditions of Indian self-government'. It would be unwise, he thought, to prejudge the considered opinion of the Commander-in-Chief in India and the Viceroy, which was not yet available.[34]

At the end of March 1945 Auchinleck accordingly prepared a briefing document on the future of the Gurkhas.[35] He noted that the future of the Gurkha units was 'one of the most difficult problems' facing the Indian Army Reorganisation Committee. India was about to get self-government, and he thought there might be 'hot competition for the privilege of serving in the [Indian] Army, as there was before the war'. It therefore might be politically impossible for an independent Indian government to 'take bread from the mouths of Indians' by recruiting 'foreigners'. The future destinies of Nepal and India were, however, linked, and the fighting strength of the Gurkhas was bound to be a military factor in the future of the subcontinent; but if India sought to recruit Gurkhas in war 'they must also recruit them in peace. All we can ask at the present stage', thought Auchinleck, it was for HMG to 'state whether they would be prepared to employ Gurkhas', and if so 'up to how many'.[36] On this basis, Wavell raised the question of the Gurkhas again with Leo Amery (Secretary of State for India, 1940–45) when he had discussions with him in London in April 1945.[37]

The future of the British officers with Gurkha units was understandably a matter of grave concern within the regiments. By October 1944 the Indian

---

32 Tuker, *While Memory Serves*, pp. 628–31; Gould, *Imperial Warriors*, p. 287.

33 War Cabinet, 5 March 1945, *Transfer of Power*, Vol. V, doc. 298.

34 Note by General Sir M. Mayne, March 1945, ibid., doc. 346; Gregorian, *The British Army, the Gurkhas and Cold War Strategy*, p. 37.

35 P. Warner, *Auchinleck: The Lonely Soldier* (1981), p. 187. See also Gould, *Imperial Warriors*, p. 286 and Bellamy, *Gurkhas*, p. 256.

36 Auchinleck to Wavell, 28 March 1945, AUC/1085.

37 Wavell to Pethick-Lawrence, 1 January 1946, *Transfer of Power*, Vol. VI, doc. 325.

Army had 11,983 Indian officers,[38] serving almost everywhere except in the Gurkha Brigade whose officer corps remained exclusively British. In July 1945 Auchinleck wrote a 'strictly confidential' letter to the Commandants of all Gurkha Rifle training centres, to reassure them that matters concerning the future of the Gurkhas were under his 'close and constant personal supervision'.[39] If it proved 'impossible or undesirable' to keep the Gurkha regiments in the Indian Army he suggested that HMG might wish to use them as a 'strategic reserve', provided that the Government of Nepal agreed. 'A solution on these lines', he suggested, might prove to be 'the best in the long run'. In these circumstances it would be possible 'to preserve the individuality and traditions of existing Gurkha Rifle Regiments' – an issue of great concern to their British officers. He did warn, however, that an autonomous Government of India might be willing and able to retain Gurkha units. Such a government 'would find it difficult if not quite impossible' to justify a situation in which Indian officers were not permitted to command Gurkha troops. He asked the Commandants to ensure that the possibility of retaining existing Gurkha units 'in a role suitable to their reputation and tradition after the war' was 'not endangered by indulgence on the part of [British] officers in thoughtless and irresponsible talk or criticism' which could do 'untold harm' if it reached 'the wrong ears'.

At the end of September 1945 Auchinleck told Lord Alanbrooke (Chief of the Imperial General Staff, 1941–46) that it was now a 'matter of urgency … to arrive at definite conclusions' as to the future size and composition of the Indian armed forces.[40] The future of the Gurkha units of the Indian Army greatly affected the issue. In May 1945 an examination of British post-war security problems had shown that all 20 pre-war Gurkha battalions could be used for service overseas.[41] Auchinleck suggested that ten battalions could be located in the Middle East, and the other ten used to garrison Singapore and Hong Kong. This, of course, would partly depend upon the attitude of the Maharaja of Nepal. Without the 'specific agreement of the Nepalese Government to the continued employment of Gurkha battalions overseas' the Gurkhas could not be made permanently available.[42] Auchinleck, however, was confident that such an agreement could be obtained, because Nepal was a 'small country and a poor

---

38 Establishment of the Indian Army Officer Cadre, L/WS/1/924, Annexure 'A'. This figure does not include VCOs.

39 This paragraph is a summary of Auchinleck to Commandants of Gurkha Rifle Training Centres, GHQ India, 19 July 1945, AUC/1095.

40 Auchinleck to Brooke, 30 September 1945, AUC/1102.

41 War Office to Auchinleck, 15 October 1945, AUC/1105.

42 Auchinleck to Brooke, 30 September 1945, AUC/1102.

one' and the 'deployment of 20,000 or 30,000 Gurkha soldiers outside Nepal' would be a 'definite advantage to the country'.

Wavell asked Auchinleck to have a 'private conversation with the Maharaja on the subject', as he did not want to alarm him with a 'formal enquiry'.[43] At the end of October 1945 Auchinleck visited Kathmandu,[44] where he privately broached the subject of the Gurkhas with the Maharajah.[45] The prospect of HMG employing Gurkhas as part of an imperial strategic reserve appealed to the Maharaja 'very strongly indeed'.[46] He repeatedly made it very clear that he would prefer Gurkhas to serve under HMG than under an Indian Dominion. 'The interview', Auchinleck wrote, 'was extremely cordial and friendly throughout, and I got the impression ... that [his] sentiments towards Britain were very warm and genuine.'[47]

In December 1945 Alanbrooke visited India. He discussed the Gurkha issue with Auchinleck who made it clear that, if Gurkha troops were to be employed by HMG, it would have to be as some sort of 'Foreign Legion', entirely independent of the Indian Army and of the Government of India.[48] Wavell considered that HMG should 'definitely decide to permanently employ as many as possible of the pre-war Gurkha battalions'. He thought that the temporary employment of Gurkhas, which had been considered, 'would not meet the case in any way'.[49] In March 1946, as the Cabinet Mission prepared to leave for India, the Chiefs of Staff made it clear that any agreement reached with the Indian government should not 'prejudice the separate negotiations' then being undertaken with a view to the future recruitment of Gurkhas into the 'Imperial as opposed to the Indian Army'.[50]

The context of European decolonisation in South-East Asia is crucial for understanding British and Indian concerns about the Gurkhas. US President Roosevelt was determined that Indochina should not return to France.[51]

---

43 Wavell to Pethick-Lawrence, 5 August 1945, *Transfer of Power*, Vol. VI, doc. 4.

44 Wavell to Pethick-Lawrence, 1 January 1946, ibid., doc. 325.

45 Auchinleck to Wavell, 6 Novembe 1945, AUC/1110; Wavell to Pethick-Lawrence, 1 January 1946, *Transfer of Power*, Vol. VI, doc. 325. See also Gregorian, *The British Army, the Gurkhas and Cold War Strategy*, p. 37.

46 Wavell to Pethick-Lawrence, 1 January 1946, *Transfer of Power*, Vol. VI, doc. 325.

47 Auchinleck to Wavell, 6 November 1945, AUC/1110.

48 Wavell to Pethick-Lawrence, 1 January 1946, *Transfer of Power*, Vol. VI, doc. 325; Gregorian, *The British Army, the Gurkhas and Cold War Strategy*, p. 37.

49 Wavell to Pethick-Lawrence, 1 January 1946, *Transfer of Power*, Vol. VI, doc. 325.

50 L.C. Hollis to Sir D. Monteath, 13 March 1946, ibid., doc. 521.

51 A. Danchev and D. Todman (eds), *War Diaries, 1939–1945: Field Marshal Lord Alanbrooke* (2001), entry for 6 April 1945.

At Potsdam in July 1945 it was agreed that the Chinese would oversee the surrender and disarmament of the Japanese in Indochina North of the 16th Parallel, while Mountbatten's South East Asia Command did the same in the South.[52] Accordingly, in September 1945 a brigade of 20th Indian Division was flown into Saigon to disarm the Japanese before French forces returned.[53] The French had wanted an all-white force, and were disappointed that Indian troops had been sent. There was some relief, however, that Gurkhas – not really 'Indians' – made up a 'significant proportion' of the Indian division.[54] For several months the Gurkha battalions helped to keep order and to effectively reinstall the French (the nationalist Viet Minh had established a provisional government in August 1945), incurring local hostility as they did so.[55] Japanese troops were also being used to keep order by October 1945, raising some awkward political questions.[56] Indian divisions, including six Gurkha battalions, were also sent to the Netherlands East Indies (now Indonesia) to accept the Japanese surrender in Java and Sumatra, but they soon became involved in fighting against local nationalists.[57] These British actions in South-East Asia were represented in India as 'European repression of [the] national risings of Eastern peoples'.[58] Wavell foresaw, correctly, that the Government of India would be criticised in India for allowing HMG to use Indian troops to 'suppress national movements'.[59] Britain's use of the Gurkhas in post-war South-East Asia was to have significant implications for Britain's attempt to acquire Gurkha regiments.

British policy also needs to be understood against the backdrop of political uncertainty in Nepal. By May 1946 there was 'evident anxiety' in Kathmandu as to the fate in store for Nepal when India became independent. There was concern that an independent India might discontinue Gurkha recruitment to the Indian Army, thereby cutting off a useful source of income.[60] The Government of Nepal attached great importance to maintaining its independence, and the link with

---

52 R. Aldrich, *Greater France: A History of French Overseas Expansion* (Basingstoke, 1996), p. 279; P. Dennis, *Troubled Days of Peace: Mountbatten and South East Asia Command, 1945–46* (Manchester, 1987), pp. 24, 39, 44; P. Ziegler, *Mountbatten: the Official Biography* (1985), p. 330.

53 Dennis, *Troubled Days of Peace*, pp. 33–5, 37–9.

54 Ibid., p. 42.

55 Ibid., pp. 25, 49–50.

56 Ziegler, *Mountbatten*, p. 332.

57 M.C. Ricklefs (ed.), *A New History of Southeast Asia* (Basingstoke, 2010), p. 340.

58 'Internal Situation in India': Appreciation by General Sir Claude Auchinleck, November 1945, AUC/1121.

59 Wavell to Pethick-Lawrence, 1 October 1945, *Transfer of Power*, Vol. VI, doc. 127. See also Dennis, *Troubled Days of Peace*, p. 188.

60 H. Weighton to Donaldson, 14 May 1946, *Transfer of Power*, Vol. VII, doc. 281.

Britain via the Gurkhas was very useful in this regard. Transferring the Gurkha regiments to the British Army might therefore bring potential economic and political benefits to Nepal after Indian independence.

In the meantime, Gurkhas were being employed on internal security duties in India. Gurkhas had always been regarded 'in the same class as British troops for the maintenance of law and order' during communal troubles because of their 'complete impartiality' between Muslim and Hindu Indians.[61] For example, in November 1945, when facing the prospect of civil disturbances in the Central Provinces and Berar, Sir Henry Twynam, the provincial governor, said 'if we cannot have British troops, we would like to have a battalion of Gurkhas'.[62] In November, Auchinleck described Gurkhas as more reliable than Indian troops because they were less influenced by Congress or by 'communal strife'.[63] The following month, he noted that nationalists were 'spread throughout the Indian Armed Forces except in Gurkha units'.[64]

By June 1946, things seem to have changed. The Chiefs of Staff considered that the reliability of the Indian Army, including its Gurkha units, was 'open to serious doubt', although they believed that an early announcement that HMG would employ Gurkhas would 'increase the chances' of the Gurkhas 'remaining loyal'.[65] In May 1946 Auchinleck told the Cabinet Mission that he thought Gurkhas could be relied upon during minor communal disturbances, but not if there were 'a major conflict' between the Muslims and the Hindus. Gurkhas were 'essentially Hindus' and 'the Nepalese Government knew that it would have to make terms with ... Congress which would control the areas in India which bordered Nepal'.[66] By September 1946 Gurkha troops were 'beginning to show signs of disquiet owing to uncertainty as to their future'.[67]

Gurkha discipline was put to the test when Gurkhas served in the Punjab Boundary Force, which was embodied between August and September 1947 to police the new India-Pakistan border in Punjab, where communal violence was at its most intense. The Boundary Force was formed from the remnants of 4th

---

61 Tuker, *While Memory Serves*, p. 632.

62 See Twynam to Wavell, 10 November 1945, *Transfer of Power*, Vol. VI, doc. 203.

63 'Internal Situation in India: Appreciation by C-in-C India', 24 November 1945, ibid., doc. 256.

64 Auchinleck to Chiefs of Staff, 22 December 1945, ibid., doc. 309.

65 India: Military Implications of Proposed Courses of Action: Report by Chiefs of Staff, 12 June 1946, *Transfer of Power*, Vol. VII, doc. 509.

66 Record of Meeting of Cabinet Delegation, Field Marshal Viscount Wavell and General Auchinleck, 6 May 1946, ibid., doc. 202.

67 Note by the Commander-in-Chief [Auchinleck] on the Military Aspect of the [Breakdown] Plan, 5 September 1946, *Transfer of Power*, Vol. VIII, doc. 286, Appendix III.

Indian Division, and it included the 4th and 7th Gurkha Rifles.[68] The Force was 40 per cent caste Hindu, 35 per cent Muslim, 20 per cent Gurkha and non-caste Hindus; and 5 per cent 'other'.[69] In June, Tuker had advocated the formation of an all-Gurkha peacekeeping force, but by July it was too late to concentrate 'neutral' battalions in troubled regions.[70] On 23 August the ration strength of the Force was only 23,000.[71] This limited force had a near-impossible task, but did as well as could be expected in very difficult conditions. Gurkhas turned out to be among the troops which 'proved of greatest value' during the August disturbances.[72]

In June 1946 Wavell learned that after 'much discussion' between the India Office, the War Office and the Treasury, the War Office were going to make a firm bid for the permanent employment of a 'minimum of eight Gurkha battalions', with the likelihood that the remaining 12 pre-war Gurkha battalions would also be required.[73] In September, negotiations started for the transfer of eight Gurkha battalions to the 'Imperial Army'. The Chiefs of Staff reiterated their wish for the other 12, but nothing could be done until the Interim Government of India had been established.[74]

The establishment of the Interim Government, however, meant that these negotiations soon ran into trouble. On 8 November the Interim Government raised the matter of the Gurkhas officially with the Secretary of State for India. They claimed that all the Indian Army's Gurkha battalions 'should be retained in the post-war Indian Army' and that they should be officered exclusively by Indian (not British) officers.[75] They sought to retain the Gurkhas 'apparently as a means of exercising political influence in Nepal'.[76] They also said that they were 'opposed' to the use of Gurkha troops by HMG 'for imperial purposes'.[77] They nevertheless recognised the difficulties inherent in the situation, and suggested a settlement by negotiation between HMG, Nepal and India.[78]

---

68 Bellamy, *The Gurkhas*, p. 264. Presumably only one battalion of each regiment.

69 R. Jeffery, 'The Punjab Boundary Force and the Problem of Order', *Modern Asian Studies*, 8/4 (1974): 498–500.

70 Ibid., pp. 518–19.

71 Ibid., p. 514.

72 Ibid., p. 518.

73 Henderson to Wavell, 6 June 1946, *Transfer of Power*, Vol. VII, doc. 467.

74 'Indian Forces Outside India', Report by Chiefs of Staff, September 1946, *Transfer of Power*, Vol. VIII, Enclosure to doc. 371.

75 GI Defence Dept. to SSI, 8 Novembe 1946, *Transfer of Power*, Vol. IX, doc. 16.

76 Gregorian, *The British Army, the Gurkhas and Cold War Strategy*, p. 38.

77 GI Defence Dept. to SSI, 8 November 1946, *Transfer of Power*, Vol. IX, doc. 16.

78 'The Future of the Gurkhas', Memo by SSI, 7 March 1947, ibid., doc. 503.

In January 1947, on looking through their records, the British Legation in Nepal discovered that Britain's right to recruit Gurkhas rested on two notifications published by Prime Ministers of Nepal in 1885 and 1888. These notifications made specific reference to 'British service' in 'British regiments' in the 'British Army' – so technically Britain's legal 'right' to recruit Gurkhas remained, although it was 'never contemplated at the time' that Britain would wish to recruit Gurkhas other than for service in the Indian Army.[79] There was also some lobbying in Britain on behalf of the Gurkhas by former Gurkha officers; for example Major-General William O. Twiss wrote to the editor of *The Times* that many ex-officers of the Gurkha regiments were 'becoming anxious' about the future of the Gurkha regiments and that of Nepal.[80]

An alternative to the transfer of the Gurkhas was briefly considered. In January 1945 Attlee proposed the creation of a 'Foreign Legion' using some of the 217,000 Polish soldiers then under British command.[81] The War Office rebuffed this idea. The Polish troops would be needed for the reconstruction of their own country, and as a 'Foreign Legion' they would become permanently excluded from Poland because of the Soviet occupation of their country. Such a legion could not be expanded in wartime, and it would be 'objectionable' to use Polish manpower for imperial policing in peacetime.

On 20 February 1947 the Labour Government announced that India was to become independent 'not later than' June 1948.[82] According to the perceptive Conservative backbencher Sir Cuthbert Headlam, Attlee's statement came 'as a shock to the whole of the House and he did not seem very comfortable about it himself'.[83] At the same time, Lord Louis Mountbatten was designated Viceroy of India.

On 5 March 1947, the Chiefs of Staff again discussed the possible transfer of Gurkhas to the British Army. Lord Montgomery of Alamein (Chief of the Imperial General Staff from 1946) said that HMG was going to bid in Nepal initially for eight Gurkha battalions to provide the infantry element of a division

---

79 George Falconer, British Legation Nepal, to E.P. Donaldson, India Office, 11 January 1947, L/WS/1/1025–7.

80 'Nepal and the Gurkha Regiments', *The Times*, 21 January 1947.

81 Gregorian, *The British Army, the Gurkhas and Cold War Strategy*, pp. 36, 39.

82 Indian Policy: Statement of 20 February 1947, *Transfer of Power*, Vol. IX, doc. 438. See also A. Inder Singh, 'Decolonization in India: The Statement of 20 February 1947', *The International History Review*, 6/2 (1984): 191–209.

83 S. Ball (ed.), *Parliament and Politics in the Age of Churchill and Attlee: the Headlam Diaries, 1935–1951* (1999), entry for 20 February 1947.

in Malaya.[84] Mountbatten said that he wished to discuss the future of the Gurkhas with the Defence Committee of the Cabinet before he departed for India. Attlee agreed to this.[85]

The Defence Committee met on 17 March. The Committee agreed to seek the transfer of 25,000 Gurkhas to the British Army for deployment anywhere in the world, and with no time limit to their engagement.[86] A few days later, Sir Terence Shone (the British High Commissioner in India) reminded the Cabinet that 'the connection of Gurkhas with [the] British Army was as least as strong as with [the] Indian Army. If India wished to use Gurkhas and deprive us and them of the advantages from that use, this would be a dog-in-the-manger attitude.'[87]

Mountbatten arrived in India on 22 March 1947. He rapidly concluded that the Cabinet Mission plan for a united India was a dead letter. On 3 June he announced that a plan had been drawn up for the partition of the subcontinent.[88] The provisional date for Indian independence was also brought forward to 15 August 1947. Attlee, at Mountbatten's suggestion, asked Montgomery to discuss the Gurkhas with Nehru when the two met in late June to arrange the final departure of British troops from India. Mountbatten thought that the meeting would be a 'very favourable opportunity for settling once and for all the question of the Gurkhas', which, he felt, had been 'hanging fire'.[89]

The main obstacle to the transfer was the Government of India's objection to the British use of Gurkha troops in suppressing Asian independence movements.[90] Montgomery, accompanied by Sir Terence Shone, had a 'long discussion' with Nehru about the Gurkhas on 23 June 1947.[91] Nehru seemed on the defensive and was worried about the political repercussions if the Gurkhas were transferred. He did not want a 'continuation of the old tradition of [using] Gurkha troops for imperial purposes', which, he thought, would cause 'adverse

---

84 Chiefs of Staff Committee, 5 March 1947, *Transfer of Power*, Vol. IX, doc. 487. See also 'Gurkhas' Future', *The Times*, 9 August 1947.

85 'The Future of the Gurkhas', Memo by SSI, 7 March 1947, *Transfer of Power*, Vol. IX, doc. 503.

86 Cabinet Defence Committee, 17 March 1947, ibid., doc. 539; Gregorian, *The British Army, the Gurkhas and Cold War Strategy*, p. 39; Bellamy, *Gurkhas*, p. 260.

87 British HC in India to Cabinet Office, 24 March 1947, L/WS/1/1021–4.

88 Text of Broadcast by Mountbatten, 3 June 1947, *Transfer of Power*, Vol. XI, doc. 44, and following documents.

89 Mountbatten to Attlee, 12 June 1947, ibid., doc. 173. See also Mountbatten to Ismay, 19 June 1947, ibid., doc. 259 and Gould, *Imperial Warriors*, pp. 296–7.

90 Brief for the British Negotiators in Discussions with the Government of India as to the Employment of Gurkha Troops under HMG, L/WS/1/1022.

91 Montgomery to Simpson, 23 June 1947, *Transfer of Power*, Vol. XI, doc. 315.

comment in India'.[92] Nehru also had strong political objections to the use of the Gurkhas in Indonesia. Furthermore, he did not want the transfer of the Gurkhas to become a precedent for Britain's employment of other South Asian units, for example, Afridi battalions, which might cause complications with Pakistan. According to Nehru, Montgomery promised that Britain required the Gurkhas, and only the Gurkhas:

> as a reserve for emergencies and to carry out British commitments in the Far East. These troops were not be used locally and certainly not against any peoples' movement for freedom. They were not to be used at all in fact, unless war came. Malaya was a suitable place for them to be stationed; otherwise they had nothing to do with Malaya. [Montgomery] told me how [the] Gurkhas had been misjudged in Indonesia, as they really helped in keeping the peace.[93]

The underlying British assumption was that the primary responsibility for internal security in Malaya would rest with troops raised and maintained locally, while the main role of the regular British Army would be the defence of the Commonwealth from external attack.[94] After two days of negotiations, Nehru 'agreed in principle' that some Gurkhas could be employed in the British Army.[95] Mountbatten pronounced himself 'so glad' that the employment of Gurkha troops in the British Army appeared to be 'on the way to a satisfactory settlement'.[96]

The Partition of the Brigade

It was not quite as simple as that. If Britain were to obtain eight battalions of Gurkhas, then the Brigade would have to be divided between Britain and India. The question of how to divide the Brigade was to become an emotive subject.[97] Auchinleck had raised the issue as early as October 1946, at a time when he assumed that division, were it to take place, would be 50/50. There were two

[92] Note on an Interview with F.M. Montgomery on the Employment of Gurkha Troops in the Indian Army, 24 June 1947, *Transfer of Power*, Vol. XI, enclosure to doc. 388.

[93] Ibid.

[94] Omissi, 'Witness Statement', docs 105–7.

[95] Montgomery to Attlee, 24 June 1947, *Transfer of Power*, Vol. XI, doc. 330; Montgomery to Nehru, 24 June 1947, *Transfer of Power*, Vol. XI, doc. 331; Gregorian, *The British Army, the Gurkhas and Cold War Strategy*, p. 40; Gould, *Imperial Warriors*, p. 297.

[96] Viceroy's Personal Report No. 10, 27 June 1947, *Transfer of Power*, Vol. XI, doc. 369.

[97] Gould, *Imperial Warriors*, p. 290.

main options. Either one battalion of each Gurkha regiment could be kept in the Indian Army and the other one transferred to the British Army; or five Gurkha regiments, each of two battalions, could be kept in the Indian Army, and the other five be transferred. Tuker believed that 'those who had the interests of the whole brigade at heart hoped that England [*sic*] would take the first battalion of all its regiments, thus preserving the identity of them all and the ... traditions of the brigade'.[98] On the other hand, those who supported the transfer of the first five regiments pointed out that the first five were not only the oldest regiments, and therefore had the longest connection with Britain, they also all had royal titles, which the last five did not.[99] Given that elements of Congress were committed to a republican state, and that India became a republic within the Commonwealth in 1949, their argument contained a certain logic. Whatever was decided, Auchinleck said that he would seek 'the best compromise in order to preserve the future of the Gurkha units'. He remarked, presciently, that 'it will not be possible ... to please everyone'.[100]

By July 1947 Auchinleck was worried that he 'had not yet had an official ruling about the Gurkhas'.[101] In early August – a week before partition – an agreement was reached 'in principle' between the governments of the UK, India and Nepal.[102] Four Gurkha regiments, each of two battalions, with their regimental centres, were to be transferred to the British Army.[103] All other Gurkha battalions were to remain in the Indian Army.

The four regiments to be transferred were the 2nd, 6th, 7th, and 10th Gurkha Rifles.[104] Why these four, and not the first 'royal' four (or five)? The choice of regiments was based on two factors. First, three of the four each had one battalion (1/6th, 1/7th and 1/10th Gurkha Rifles) still based in Burma, so it would be easier to move these regiments to Malaya.[105] Second, it was considered desirable that the British Gurkha regiments be able to draw their recruits from

---

98 Tuker, *While Memory Serves*, p. 636.

99 *Indian Army List*, July 1939.

100 Auchinleck to Slim, Scoones, Tuker et al., 21 October 1946, AUC/1197.

101 Record of Interview between Mountbatten and Auchinleck, 15 July 1947, *Transfer of Power*, Vol. XII, doc. 113.

102 Mountbatten to Listowel, 7 August 1947, ibid., doc. 370.

103 'Gurkhas' Future', *The Times*, 9 August 1947; Gregorian, *Britain, the Gurkhas and Cold War Strategy*, p. 40.

104 GHQ India to Military Department, India Office, 12 August 1947, L/WS/1/956.

105 Gregorian, *The British Army, the Gurkhas and Cold War Strategy*, p. 246, fn. 56; Bellamy, *Gurkhas*, p. 262.

both Western and Eastern Nepal; and the 7th and 10th Gurkha Rifles were the only two of the pre-war regiments to recruit from the East[106]

The outcome did not please everyone.[107] 'As expected', wrote Auchinleck, the choice of Gurkha regiments caused a 'lot of pother [*sic*] and fuss amongst the retired officers of Gurkhas. ... I wish the few gentlemen ... could be made to take a more realistic view of the situation out here.'[108] Supporters of the older regiments complained that the newer regiments had 'jumped the queue'.[109] 'Thus the Gurkha Brigade, with all its traditions', Tuker somewhat ruefully recalled, 'ceased to exist.'[110]

The Gurkha other ranks were given some say in their future, and various polls, or 'opts' as they became known, were held in different units at different times.[111] The early results were quite encouraging from the point of view of HMG, but some of the later results surprised Auchinleck and others. In the Regimental Centre of the 6th Gurkha Rifles there was a relatively narrow majority (60:40) in favour of HMG; but in the 5th Royal Gurkha Regimental Centre, 91 per cent opted for India; and in the 2/7th Gurkha Rifles 95 per cent did so. Auchinleck regarded the results as 'absolutely opposite to the opinion generally held by officers of Gurkha regiments', and 'really extraordinary and most significant'.[112] His analysis is worth quoting at length:

> The pre-conceived idea, held generally by British officers of Gurkha units, serving and retired, that there could be no question that the Gurkha soldier would opt to serve Britain rather than India, has been completely upset by the referendum to ascertain the wishes of the Gurkha soldiers. There is very far from being any universal or general wish to serve under HMG, and it is possible that the required number of volunteers to fill the eight allotted battalions may not be forthcoming.[113]

---

106 C.J. Morris, *Handbook for the Indian Army:* Gurkhas (2nd ed., 1936), pp. 86, 133; Tuker, *While Memory Serves*, p. 638.

107 Gould, *Imperial Warriors*, pp. 298–9.

108 Auchinleck to Scoones, 15 September 1947, AUC/1259.

109 Bellamy, *Gurkhas*, p. 262.

110 Tuker, *While Memory Serves*, p. 637.

111 For some of the poll results see Gould, *Imperial Warriors*, pp. 308, 310, 314–15.

112 Auchinleck to Scoones, 15 September 1947, AUC/1259.

113 'Report on the Situation in India and Pakistan' for the information of the Cabinet and Chiefs of Staff, 28 September 1947, AUC/1262.

Auchinleck felt, however, that there was a distinct possibility that the men had been subject to propaganda dissuading them from opting for British service.[114] The Interim Government, in Auchinleck's view, were opposed to the whole idea of the transfer and would have welcomed its abandonment. It seems probable, too, that the men were reluctant to be based overseas during peacetime.

On 3 November 1947 there was a 'significant incident', amounting to a near-mutiny, in 1/2nd Gurkha Rifles. Practically the whole battalion refused to parade and instead assembled outside the quarterguard. The men told the CO that they would rather serve in India than serve the British in Malaya, and they asked to be allowed to make their opt immediately in the presence of their Indian officers. The trigger for the incident appears to have been a warning order (issued in error) of a move to the Punjab. The men read this as a 'sign that they were being posted to Malaya before they had even opted'. The 1/2nd Gurkha Rifles was Tuker's old battalion, and he addressed the men in person later that month. He told them that, if they opted for India *en masse*, the truncheon on which, as new recruits, they had sworn their allegiance to the crown, would have to be returned to the grandson of Queen Victoria, King George VI. 'His intervention proved effective', and when the battalion opted in December, 340 out of 717 men chose British service.[115]

A Tripartite Agreement between Britain, Nepal and India was signed on 9 November 1947. The Maharajah allowed India to retain some of the war-raised battalions 'in view of the existing political situation in India'.[116] After the agreement, a further referendum was held in all four regiments earmarked for British service. The men could choose to remain in the Indian Army, to transfer to British service or to be discharged.[117] The overall results of this 'opt' have been described as 'dismal' – by 20 January 1948 only 124 Gurkha officers and 3,432 Gurkha other ranks had opted for British service.[118] The proportion that opted for the British army was much higher in those battalions stationed in Burma than in those stationed in India or Pakistan, presumably because the former were less exposed to propaganda. The full 'opt' was offered only in those regiments destined for British service: in the other six regiments the only choice offered

114 On the question of propaganda amongst Gurkhas see Gould, *Imperial Warriors*, pp. 320–22.

115 Ibid., pp. 312–14.

116 Gregorian, *The British Army, the Gurkhas and Cold War Strategy*, pp. 41–2.

117 GHQ India to Military Dept, India Office, 12 August 1947, L/WS/1/956.

118 Gregorian, *The British Army, the Gurkhas and Cold War Strategy*, p. 42. 'Gurkha officers' refers to Gurkhas holding the Viceroy's commission. No Gurkhas at this date held the King's commission.

was to stay in the Indian Army or to accept discharge without compensation.[119] For professional soldiers from a poor country this 'choice' was effectively no choice at all.

There had long been an understanding that Gurkha units would be officered only by British officers.[120] This was about to change. In the Gurkha regiments that were to remain in the Indian Army, British officers now had to make way for incoming Indian officers transferred from other regiments of the Indian Army. In some units (notably the 4th Gurkha Rifles) the transition went smoothly enough, but in others the outgoing British officers made it clear that they did not relish handing over their regiment to Indian newcomers. There were a few unpleasant incidents in some units. At the Regimental Centre of the 5th Gurkha Rifles, for example, the mess was stripped of virtually all moveable goods – furniture, paintings, crockery and cutlery. Even the mess silver 'had been packed away and sent to Britain'.[121] Some British officers feared that the regiments allocated to India would lose their titles and identity. Ironically, the regimental traditions of Gurkha regiments have been better preserved in the Indian than in the British Army, where separate Gurkha regiments have been merged into one, whose future is uncertain.[122]

The Tripartite Agreement became effective from 1 January 1948, when the four Gurkha regiments were formally transferred to the British Army.[123] The War Office planned to form the Gurkhas (with some additional British Army units) into an infantry division to use as a strategic reserve in the Middle East in the event of war with the USSR: they were stationed in the Far East mainly as an administrative and logistical convenience. The British Gurkhas began their move to Singapore, Malaya and Hong Kong after Burmese independence on 4 January 1948. The troops arrived, battalion by battalion, between January and March 1948. There was little suitable accommodation in Malaya, and for many months the Gurkhas and their families had to live in tents. They did, however, become collectively, and formally, recognised as Britain's Brigade of Gurkhas.[124]

---

119 Gregorian, *The British Army, the Gurkhas and Cold War Strategy*, p. 42; Gould, *Imperial Warriors*, p. 316.

120 'The Future of the Gurkhas', Memo by SSI, 7 March 1947, *Transfer of Power*, Vol. IX, doc. 503.

121 Gould, *Imperial Warriors*, p. 318.

122 Bellamy, *Gurkhas*, pp. 262–3.

123 'Gurkhas Transferred to British Army', *The Times*, 2 January 1948; Gould, *Imperial Warriors*, p. 322.

124 Most of this paragraph is based on Gregorian, *The British Army, the Gurkhas and the Cold War*, pp. 42–3, 46, 48.

Conclusion

Was the story of partition of the Gurkha Brigade indeed a 'dismal one', as Sir Francis Tuker claimed? Some historians seem to think so. For example, in his fine book on the Gurkhas in this period, Raffi Gregorian argues that the whole 'business of enlisting Gurkhas into the British Army ... was not ... very successful', and that the entire transfer was 'botched'.[125] There is, however, another way of looking at it. The transfer of eight Gurkha battalions to the British Army was but a footnote to the great human tragedy of partition; and against the backdrop of partition's horrors – the seventeen million refugees, the derailed trains, the massacres, rapes and abductions – the problems experienced during the transfer of the Gurkhas (unfavourable poll results, a peaceful 'mutiny', and some unpleasantness concerning mess funds and silver) do not really add up to very much. A more positive reading of the transfer is certainly possible. Britain, India and Nepal did negotiate a workable agreement concerning the future of the Gurkhas. Furthermore, enough Gurkhas did eventually rally to the British cause to enable the formation of a British Brigade of Gurkhas. In February 1948, Brigadier Osborne Hedley estimated that by 1 April 1948 the British Gurkhas would consist of 7,400 men (optees, recruits, volunteers from Indian regiments, and men on leave who had yet to opt). His prognosis was optimistic:

> Since 1 [January] 1948, the day of transfer to HMG, there has ... been a change of spirit and outlook amongst British Gurkha units towards the whole scheme. There is now marked enthusiasm. The child has not been born without labour, and if the weaning is done patiently and thoroughly, there is no reason why it should not prosper.[126]

British policy makers certainly did not achieve everything they hoped for, but it could have been so much worse. The Gurkhas, after all, fared much better than some other indigenous imperial forces at decolonisation, such as the Assyrian Christians in Iraq in the 1930s, and the Algerian *harkis* in the 1960s, both of whom faced violent reprisals after independence as supposed 'collaborators'.

In June 1948, shortly after the British Gurkhas had moved to the Far East, three British planters were killed by Communist insurgents in Malaya. Sir Edward Gent, the High Commissioner of Malaya, declared an Emergency on 18 June.[127] Gurkha troops were to hand, and they were soon being employed to

---

125 Ibid., pp. 42, 50.

126 Quoted in Gould, *Imperial Warriors*, p. 322.

127 Gregorian, *The British Army, the Gurkhas and the Cold War*, p. 50.

counter the insurrection. Was this a breach of Montgomery's personal promise to Nehru, made only a year earlier, that the troops 'were not to be used locally'? The British Ambassador to Nepal, Sir George Falconer, did not say so in as many words; but in August 1948 he told the Foreign Office that it would be 'unwise' for the BBC to draw attention to the Gurkhas' counterinsurgency role in Malaya because it could 'embarrass' both India and Nepal.[128]

---

128 Gould, *Imperial Warriors*, p. 320; Bellamy, *Gurkhas*, p. 270.

Chapter 11

Small Wars and Internal Security: The Army in India, 1936–1946

Robert Johnson

The Army in India's approach to frontier operations in the Inter-War Years was shaped by its experiences in the nineteenth and early twentieth century.[1] British techniques in maintaining order, drawn from across the Empire, were gradually brought together into a coherent *modus operandi* by 1914. These were then influenced by new expectations about the character of colonial governance after the First World War, particularly in light of low-intensity politicised violence from Ireland, Palestine, Egypt and Iraq.[2] The Army in India, acting in support of the civil authorities in the subcontinent, made its own contribution to the development of ideas and techniques through its operations on the North West Frontier and through internal security duties known as 'Military Aid to the Civil Power'.[3]

---

1 Ian F.W. Beckett (ed.), *The Roots of Counter-Insurgency: Armies and Guerrilla Warfare, 1900–1945* (London: Blandford Press, 1988); Ian F.W. Beckett, *Modern Insurgencies and Counter-Insurgencies: Guerrillas and their Opponents since 1750* (London and New York: Routledge, 2001); Douglas Porch, *Wars of Empire* (London: Cassell, 2000); Charles Townshend, *Britain's Civil Wars: Counterinsurgency in the Twentieth Century* (London: Faber, 1986); Thomas Mockaitis, *British Counter-Insurgency, 1919–1960* (Basingstoke and New York: Palgrave Macmillan, 1990); David A. Charters and Maurice Tugwell (eds), *Armies in Low Intensity Conflict: A Comparative Study of Institutional Adaptation to New Forms of Warfare* (London: Brassey's Putnam Aeronautical, 1989).

2 David M. Anderson and David Killingray (eds), *Policing the Empire: Government, Authority and Control, 1830–1940* (Manchester: Manchester University Press, 1991); Martin Thomas, *Empires of Intelligence: Security Services and Colonial Disorder after 1914* (Berkeley and London: University of California Press, 2008); Keith Jeffrey, *The British Army and the Crisis of Empire, 1918–1922* (Manchester: Manchester University Press, 1984). See also Robert J. Blyth, *The Empire of the Raj: India, Eastern Africa and the Middle East, 1858–1947* (London and New York: Palgrave, 2003) and Ranajit Guha, *Elementary Aspects of Peasant Insurgency in Colonial India* (New Delhi, 1983).

3 Gyanesh Kudaisya, '"In Aid of Civil Power": The Colonial Army in Northern India, c. 1919–1942', *Journal of Imperial and Commonwealth History* 32, 1 (2004): 41–68; Tim

The imperative of the colonial period was to maintain the imperial order and to preserve prestige by instilling a fear of the force at the British Empire's disposal, without, it was hoped, having to actually use that force. The civil police were designed to deal with low-level disturbances while the army was held in reserve. By minimising disorders and military deployments the aim was to keep costs down and avoid antagonising the population. Much of the unrest in the 1930s and 1940s stemmed from a challenge to the colonial dispensation, but it was also the result of some far older sources, particularly communal violence, food riots and fighting for the preservation of traditional ways of life on the North West Frontier. It is worth noting that both the nature of unrest and resistance, and the measures to deal with them, were peculiar to each historical era.

The Army in India had competing roles to prepare for, which it tended to prioritise as conventional war fighting, frontier warfare, and internal security.[4] In terms of the conventional threat, the army had to prepare itself for a potential attack across Afghanistan by the Soviet Union, a continuation of the Russian menace which had so exercised the minds of British strategists in the nineteenth century.[5] Afghanistan too had confronted the British with a conventional security problem in the brief Anglo-Afghan War of 1919 and there was a probability it would do so again. Expeditionary warfare was a role for which the Army in India had also to prepare. The experience of the First World War had also reinforced the possibility that the Army in India would have to send forces overseas at short notice to the Persian Gulf, East Africa and South East Asia – and it was indeed compelled to do again in the Second World War. At the same time, the army had to train to meet the low intensity threat. The Army in India was frequently confronted with internal security problems which required quite different force structures and tactics.

In India during the Inter War Years, the Indian National Congress (INC) had begun to disrupt British authority and built up a base of support amongst large sections of the population, but it took the crisis of the war in 1939, and the widespread agitation of the 'Quit India' campaign from 1942, to change

Moreman, '"Small Wars" and "Imperial Policing": The British Army and the Theory and Practice of Colonial Warfare in the British Empire, 1919–1939', *Journal of Strategic Studies* 19.4 (1996): 105–31.

4 *Expert Investigation of the Strength, Composition and Functions of the Army in India, 1931* (Simla, General Staff India, 1931).

5 Robert Johnson, '"Russians at the Gates of India": Planning the Strategic Defence of India, 1884–1899', *Journal of Military History*, 67 (July 2003): 697–743.

attitudes towards the Raj significantly.[6] British political concessions, albeit half-hearted before 1939 and delayed for the duration of the war, gave rise to frustration and anger on the part of Congress, and further extended the numbers that supported *swaraj* (self-government). Although its official goal was independence by non-violent means, not all adhered to this principle, and terrorism and sabotage compelled the British to introduce more comprehensive internal security measures.[7] The Defence of India Act (1939) gave the Army in India considerable licence to maintain order but this too added to the weight of opinion that the British security apparatus was unjust and heavy-handed. Of course, the paradox of the war years is that India fielded a vast volunteer army, which was, in essence, fighting Britain's war. The Quit India campaign, the INC's path towards independence, and British political machinations in the late Raj have been well-charted, and the performance of the British and Indian Armies in conventional operations have been thoroughly scrutinised. Yet internal security and low intensity conflict in the inter war years, which lay the foundations of doctrine that was to come into play in other parts of the Empire later, merit further attention. Such an examination reveals the levels of integration and disjunction between political and military approaches to defeating insurgency or quelling internal unrest.

The long-running security problem of the North West Frontier and Baluchistan in the Inter-War Years, and in particular the unrest caused by the Faqir of Ipi in Waziristan in the years 1936–39, necessitated military operations on a significant scale. Surprisingly perhaps, the frontier was relatively quiet during the war itself. One might have expected the Pashtuns to have taken advantage of the weakened British security apparatus after 1939, but a combination of military and political measures proved effective. Paradoxically, even as the frontier became quiet, internal security within India became a significant problem and necessitated considerably more forces to manage it.

Within the limits of a short chapter it is not possible to give a full history of all the methods used to tackle unrest in India or on the Frontier, but a few important areas can be highlighted in order to produce a broader understanding of the way the Army dealt with the range of low-intensity warfare between 1936 and 1946, the crucial decade before Britain's departure from South Asia. The chapter is thus divided into two sections. The first examines British approaches to low intensity operations as applied to the North West Frontier; the second

6 Judith Brown, *Modern India: The Origins of an Asian Democracy* (Oxford: Oxford University Press, 1994), p. 324.

7 Home Political File, 3/52/43(1) cited in F.G. Hutchins, *India's Revolution: Gandhi and the Quit India Movement* (Cambridge, Massachusetts, 1973), pp. 230–31.

attempts to assess specifically internal security methods in this period, with remarks about the emerging doctrine and its limitations throughout.

Low Intensity Warfare on the North West Frontier

Britain's experience of fighting irregular opponents in its colonial wars in the late nineteenth century prompted Colonel Charles Callwell, the author of the famous *Small Wars: Their Principles and Practice* (1896), to admit that guerrilla wars were: 'the most unfavourable ... for regular troops' and at times required measures that would 'shock the humanitarian'.[8] When the enemy engaged in hit-and-run attacks, Callwell argued that the destruction of property, crops and livestock would invariably tempt them into battle where force could be concentrated against them 'which will probably bring the war most rapidly to a conclusion'. The object in suppressing rebellion was to 'inflict punishment on those who had taken up arms', so as to leave the refractory subjects 'chastised and subdued'. Decisive and destructive action, he argued, was more likely to forestall any chance of long term rebellion. However, he warned against unlimited devastation and violence, suggesting that the purpose was to 'ensure a lasting peace' and not the 'exasperation of the enemy'. He concluded that a 'moral effect was often far more important than material success' and he drew a clear distinction between civilised European theatres and 'savage' enemies in the application of his theory. Callwell highlighted the importance of intelligence, the use of local auxiliaries and the need for mobility in low-intensity operations, but the focus of his interest was really conventional warfare in the setting of Africa and Asia. His guidance, in keeping with other works of the period, was designed to simply avoid protracted operations altogether.

The fighting on the North West Frontier of India went through several phases of development and variations in policy, but there were consistent characteristics involving either deterrence by the presence of large forces, or limited expeditions to carry out punitive destruction of elusive tribal *lashkars* (war parties) or their villages and crops, euphemistically known as 'butcher and bolt'.[9] These were invariably in response to 'outrages' of raiding, kidnapping and murder by the tribesmen. In the Inter-War Years the Army in India could use the methods of 'air policing' to augment their ground forces, although the terrain meant there were limits to the use of air power alone. The topography also hampered the use

[8] C.E. Callwell, *Small Wars: Their Principles and Practice* (London, 3rd edn, 1906), pp. 99 and 40–42.

[9] *Report on the Administration of the Border of the North West Frontier Province* (Peshawar: Government Press, 1921–38).

of Field Artillery and tanks. Movement of burdensome supply columns through the valleys meant that infantrymen had to 'crown the heights' to protect them. The lack of infrastructure meant that pack mules and light machine guns or mountain artillery were essential, although roads were used for wheeled transport whenever they were available. Despite the greater firepower available to the Indian Army of the 1930s and 1940s, it was confronted by the same problems that had plagued their forebears.[10] Severe logistical problems were created by the vast distances. Heat, the mountainous nature of the ground and fatigue limited the troops' mobility still further. Moreover, the tribesmen fought as guerrillas in small dispersed bands, with knowledge of the terrain, which made it difficult to concentrate against them. Although obsolete in the West, cavalry and light infantry could still match the speed and agility of the *lashkars* in the hills in a way that mechanised formations could not.[11] Thus traditional methods were still relevant in many frontier actions. The Waziristan Campaign, which was the last major operation on the North West Frontier before the Second World War, highlights particularly well the challenges this theatre presented and the solutions, old and new, that were found to low-intensity resistance.

The Waziristan Campaign, 1936–1937

In Waziristan in 1936, Mirza Ali Khan, a pious Tori Khel Wazir, stirred agitation against the British. When the verdict of a high profile legal case which ran contrary to the interests of the Waziris was announced, there was a wave of raids, arson and murder.[12] Mirza Ali Khan, or the Faqir of Ipi as he became known, was able to draw on existing grievances as well as fresh fears about British encroachments into tribal areas to lend credibility to his cause. His claim that Allah made him immune from the British seemed more persuasive when the authorities initially failed to take action against him.[13] With volunteers flocking to him, he implored the tribesmen to fight a Jihad against the British. When the Political Officers of the frontier asked the local elders and maliks to expel him, they refused, since this

---

[10] See, for example, *Waziristan and the Lessons of the Last 60 Years* (Simla: Government Central Press, 1921).

[11] Moreman, *The Army in India and the Development of Frontier Warfare* (London: Macmillan, 1998), pp. 129 and 135.

[12] There were 39 raids, 31 kidnappings, and the murder of ten Hindus, as well as the razing of 60 houses, the theft of cattle and sheep, and the looting of trucks on the road.

[13] 'Note on the Faqir of Ipi', File 514/VII, IOR R/12/72; Supplement 3 to Intelligence Summary 6, 17–23 June 1937, Appendix A, IOR L/Mil/5/1065; Alan Warren, *Waziristan, The Faqir of Ipi and the Indian Army: The North West Frontier Revolt* (Oxford, 2000), pp. 98–9.

would have been a breach of *melmastia* (hospitality), a feature of the tribal code of *Pushtunwali* (code of the Pashtun).[14] The British decided to 'show the flag' to impress the tribesmen with the force at their disposal and sent two columns ('Razcol' and 'Tocol') up the Khaisora Valley in November 1936. However, far from overawing the tribesmen, the troops provided a focus of resistance.[15] Razcol was attacked by the Faqir of Ipi's followers on 25 November, resulting in 14 killed and 43 wounded by the day's end.

Post operational analyses stated the situation had been the result of insufficient artillery, too little route security by piqueting caused by the imperative to link both columns up, and a lack of experience amongst the units involved. However, it also revealed a fatal miscalculation about the psychology of the Waziris: the advance of the British columns seemed to confirm the Faqir of Ipi's assertions that roads and new garrisons were but a prelude to the full occupation of the tribal areas, the destruction of Islam and the expropriation of their lands.[16] From the British perspective, there was a requirement for greater mass: a brigade with 11th Light Tank Company, armoured cars, artillery and a further two infantry battalions were deployed to reinforce the area. Their objectives were to forestall the trouble spreading, punish the Tori Khels, and construct a road through the Khaisora Valley to facilitate future pacification. To unify the direction of operations, General Sir John Coleridge was given the command of all the military forces, Civil Armed Forces and the RAF assets. Note that having provoked the fighting, the solution was seen in entirely military terms. The road was built in just two months whilst the fortified houses of known insurgent leaders were destroyed. The entire region was saturated with troops to concentrate force, but air operations were limited to an area five miles ahead and either side of the subsequent advance by 'Khaicol', another well-armed column. The headquarters of the Faqir at Arsal Kot were destroyed and Afghan volunteers who had come to the aid of the Waziris were driven off. British civilian control was then re-established when the Tori Khel submitted, but not until a total of 166 casualties had been sustained.[17]

However, the fighting was far from over. The Faqir kept on the move and did his best to encourage further resistance. In northern Waziristan in the spring of 1937, hostile parties attacked villages in the settled area of Derajat. Political

---

14 Warren, *Waziristan*, p. 86.

15 7–11 November 1936, IOR L/PS/12/3230.

16 Maj. J.A. Robinson, 'The Disturbances of 1936–7 in Waziristan', North Waziristan Affairs, Waziristan Disturbances, 1936–38, IOR L/PS/12/3232. *Operations on the North West Frontier, Intelligence Summaries, 1936–37*, p. 16, IOR L/PS/12/3192.

17 Report on the Operations in Waziristan, 25 November 1936 to 16 January 1937, 21 June 1937, IOR L/Mil7/16971; Moreman, *Army in India*, p. 156.

Officers negotiated and demanded submission, and there were limited punitive air operations, but these had no effect.[18] A low intensity campaign manifests itself in the form of sniping at piquets, or attacks on bridges, culverts and telephone lines. Two brigades were sent to reinforce the garrison of North Waziristan, but the local *Khassadars* (auxiliaries) looked unreliable and so regular troops were soon tied down in route protection. To improve road security, permanent piquets were established, and sweeps conducted to open the road every day. Avoiding a direct confrontation, the Faqir's men made isolated and intermittent attacks, although some were far more serious. At Damdil on 20 March 1937, for example, a determined night attack was made on 1/6th Gurkhas' camp piquet.[19] Swordsmen, supported by riflemen laying suppressive fire, rushed the Gurkhas' sangars, flinging hand grenades as they approached. The attacks were beaten off, and, with daylight, the machine gun fire of armoured cars, artillery, and strafing by aircraft compelled the Faqir's raiders to withdraw.

However, as so often in low intensity operations, guerrilla losses were replaced, and, over the summer of 1937, the Faqir's *lashkar* strength increased to approximately 4,000 men. There were further raids into settled areas, with more attacks on bridges, culverts and piquets along the new road. Sniping against patrols was also frequent. The most successful and audacious ambush for the tribesmen occurred at Shahur Tangi on 9 April 1937.[20] A mixed Mahsud and Bhittani force, numbering somewhere between 100 and 300 men, knocked out the head of the column and the last vehicle which hemmed in the rest. The armoured cars couldn't elevate their guns and the Indian escort was subjected to intense fire, losing approximately 80 men in the action. As a result, all road traffic was halted unless it was traversing a protected route, and permanent piquets were established, surrounded by barbed wire entanglements, on high ground above the roads. On 22 April, a new drive by ground forces took place in the Khaisora and Shaktu areas, operating where it was relatively easy for armour and for aircraft to co-ordinate with ground attacks, but the *lashkars* carefully avoided fighting the full might of the Army in India. Instead, the tribesmen waited for the opportunity to inflict heavier losses and perhaps deter any further encroachments into their territory. They made a determined night attack on one encampment, but two days later, the same *lashkar* was caught in the open by artillery fire and air attack, while, on the 30th, another group of 100 tribesmen

---

18 *Operations on the North West Frontiers, Intelligence Summaries, 1936–7*, IOR L/PS/12/3192; File 514/IV, Resident to Governor North West Frontier Province, 18 February 1937, pp. 38–41, IOR R/12/69.

19 Warren, *Waziristan*, pp. 146 and 148.

20 'Attack on the convoy at Shahur Tangi on 9th April, 1937', *Journal of the United Services Institution India*, 67/288 (April and July 1937), pp. 261–5.

was ambushed as they tried to move positions. By the beginning of May, the tribesmen around Khaisora had suffered significant losses. To administer the *coup de grace*, 'WazDiv' (Waziristan Division), the formation based at Dosalli, intended to strike against the Tori Khels in Shaktu, the Faqir's stronghold. On 11 May the column made an unorthodox overnight advance over the Iblanke Range led by the Tochi Scouts.[21] Another brigade advanced in a converging arc, and, after a brief firefight, the *lashkar* was cut down by aircraft as it tried to escape across the Sham Plain.

Although the Faqir escaped, the accumulated losses ensured that many tribesmen gave up the campaign at this point and a proportion of the Afghan volunteers left the Faqir's cause. When his base at Arsal Kot was taken, and his cave complex destroyed, the Faqir's prestige and credibility was further reduced.[22] Many of his promises that the British would be turned back had been proven false, and, although he maintained a small group of acolytes, the worse of the fighting was over. In fact, the majority of the Tori Khel's had obeyed their maliks, under the pressure of the British Political Officers, to keep out of the fighting. This was evidence of the weakness of the Faqir's cause and exemplified the importance for the British of a political effort alongside the military one.

A new circular road was constructed during the summer and autumn of 1937 and mopping up operations were carried out against the remaining hostiles, with a column making its way through Bhittani country following tribal raids on settled areas. Small ambushes, the cutting of telephone lines, and the destruction of bridges and culverts continued, but these were regarded as a nuisance rather than events of any significance. In November 1937, British and Indian troops again swept through the Khaisora. The Faqir had to keep on the move to avoid capture making it harder for him to maintain resistance and the momentum of support, and, as a result, raiding fell off to practically nil by the year's end.

The Waziristan campaign had been fought by only a few thousand tribesmen but it had required 61,000 troops to suppress it, a ratio not uncommon in other low intensity campaigns.[23] The Army in India had lost 245 killed and 684 wounded, with a further 73 deaths from diseases. From a military point of view, the Army in India was able to assert control of the area of operations and to limit the mobility of the tribesmen to some extent. They were able to inflict substantial

---

21 *Operations North West Frontier, Intelligence Summaries*, 1936–37, pp. 90–93, IOR L/PS/12/3192; Warren, *Waziristan*, pp. 178 and 180–81.

22 John Masters, *Bugles and a Tiger* (London: Michael Joseph Ltd, 1956), pp. 225–31.

23 Robert Taber, *War of the Flea* (New York: L. Stuart, 1965; new edn, Washington DC: Potomac Books, 2004), p. 11; American doctrine suggests there must usually be 20 to 25 counterinsurgents for every 1,000 residents in an operational area. *Counterinsurgency Field Manual* FM3-24 (University of Chicago Press, 2007), p. 23.

casualties, despite their opponent's guerrilla tactics, because the tribesmen were determined to fight every physical manifestation of the occupation and that made them 'visible'. However, the greater strength and firepower of the Army in India made the tribesmen more reluctant to expose themselves to battle. It is for this reason they resorted to sniping and night ambushes wherever possible in the latter stages of the campaign.

The principle of letting local forces lead where possible, to reduce costs, to make full use of their knowledge, and to avoid the antagonism created by the presence of 'foreigners', was well understood. The auxiliaries, namely the Tochi Scouts, who were about 5,000 strong, had proved useful when deployed with regulars or on independent pursuits. They were mobile, had local knowledge, and could operate on the flanks and rear against a tribesmen's attack, although they were too lightly armed for sustained battles. It was even suggested the Indian Army should recreate a specialised frontier unit which would be made up almost entirely of this sort of light infantry. However, the idea was rejected as impractical, on the grounds that the army needed to be prepared to fight in Afghanistan against regular forces, although concerns about the reliability of the existing locally-recruited auxiliaries in certain cases may also have played a part in the decision.[24]

The Army had been restricted in the campaign by political considerations. Rules of engagement were considered irksome, and John Masters, a subaltern in the 4th Gurkhas who went on to become an accomplished author, complained: 'we fought with one hand tied behind our backs'.[25] The area of operations was strictly limited to a defined 'proscribed area'. Outside of this zone, they could not fire unless shot at. Within the zone they could only engage groups of more than ten men if they were armed and not on a path. Given that tribesmen dressed the same as the inhabitants and could conceal their weapons, and that the nature of the country defied any neat definition of the term 'path', the rules were not adhered to if 'there was no Political around'. Inexperienced units inflicted their own punitive measures against those closest to routes where hostile action had occurred. The tribesmen would often mine roads and construct booby-traps with grenades, but the tribesmen's practice of mutilating the dead or wounded elicited the strongest reactions. In one incident, the troops retaliated by refusing to take prisoners.[26]

---

24 Moreman, *The Army in India*, pp. 179–80.

25 Arthur Swinson, *North West Frontier* (London: Hutchinson, 1967), p. 377.

26 When a British officer was captured, castrated and flayed – his skin being pegged out nearby – his Indian troops were ordered to beat a wounded Pathan. Swinson, *North West Frontier*, p. 378.

Masters parodied the rules of engagement by citing military maxims. In response to the traditional idea to: '*shoot first, shoot fastest, shoot last and shoot to kill*', he wrote the new rules implied: 'Do not shoot unless you have been shot at, and then try not to hurt anyone, there's a good chap!', and furthermore, to the maxim: '*Mystify, mislead and surprise your enemy, then never leave him a moment to gather himself again, but fall on him like a thunderclap and pursue him to his utter destruction, regardless of fatigue casualties or cost*', Masters wrote: 'Announce your intentions to the enemy, in order that he may have time to remove his women and children to a place of safety – and time to counter your plan. At all events, stop what you are doing as soon as he pretends to have had enough, so that he may gather again somewhere else.'[27]

However, the most controversial rules governed the use of air power. The older *Manual of Operations on the NWF of India* was eventually replaced in November 1938 by *Frontier Warfare (Army and RAF) 1939* but the publication was delayed because of sensitivity about the issue of bombing, especially of villages.[28] Warnings were always issued by dropping leaflets prior to a bombing run on property, usually twice; although in certain circumstances it might only be once. The length of time between warnings and a bombing was determined by how long it would take for a village to convene, discuss and then present a response or submission, but was never under 24 hours. The warnings had to specify which tribe and section was affected, and an outline of the circumstances that led to the threat. Clear instructions including the precise course they had to follow, and the place and date where a submission was to be made, were also to be included. The final note was printed on red paper, which included the same details and the explicit reason why air action was about to be taken against them, and a description of the nearest place of refuge. To avoid the risk that civilians might not get the warnings, ground messages were also delivered if possible. After the action, white leaflets were dropped, and efforts would be made to destroy any unexploded ordnance less the tribesmen try to make use of them as road mines.

---

27 Masters, *Bugles and a Tiger*, p. 205. If withdrawing, troops had to maintain continual observation of the hostile tribesmen throughout, and only then could they attack. Usually they had to be in contact for 30 minutes to take firm action from the air, but an area of two miles around could be considered a combat zone. *Instructions Governing the Employment of Armed Forces in the Maintenance of Tribal Control of the NWF of India and in Baluchistan, 1940*, Confidential (Government of India, Defence Dept) IOR L/PS/20/B308.

28 *Instructions Governing the Employment of Armed Forces in the Maintenance of Tribal Control of the NWF of India and in Baluchistan, 1940*, Confidential (Government of India, Defence Dept) IOR L/PS/20/B308.

In certain circumstances, action could be taken by ground and air forces without the sanction of the Government of India, but all 'Deliberate Operations' had to have official sanction with clearly defined political objectives. In periods of Watch and Ward, including maintaining the security of communications or action against gun runners and raiders, the civil authority could call on the Army for support, but when a situation arose which could not be controlled by the Civil Armed Forces, the deployment of regular troops became imperative and control would naturally shift to the local military commander. Nevertheless, the Government of India insisted on the full cooperation of the civilians and the military, and 'political control' could be transferred *only* by the government of India. The army were expected to consult the Political Officer before entering tribal areas, except in maintenance of security in 'road open' days, although the army and air force could be deployed in readiness for action.

Although major operations had ceased in 1937, the Faqir of Ipi remained at large, and, between 1938 and 1939, 'irreconcilable tribesmen' continue to snipe at troops and posts, attack roads, rob traffic and cut telephone lines.[29] Villages in Derajat were raided and special defensive arrangements had to be made. Troops were called in and a line of communication established to provide platforms of observation using the regulars, Tochi Scouts and aircraft patrols. However, the various divisions of the Masud and Waziri tribesmen did not necessarily recognise any settlement made by their neighbours and continued their resistance independently, leading to a fragmented peace, whilst some simply resumed their fighting once the pressure was off. On 23 July 1938, there was a serious raid on Bannu in which several civilians were killed and properties burned.[30] Many tribesmen were killed and 20 were captured, but the rest stayed in the hills nearby and hundreds of civilians left their homes in fear of further violence.

The Frontier during the Second World War

At the outbreak of the Second World War in 1939, there were 48 British and Indian battalions on the North West Frontier, which represented 38 per cent of the Army in India's peacetime strength. With the Faqir of Ipi still raiding Derajat, in December 1940 it was decided to build frontier posts in Waziristan. However, intelligence that the Faqir of Ipi was the object of some interest to German and Italian envoys in Afghanistan, and the success of the Wehrmacht

29 Weekly Summaries North Waziristan 1938–43, Edward Lydall Papers, IOR MSS Eur D923.

30 Swinson, *North West Frontier*, p. 388.

against Russia in 1941 caused concern.[31] In an unwitting form of flattery for the tribesmen, it was suggested the Army in India would stop the Axis forces in Afghanistan's mountains using Pathan (Pashtun) tactics and mountain warfare techniques: 'The Army in India starts with having studied the Pathan and his ways and having acquaintance with the conditions, tactical and administrative, of fighting in the mountains. It should ... be able to adapt the Pathan's harassing tactic to worrying a more stereotyped opponent both near the battlefront and on the L[ine] of C[ommunication].'[32]

By 1943, there were 57 British and Indian infantry battalions and four armoured car regiments committed to the North West Frontier, although, by then, it was the threat of invasion on the north-eastern border that was absorbing the lion's share of the wartime expansion of the Indian Army. The NWFP governor's fortnightly intelligence reports provide an interesting assessment of the falling away of tribal resistance during the conflict and the tribesmen's interest in the war. Initially, the Faqir of Ipi and the tribesmen kept up their routine of raids and 'outrages'.[33] By February 1942, the situation had changed and the Governor wrote: 'I believe that the efforts we have been making for some time to influence the Faqir through two or three important mullahs are bearing some fruit.'[34] In August 1942, it was estimated there had been 57 incidents for the year to date, which compared with 59 incidents in 1941, and 176 in 1940.[35] The steady decline in violence continued so that by 1944–45 the frontier was relatively quiet, and the number of incidents had fallen to single figures.

There were multiple explanations for this trend. The Governor admitted that during the war 'we have a large number of local people of influence, including

---

31 Milan Hauner, 'One Man Against the Empire: The Faqir of Ipi and the British in Central Asia on the Eve of and During the Second World War', *Journal of Contemporary History*, 16, 1 (January 1981), pp. 183–212.

32 *Military Training Pamphlet No.7 (India) Extensive Warfare (Notes on Warfare in Mountainous Country between Modern Forces in Eastern Theatres)* (Simla, 1941), p. 3, IOR L/MIL/17/5/2248 cited in Moreman, *Army in India*, p. 180.

33 In January 1942, an ambush of the Assistant District Officer, Mr Morgan and his frontier constabulary escort, resulted in the death of Morgan and a Havildar. In the subsequent skirmish, two more frontier Sepoys were also killed, but the raiders lost 12 killed and wounded, largely because of the hot pursuit of the frontier forces, including a running battle through crops of sugar cane. *NWFP Governor's Fortnightly Intelligence Reports*, Secret, 24 January 1942, IOR L/PJ/5/219.

34 *NWFP Governor's Fortnightly Intelligence Reports*, Secret, No. 4, 23 February 1942, IOR L/PJ/5/219.

35 *NWFP Governor's Fortnightly Intelligence Reports*, Secret, Report for first half of August 1942, IOR L/PJ/5/219.

many of the best known mullahs, working for us'.[36] Newspapers were carefully monitored for signs of propaganda.[37] Recruiting was also more problematic for both the Indian Army and the Faqir during the late summer when labour was needed for wheat cutting, but this also absorbed the numbers of young raiders. The Governor noted that: 'In all the country through which I have toured the paucity of young men of military age is now very noticeable.' The decline in raids may also have been in response to the British themselves assuming a defensive posture.

A confidential report in December noted that in Kurram and Dera Ismail Khan, 'the general attitude of the people [was] excellent'.[38] The same report noted that at all the *jirgas* (councils), the tribesmen expressed pleasure in the Allied victories in North Africa and Stalingrad, whilst the Indian National Congress (INC) was 'rarely mentioned'. They were 'far more interested in their own small problems of irrigation' and the rising cost of foodstuffs, but the report noted that it was remarkable how well informed the average villager was regarding the general trend of the war. Swabi Tehsil in Mardan district was one of the 'bad spots' in 1930, and the report stated: 'It is difficult to picture it as ever having been in that condition. It is a great recruiting area, and has a very fine record during this war. One village which has produced 550 recruits in the last three years has got a war memorial of the last war which shows only 112 were enlisted between 1914 and 1918'.[39] In the *Review of Frontier Defence* in 1944, in a tacit acknowledgement that forward garrisons tended to encourage resistance, there was a recommendation to revert to Curzon's policy of 1901, namely to withdraw the Army from its garrisons inside tribal areas to be replaced with smaller bodies of frontier Armed Civil Forces. It was a policy decision that Pakistan itself adopted in 1948.

Military Aid to the Civil Power

Charles Gwynn, the Commandant of the Staff College (1926–30), tackled something of the political dimension to unrest in the British Empire in his

36 *NWFP Governor's Fortnightly Intelligence Reports*, Secret, No. 18, 23 September 1942, IOR L/PJ/5/219.

37 *NWFP Governor's Fortnightly Intelligence Reports*, Secret, No. 10, 23 May1942, IOR L/PJ/5/219.

38 *NWFP Governor's Fortnightly Intelligence Report*, Confidential, No. 23, 8 December 1942, IOR L/PJ/5/219.

39 *NWFP Governor's Fortnightly Intelligence Report*, Confidential, No. 2, 19 November 1942, IOR L/PJ/5/219.

influential *Imperial Policing* and an official manual which carried the same title.[40] In light of Britain's experiences in Egypt, Iraq and during the Moplah Rebellion (1921) in India, Gwynn argued there should be four governing principles: primacy of the civil power, the use of minimum force, firm and timely action, and, cooperation between civil and military authorities. The very fact that Gwynn had written such a study was an acknowledgement that the suppression of unrest, when it was serious enough to warrant troops, was being played out in front of a regional, national and international audience. With the exception of Moplah, which was a revolt in favour of a creation of an Islamic Khalifat, the nationalist character of the riots had given Gwynn and his contemporaries pause for thought. However, Gwynn did not advocate political concessions to head off trouble: his focus was entirely on the means to restore order, and at times that still involved considerable coercion and collective punishment. He wrote: 'The principal police task of the Army is no longer to prepare the way for civil control, but to restore it when it collapses.'[41] A soldiers' pamphlet, entitled *Duties in Aid of the Civil Powers*, was blunt: 'when soldiers are called upon to act, they act as soldiers and not as policemen'.[42]

Nevertheless, Military Aid to the Civil Power was the least popular amongst the troops because it was regarded as glorified policing and a far cry from real soldiering. Most deployments were by British units because of concerns about the loyalties of Indian troops, although, on the occasions that Indian soldiers were put on the streets, as in 1942–43, they were wholly impartial and professional. Yet, in military circles in India, there was some concern, in light of the treatment of Brigadier General Dyer after the infamous shootings at Amritsar in 1919, about how civilian authorities might treat officers who used force, and who might deem their actions 'excessive'. Army regulations in 1904 insisted that officers: 'apply as little force, and do as little injury, as may be consistent with dispersing the assembly' and there had to be a clear warning.[43] The *Manual of Military Law* (1914) had stipulated that 'so much force is to be used as is sufficient to effect the object in view'.[44] Yet Dyer had argued that his actions

[40] Gwynn, *Imperial Policing* (London: Macmillan, 1934).

[41] Gwynn, *Imperial Policing*, p. 5.

[42] *Duties in Aid of the Civil Powers*, The Nigeria Regiment (Lagos, 1934), p. 6.

[43] *Army Regulations India, 1904*, II, p. 76; David Omissi, *The Sepoy and the Raj: The Indian Army, 1860–1940* (London: Macmillan, 1994), p. 217. See also Rod Thornton, 'The British Army and the Origins of the Minimum Force Philosophy', *Small Wars and Insurgencies*, 15, I (2005), pp. 83–106 and Charles Townshend, 'Martial Law: Legal and Administrative Problems of Civil Emergency in Britain and the Empire, 1800–1940', *The Historical Journal*, 25 (1982), pp. 167–95.

[44] *Manual of Military Law* (London: War Office, 1914), p. 219.

had been justified 'from a military point of view' in that they neutralised any prospect of rebellion in the Punjab.[45] The number of deaths may not have been proportional to the situation in Amritsar, but in the minds of the authorities there was some doubt about the balance between restraint and violence that would be deemed acceptable to achieve the restoration of order. As a result, the Indian Disorders Committee ruled that civilian authorities, namely magistrates and governors, had to be a part of the martial law apparatus.[46] It also specified that the formation of additional armed police would mean there was less need for troops. The committee stipulated that troops were to be deployed as a last resort. To open fire, officers had to have the written support of a magistrate, unless their lives were actually in danger.

The army's guidance, *Duties in Aid of the Civil Power* (1934), specified 'necessary force' as the guiding principle, rather than 'minimum force', although by 1948 the Staff College course advised that minimum force was 'the single most important principle' in internal security operations.[47] Thomas Mockaitis has argued that the British Army inculcated the guidance, not merely in a legal sense but as part of its military ethos, forming a 'culture of restraint'.[48] However, in the inter-war years there was little attempt to distinguish the great variety of scenarios that would confront the soldier to distinguish between 'minimum' and 'necessary'. There was a vague conception that peaceful protests, even 'unlawful assemblies', should proscribe the use of force, while riot and insurrection would merit it.[49] Getting the balance right was a matter of judgement. In the Moplah Rebellion of 1921, the army had been criticised for using too little force and not acting decisively.[50] Dyer had argued that he understood the principle of necessary force and 'had this principle very clearly before me during the whole time I was in Amritsar'.[51] Much depended on the experience and decision of the most senior commander present, but as expectations about the use of force

45 HMSO and D. George Boyce, 'From Assaye to *The Assaye*: Reflections on British Government, Force and Moral Authority in India', *Journal Military History*, 63, 3 (1999), pp. 643–68.

46 Indian Disorders Committee, Conclusions, 6 May 1919, CP1240, National Archives, CAB 24/105.

47 Cited in Huw Bennett, 'The Mau Mau Emergency as Part of the British Army's Post-War Counter-Insurgency Experience', *Defence and Security Analysis*, 23 (2007), p. 145.

48 Thomas Mockaitis, *British Counter-Insurgency in the Post-Imperial Era* (Manchester, 1995), pp. 17–27, 40 and 180.

49 *Manual of Military Law* (1914), pp. 216–17.

50 Charles Townshend, *Britain's Civil Wars: Counterinsurgency in the Twentieth Century* (London, 1986), p. 20.

51 Nick Lloyd, 'The Amritsar Massacre and the Minimum Force Debate', *Small Wars and Insurgencies*, 21 (2010), p. 389; Purnima Bose and Laura Lyons, 'Dyer Consequences: The

against civilians in the United Kingdom changed, so the officers of the Army found themselves on shifting sands.[52]

For the Army in India, the picture was far clearer by the time of the outbreak of war. The official manual *Duties in Aid of the Civil Power* (1937) identified six principles for military action in Internal Security operations: provision of adequate forces, necessity for offensive action, coordinated intelligence under military control, efficient 'inter-communication' [between agencies], mobility, and security measures to conceal preparations and movements of troops.[53] The manual also detailed specific tasks such as cordons, searches, 'drives' (sweeps through particular areas) and the provisions of martial law. Yet, more importantly it established that the guidelines should be civilian leadership with the army acting in support, the application of minimum force, and that the ultimate objective should be the maintenance of the rule of law. In practical terms, the army would operate in three phases.

Phase 1 would be the period of 'immediate action'. The army would attempt to conceal their arrival so that their deployment, when it came, was concentrated, rapid and would achieve surprise, with all the psychological effect that implied. The priority was to disperse the rioters, to carry out arrests (particularly of the ringleaders), order summary trials and make immediate punishments. If hostile crowds refused to heed verbal warnings, the military commanders would open fire, but, if they did so, it was never over the heads of the crowd, but always at them – the intention being to inflict casualties and cause their flight. Control of key areas (such as bridges, communications and police stations or other buildings owned by the authorities) was essential in this phase to provide a secure base for future operations.

In phase 2, the objective was to clear and extend areas of control and to gather intelligence on any remaining leaders. Phase 3 would entail preparations for the handover to the civilian authorities whereupon fines and other collective punishments might be imposed. Clearly the army understood the importance of psychology. In urban areas, during riots, troops adopted a dense 'box' formation' to create an impression of solidity and strength. The idea of shooting a handful of rioters was to have a salutary effect on very large crowds, a point that seemed imperative when the army was often heavily outnumbered. Moreover, once the key buildings and symbols of authority were secure, it was

Trope of Amritsar, Ireland and the Lessons of the Minimum Force Debate', *Boundary* 26 (1999), pp. 199–229.

52 See Stephen Miller, 'Duty or Crime? Defining Acceptable Behaviour in the British Army in South Africa, 1899–1902', *Journal of British Studies*, 49 (2010), p. 311.

53 See also C/417 *Procedure for Employment of Troops in Indian States in Aid of the Civil Power, 1932–1937*. IOR/R/2/631/224.

believed that patrolling would help to assert control of the streets, protect property and provide reassurance for those who had not been involved. For all these military solutions, the Commander in Chief, Henry Rawlinson, still acknowledged that the army was usually ineffective in the face of long-term civil disobedience, noting: 'you cannot collect taxes everywhere at the point of a bayonet'.[54] Whilst the Army in India could ensure security, it could not guarantee the functioning of the state.

'Quit India', 1942–1944

The major wartime challenge to British internal security in India broke out at precisely the moment that India faced the prospect of a Japanese invasion. In August 1942, Gandhi's 'Quit India' campaign was supposed to be a mass movement of non-violence, where the retraction of cooperation with the British would force the Raj to collapse. Assuming the self-sacrifice of Gandhi and his supporters would shame the British into halting their operations, the INC argued that brutality would be met with *satyagraha* (non-cooperation). Alerted to this imminent campaign and in a classic move to isolate the ringleaders, the British arrested the INC's most senior members. Eventually some 66,000 were detained. There was a press black-out.

With its Committees outlawed and its offices and papers seized, the left wing of the movement advocated a campaign of sabotage, but the remaining INC leaders knew that, while the Indian Army remained loyal to the British, there was no chance of a violent campaign succeeding.[55] Nevertheless, as previous campaigns had shown, it proved difficult for Gandhi and the moderate INC leaders to persuade all their followers to adopt an entirely non-violent path. News of Gandhi's arrest sparked two weeks of rioting whilst boycotting and civil disobedience spread. Disruptions to food supply caused acute shortages in some areas. Telephone lines, post offices, courts, revenue offices and even police stations were the targets for attack and arson. In extreme cases, railway

---

54 Rawlinson Diary, 28 December 1921, Rawlinson Papers, 5201/33/23.

55 An assessment of the unrest by Congress was intercepted by Military Intelligence. National Archives, WO 208/819A, 25C. The same conclusions had already been reached by the British a decade before, see Memorandum by Deverell, Chief of Staff, 26 May 1930, National Archives WO 106/5443. The British Central Intelligence Department was very well informed about INC plans, having intercepted mail and penetrated the organisation at various levels. CID briefings were held daily or every two days at height of the crisis. Home Department: History of the Congress Rebellion, Part 1, 1942–3, *Gandhi's Independence Campaign: Statistics to Assist the S[ecretary of] S[tate] to reply to P[arliamentary] Questions]* IOR L/PJ/8/628.

tracks were torn up. At its height, the Quit India campaign required an entire British division to be diverted to Bombay to quash the unrest. But it was the vulnerability of the strategic railways that really alarmed the British authorities, and the Viceroy, Lord Linlithgow, authorised the RAF to fly sorties over crowds that appeared to menace railway lines running across the Eastern Provinces and Bihar.[56] Their instructions were to fly low, fire Verey light flares and warning shots. Congress accused the British of machine gunning the demonstrators.[57] Linlithgow felt that saboteurs of railways deserved to be shot down by aircraft, and the authorities were prepared to take every measure necessary to crush the unrest in order to release the 35,000 troops that they might need as a strategic reserve to confront a Japanese offensive. The calculation was that they had a window of opportunity of just six weeks before that attack came.

Linlithgow informed Churchill that he was: 'engaged here in meeting by far the most serious rebellion since that of 1857, the gravity and extent of which we have so far concealed for reasons of military security ... Mob violence remains rampant over large tracts of the countryside and I am by no means confident that we may not see in September a formidable effort to renew this widespread sabotage of our war effort.'[58] When the idea of strafing saboteurs from the air was raised in the House of Commons on 8 October 1942, there was support for a firm line.[59] Gone were the qualms of Amritsar: Britain was on the defensive in Europe, had suffered at Dunkirk and during the Blitz, and, as a result, attitudes towards Congress had hardened. Churchill was particularly defiant, claiming he had: 'not become the King's first minister in order to preside over the liquidation of the British Empire'.[60]

British and Indian Army troops were deployed wherever the police had either lost control or were hard pressed. *Lathis* and canes were wielded to discipline those that sought to obstruct them, and in Bihar and Bengal, where the violence

56 Interestingly, the General Staff and Home Department had already discussed the possibility of creating a paramilitary force for internal security police in 1941, especially for strategic railway protection, 174/44/41, *Gandhi's Independence Campaign: Statistics to Assist the S[ecretary of] S[tate] to Reply to P[arliamentary] Questions]* IOR L/PJ/8/628.

57 Lawrence James, *Raj: The Making and Unmaking of British India* (London: Little Brown and Company, 1997), p. 566; P.N. Chopra, '"Quit India" Movement of 1942', *Journal of Indian History*, 49 (1971), pp. 39–40 and P.N. Chopra, *Quit India: British Secret Documents* (New Delhi, 1986). The crew of one of these aircraft that crash landed was murdered by a mob.

58 N.M. Mansergh, E.W.R. Lumby and P. Moon (eds), *Constitutional Relations between Britain and India: The Transfer of Power: 1942–47*, II (London: Allen and Unwin, 1970), pp. 853–4.

59 Hansard, 5th Series, 383, 1342.

60 Leo Amery, ed. J. Barnes and D. Nicholson, *The Empire at Bay: The Leo Amery Diaries, 1929–45* (London: Hutchinson, 1987), p. 830.

was worst, pacification measures included floggings and shootings. However, the troops had other solutions short of violence. INC activists were known to court gaol terms as a badge of honour, so the authorities took to dumping them naked after a short period of detention to humiliate them in the eyes of the population. One soldier recalled: 'When the crowd was getting very angry and very unruly and pressing up against us we would ease them back by gently dropping the butts of our rifles on their toes.'[61] There were plenty of efforts to portray the British as brutal thugs: it was alleged that rifles were fired at the ground to cause a ricochet that would inflict more casualties. Yet, the troops had always had a shoot to kill policy albeit one that was strictly prescribed, and were always instructed to aim directly at the rioters.[62] More often than not the British were simply outnumbered. At Sasaram, on the line from Lucknow to Calcutta, thousands of students, protestors and opportunists set fire to the railway station and signal box, and then occupied the local court house. The Hindu policemen, fearing for their lives, retreated to the gaol, whereupon 20 British soldiers arrived to reinforce them, but it was not until the Bedfordshire Regiment appeared in strength that the crowds began to disperse.[63]

Although outnumbered, the British possessed the ability to manage the unrest. During the Quit India campaign, the police and the army had been compelled to open fire 369 times, killing an estimated 1,000 and wounding a further 2,000.[64] However, there had been some problems. The army, which did not wish to prioritise internal security over the campaign in Burma, was reluctant to be involved, whilst the civilian provincial authorities were just as reluctant to admit they had lost control. New police forces that were drafted tended to be inexperienced and there was a shortage of firearms because of the competition of resources caused by the war. Over 200 police stations had been razed. Some 332 railway stations had been destroyed and 268 rolling stock damaged which had delayed troop movements, the construction of air bases and the delivery of essential coal supplies by approximately three weeks. Strikes had resulted in the reduction of vital steel production by ten per cent. Neverthless, the Indian Army, swelled by the war, had the manpower and the weaponry to contain the violence. The civilian intelligence network remained largely intact and the

61 WOII Charles Wright, *The Black Watch*, cited in Charles Allen, *Plain Tales from the Raj* (London: Faber, 1975), p. 249.

62 PRO Air 23/2053, 5, 13, National Archives.

63 Martin Papers, IOR Mss Eur F180/21, 34–6.

64 Mansergh, Lumby and Moon, *Constitutional Relations between Britain and India*, II, p. 933.

morale of Indian personnel was described as 'steadfast'.[65] Nevertheless, officers were cautioned to avoid suggestions of 'scorn for the "unenlightened Indian" who wants independence ... since freedom and independence are probably sought after by the troops themselves'.[66] The problem was to be framed solely in terms of the restoration of order. The Viceroy and the Commander in Chief were in accord on the security measures necessary, and the troops were deployed in small groups for their 'policing' tasks, rather than as concentrated units as the Indian Army would have preferred.

Nevertheless, before any success is attributed to purely military measures, an assessment must take account of other contextual factors. The fact is that many had a stake in the survival of the Raj. The Muslim League, fearing a Hindu-dominated successor state to the Raj, had sided with the British against Congress. The high percentage of Muslims in the Indian Army meant that they not only felt less sympathy with the Congress rioters, but they expected to benefit from their loyalty in the future. The Princely States also remained in league with the British, particularly when they faced Congress unrest in their own principalities. Many 'supporters' of Congress during the unrest were in fact politically neutral, but for their own safety made declarations that favoured Congress only for the duration of the troubles. Some *ryots* (peasants) and workers, who had suffered the higher wartime prices, also used the political unrest as a means to raid granaries and stores for material gain, but quickly abandoned their opportunism when the police and army appeared in force.

Moreover, as far as internal security was concerned, across the country as a whole, communal unrest was more common than the short-lived political violence of the Quit India campaign. In the period July 1937 to October 1939, the army was called out on 25 occasions to deal with communal unrest, and in the first three months of the war in 1939, the army was called out 15 times, with deployments lasting from one day to two weeks.[67] Between October 1939 and March 1943, it was estimated that 492 people had been killed in communal rioting with 1,902 injured. A small proportion of these casualties were inflicted by the police or the army when riots got out of hand.[68] A District Magistrate

---

65 Home Department: History of the Congress Rebellion, Part 1, 1942–43, *Gandhi's Independence Campaign: Statistics to Assist the S[ecretary of] S[tate] to Reply to P[arliamentary] Questions]* IOR L/PJ/8/628.

66 Brig. Gen. Cawthorn, Director of Military Intelligence (DMI), 31 August 1942, secret, IOR L/WS/1/1337.

67 *Use of Troops for Maintenance of Essential Services in Case of an Emergency*, IOR L/PJ/8/571.

68 *Official Reports of Riots and Disturbances in India*, January 1940–July 1944, IOR L/PJ/8/572A.

explained: 'Some stupid little thing would happen, a rumour that Pathans were abducting Hindu girls, or that somebody had killed a Mohammedan. Usually it was quite untrue, but then the trouble, which was always smouldering in certain cities, started ... you couldn't prevent it, but you might, if you were sufficiently prompt and on the spot at the time, prevent it assuming a serious form. I was a great believer in the maximum display of force at the very beginning to try and overawe people. I was also a great believer in using force effectively if you had to use it at all. I didn't believe in firing one or two rounds; I used to say to my magistrates: "if ever you have to open fire, fire at least five rounds. If you open up make sure that it is effective, so that people are seen to fall and the mob takes fright." It didn't occur to me as ruthless. It occurred to me as plain commonsense.'[69]

The nadir of British fortunes came in 1943. In Burma, the Indian Army's attack at Arakan failed. Morale was so low that some Indian troops talked of simply giving up, although this was against a background of difficult conditions, insufficient equipment and the memory of the defeats in Malaya and Burma. There were already large-scale defections by prisoners of the Japanese to the INA (Indian National Army) which at this stage numbered 12,000. Anxiety about Indian loyalties were revealed not just by the effort put into orchestrated morale-building measures in the Indian Army, but also by the correspondence surrounding the Special Powers Ordinance for the Military Operational Area passed in 1943.[70] The Ordinance provided for the setting up of measures to deal with fifth column activity in the zone behind the front line. An Ordinance of Special Powers was seen as preferable to martial law, since a friendly rural population was more likely to turn in enemy agents than a frightened and resentful one.[71] Moreover, the Viceroy was concerned that, in previous episodes of martial law, the army in Bihar had established special courts 'untrammelled by the usual controls', which tended to be 'hasty in decision and inadequate in record

69 Penderel Moon, Indian Civil Service and District Magistrate, cited in Allen, *Plain Tales*, p. 246.

70 On Indian Army morale see, for example, 'Secret Appreciation of Indian Morale', Overseas Planning Committee, Ministry of Information, 1942, National Archives, INF 1/556. The situation was assessed by Brig. W.J. Cawthorn, DMI, in 'Reactions in Indian Units to Japanese Propaganda', Most Secret, Weekly Intelligence Survey, India Internal, 31 March 1944, IOR L/WS/1433 and 'The Future of the Internal Security Situation in India', 31 August 1942, IOR L/WS/1/1337. Measures had already been designed from the outbreak of the war, see J.A. Thorne, *Confidential Report on the Control during the War of the Press, Broadcasting and Films, and on Publicity of the Purpose of the War* (Delhi, 1939), IOR L/I/1/1136.

71 Viceroy to Secretary of State for India, telegram, Secret 38421, 9 October 1943, and Viceroy to Secretary of State for India, telegram, Secret 38463, 13 October 1943, IOR L/PJ/8/566.

of summaries of evidence', adding 'I fear the same results if the army is given *carte blanche*'. However, he admitted that 'speed of trials in the circumstances [are] essential'.[72] His solution was to attach the Deputy Judge Advocate on the military staff in the operational area. The army too wanted assurances. General Molesworth wanted careful drafting of what the limits of military authority and territorial jurisdiction were.[73] It seems that both the army and the government were eager to maintain the primacy of political leadership and to ensure the close cooperation of military and the civilian authorities.

The famine of 1943 was another crisis with implications for the maintenance of security and order at a critical stage in the war. Subhas Chandra Bose, the INA leader, exploited the propaganda potential of the situation and offered rice 'as a gift to the people' from the Japanese.[74] The British responded by intensifying their efforts to sustain the morale of Indian soldiers.[75] When Archibald Wavell became Viceroy (1943), he injected a new energy into the relief effort.[76] He was ably supported by General Sir Claude Auchinleck as C-in-C who expanded the Indian officer corps and gave them more responsibilities, including the command of British troops.[77] Indian soldiers were entrusted without British officers, and wherever possible racial divisions were brought to an end. He increased rates of pay for Indian troops, visited their villages and talked with small groups to lift morale. His personal style left a legacy of greater consensus. He made visits to particular Indian princes to enlist their people for the war effort, but he also met Muslim and INC leaders to hear their grievances. He would not allow the authorities to condemn INC leaders, and aimed for their political neutrality. This approach paid off. Although still censored, letters by soldiers reveal that they felt new skills could be learned by military service. Military equipment, which had always been limited in quality and quantity before the war, now arrived in abundance. These new weapons and vehicles gave the men confidence, and was

72 Viceroy to Secretary of State for India, telegram, Secret 36616, 23 September 1943, IOR L/PJ/8/566.

73 Note by Under Secretary of State, 29 September 1943, IOR L/PJ/8/566.

74 See Peter Ward Fay, *The Forgotten Army: India's Armed Struggle for Independence* (University of Michigan Press, 1993), pp. 419–22.

75 See Sanjoy Bhattacharya, *Propaganda and Information in Eastern India, 1939–45: A Necessary Weapon of War* (London: Curzon-Routledge, 2001).

76 Wavell had been C-in-C India from December 1941, and had sent Indian 10th Division to Iraq, but served as Viceroy 1943–47 having been ousted from the North African theatre and C-in-C Middle East by Churchill.

77 Daniel Marston, 'A Force Transformed: The Indian Army and the Second World War' in Daniel P. Marston and Chandar S. Sundaram, *A Military History of India and South Asia: From the East India Company to the Nuclear Age* (Bloomington, IN: Indian University Press, 2008), p. 121.

a useful propaganda tool. It was also arranged that women could serve, greatly enhancing their status. It seems the British understood that an essential element of low intensity warfare was the need to 'localise', in this case to 'Indianise', the military forces, but equally, Wavell and Auchinleck both knew that the British had to be able to rely on the police and the Indian Army to maintain security and to sustain the war effort: they simply could not afford further shocks like the famine and the Quit India campaign.

The mobilisation of the Indian population, in the armed services but also in war industries, was important in creating a temporary alliance between the Indian people and the British authorities. Moreover, the war created a stimulus from which many could benefit in terms of opportunities and material gain. Unsurprisingly, many were concerned about the consequences of a Japanese invasion and occupation. Either the Japanese might destroy everything in their conquest, or the British might be tempted to repeat the scorched earth policy they had used in Burma. Indians were therefore prepared to fight for a stake in the future. Anglo-Indians thought of themselves as inherently loyalist despite all the pre-war prejudices against them, while the Hindu right and the Muslim League shared an ideological dislike of the Axis powers with the British, and the Punjab was on the verge of declaring Jihad against Japan for mistreatment of Sikh prisoners of war. For the communists, the Soviet Union was an ally of Britain and their orders from Moscow dictated they should work with Raj, but many on the political left genuinely hated the idea of Japanese imperialism as much as they disapproved of the British. Even the INC was wary of a break with Britain when the Japanese threat was so grave; not only might it lead to chaos and occupation, but it would jeopardise the moral imperative to support their own Indian troops. Some, of course, felt Britain's presence might actually cause a Japanese attack, but Gandhi expected the British to leave *and* to defend India, which did not resolve their dilemma. In light of these considerations, potential insurgents were neutralised, which perhaps helps to explain why there was no widespread insurrection between 1944 and 1945. Yet, from 1942 onwards, the authorities anticipated that the end of the war would mean a return to widespread violence that the Army in India would be unwilling to contain. A secret dispatch from Headquarters informed the Military Secretary: 'It is fair to say that, as the war draws to its close ... the general I[nternal] S[ecurity] position is bound to deteriorate, as interested parties begin to prepare (as they are now preparing) for the eventual struggle for power.'[78] In 1945, plans drawn up to deal

[78] GHQ (India) to the Military Secretary, India Office, Most Secret, 20 December 1942, IOR L/WS/1/1337.

with political agitation and violence showed that everything depended on the loyalty of the Indian troops, but since 1943, this had been in doubt.[79]

Conclusions

From their experience of previous wars, the British knew that the first component of pacification was to use force to establish security. They also knew that enlisting the local population in various capacities, from military service to political responsibility, gave them a stake in the continuation of the occupation.[80] In the initial stages of an occupation, the aim was to inflict heavy casualties, and to find measures to bring an elusive enemy into battle. The army would then seek to establish control of the area and limit the mobility of their irregular enemies. To minimise the expense of occupation, auxiliaries were deployed in the place of regular troops, and they could bring in vital intelligence and local knowledge. In the Inter-War Years, air policing at first offered the possibility of being able to dispense with some ground troops altogether. However, operations on the North West Frontier had indicated that a combination of these arms was essential.

Force could not, however, be used in an unlimited fashion. Whilst the principle of 'minimum necessary force' had long been established, ways had to be found to incorporate this principle in the use of new technologies without entirely jeopardising the ability of the army or the police to operate. On the North West Frontier, respect for force (potential and actual) was more important since there was no illusion that the British would ever be accepted as occupiers. The British used force as the means to create favourable conditions for negotiations by Political Officers. 'Insurgent' activity ebbed and flowed, but was never entirely prevented, so the aim was to re-establish an equilibrium and order. From the end of the First World War it was already recognised that

---

79 Defence HQ Outline Plan, Operation Asylum, Most Secret, 9 December 1945, IOR L/WS/2/65; Chiefs of Staff Committee, Indian Army, 'Subversive attempts on the loyalty of the Indian Army', Secret, 10 May 1943, IOR L/WS/1/707.

80 In the operations in India, security was regarded as the first priority and it was dependent on four factors. The first was the military (made up of local forces, garrisons and 'strike forces', namely columns, with a strategic reserve in the form of ground and air forces). The second were the frontier militias and the police (which were essentially paramilitary police staffed by locals). These local agencies brought in intelligence, whilst British personnel provided command and control. The third was the element of human security, particularly economic factors such as food and employment, but also of established beliefs and way of life. The fourth element was the control of resources and the population, effected through access controls, reporting systems, and collective responsibility, but also by working through local elites (such as the *maliks*, Princes and Indian middle classes).

frontier warfare and conventional warfare were distinct, and even required 'contradictory' approaches.[81]

For internal security within India, certain steps were taken. First, the army concentrated enough force to destroy or disperse the main body of armed insurgents, and, in the initial stages, inflicted heavy losses. Second, they established contact with the population on a frequent or permanent basis through political officers, and controlled movements and resources in order to cut off any links with local fighters. Third, they destroyed or discredited the local insurgent political organisations, which included the promises of the Faqir of Ipi or the promise of the INC that the Quit India campaign would induce the British to abandon the sub-continent. Fourth, they used local authorities, and supported alternative but credible interlocutors overtly or covertly. These included the *maliks* on the frontier, the Muslim League and a range of personnel in India itself. Fifth, local defence units (such as the Tochi Scouts) were organised and assigned areas of responsibility. Sixth, local leaders were encouraged to pursue their grievances peacefully through the colonial authorities. Linlithgow attempted to permit the INC to function during the war, but it was Wavell who worked hard to establish a consensus that the British would relinquish power after the war in return for support against the Axis powers. The final step was to win over or suppress the last insurgents. On the frontier, this was achieved only temporarily, but in India there was at least enough goodwill or shared aspirations to sustain the war effort.

The idea of political concessions in British thinking about the security of India had existed before the war, but emerged more strongly after 1942. If the British had relied only on security measures to maintain their rule, they would have had to ensure the Indian armed forces remained loyal. However, after the trial of INA officers and the mutiny in the Indian Navy, it was clear that the British could no longer rely on their security apparatus. Sir Stafford Cripps noted in a Commons debate in 1947 that the only way to hang on to India was through 'total repression' which would be possible only with the deployment of a large number of British troops and that, under the financial and international climate of the time, was impossible.[82] Wavell had recognised the need to combine the British and Indian views of the conflict to create a united war effort and his successor, Lord Louis Mountbatten, avoided a protracted and futile British counter-insurgency campaign by recognising that the end had come, and a political solution was the only option.

---

81 Moreman, *The Army in India*, p. 178; compare similar comments in the introduction of the American *Field Manual on Counterinsurgency*, FM3-24, (University of Chicago Press, 2007).

82 V.P. Menon, *The Transfer of Power in India* (Bombay: Orient-Longmans, 1950), p. 346.

Index